Teaching for Intelligence II: A Collection of Articles

edited by
Arthur L. Costa

Arlington Heights, Illinois

Teaching for Intelligence II: A Collection of Articles

Published by SkyLight Professional Development
2626 S. Clearbrook Dr., Arlington Heights, IL 60005-5310
Phone 800-348-4474, 847-290-6600
Fax 847-290-6609
info@skylightedu.com
http://www.skylightedu.com

Director, Product Development: Donna Nygren
Acquisitions Editor: Jean Ward
Editor: Barb Lightner
Cover Designer and Illustrator: David Stockman
Book Designer/Formatter: Christina Georgi
Proofreader: Donna Ramirez
Indexer: Candice Cummins Sunseri
Production Supervisor: Bob Crump

Printed in the United States of America.

ISBN 1-57517-266-6
LCCCN: 00-130211

2611V
Item number 1927

Z Y X W V U T S R Q P O N M L K J I H G F E D C B A
06 05 04 03 02 15 14 13 12 11 10 9 8 7 6 5 4 3 2

Contents

New Perspectives on Intelligences

As Edward deBono once said, "If you never change your mind, why have one."

Traditional perspectives about intelligence have imprisoned educational thought and practices long enough. While changing the conception of intelligence is a relatively recent event, this change is one of the most liberating and powerful forces in the restructuring of schools, education, and society.

At the turn of the century in the United States, society was undergoing great shifts. Masses of foreign immigrants poured into coastal ports and moved inland to compete for positions in the job-hungry industrial revolution. A means was needed to separate those who were educable and worthy of work from those who should be relegated to menial labor. Based on the machine-model of the times, it was thought that intellectual capacity could be measured by a test yielding a static and relatively stable score, and that intelligence was inherited through genes and chromosomes—some people had it, while others missed out.

In retrospect, society now realizes that this was an elitist, racist, and sexist way of thinking, fueled by the fear of diluting "Anglo-Saxon purity." However, such theories still serve educators as a rationale for justifying such standard operating procedures as tracking students according to high and low aptitude, the bell curve, drill and practice, competition, frequent testing, ability grouping, using IQ scores as a basis for special education, task-analyzing learning into separate skills, and reinforcing learning by rewards and external motivations. The contributors to this volume implore us to think of intelligence otherwise.

The theory of growing intelligence began to take shape in the mid-70s, when Arthur Whimbey (Whimbey and Whimbey 1975), who was ahead of his time, urged society to reconsider its basic concepts of intelligence and to question the assumption that genetically inherited capacities were immutable. He argued that intelligence could be taught and provided evidence that certain interventions could enhance cognitive functioning. Through instruction in problem solving, metacognition, and strategic reasoning, his students not only increased their IQ scores, but also displayed more effective approaches to their academic work.

The theory of growing intelligence has been further supported by evidence that average IQ scores have risen over the years (Kotulak 1997). These increases demonstrate that instead of being fixed and immutable, intelligence is flexible and subject to great changes, both up and down, depending on the kinds of stimulation the brain gets from its environment.

David Perkins (1995, 264) further supports the theory that intelligence can be taught and learned. He believes that while neural intelligence is "genetically determined," experiential intelligence, the context-specific knowledge that is accumulated through experience, can be expanded. He believes that reflective intelligence, self-managing, self-monitoring, and self-modifying, can and should be cultivated.

It has been shown that intelligence is multifaceted. To represent this, the term *intelligences* should be pluralized. J. P. Guilford and his associates (Guilford and Hoeptner 1971) discerned 120 factors of the intellect. They believed that all students have intelligence, but asked "What kind?" instead of "How much?". They theorized that these 120 factors of the intellect were combinations of *operations, contents,* and *products.* They defined *operations* as including such mental capabilities as comprehending, remembering, and analyzing; *contents* as referring to words, forms and symbols; and *products* as referring to complexity—single units, groups, and relationships. Guilford believed that through various targeted interventions, a person's intelligence could be amplified.

Howard Gardner (1983) adds support to the belief that intelligence is multifaceted with his theory that there are many ways of knowing, learning, and expressing knowledge. Gardner identified several distinct intelligences: verbal, logical, bodily/kinesthetic, musical, spatial, naturalistic, interpersonal, and intrapersonal, which function in problem solving and in the creation of new products. Gardner also believes that these intelligences can be nurtured in all human beings, and, although each individual may have preferred forms, with proper mediation and experience all people can continue to develop these capacities throughout their lifetime.

More recently, intelligence is being defined as what people do, not who they are. Steven Jay Gould (1981) supports this idea when he suggests thatintelligence is the ability to face problems in an unprogrammed (creative) manner, and the notion that such a nebulous socially defined concept as intelligence might be identified as a "thing" with a locus in the brain and a definite degree of heritability.

Mythological IQ scores (Sternberg, Torff, and Grigorenko 1998) were found to have little predictive quality in regard to success in later life. Sternberg argues for three types of intelligence: analytical intelligence in which comparisons, evaluations, and assessments are made; creative intelligence involving imagination, design, and invention; and practical intelligence in which use, practicality, and demonstration are paramount. Sternberg believes that all human beings have the capacity to continue growing in these three domains and encourages educators to enhance them all.

By definition, a problem is any stimulus, question, task, phenomenon, or discrepancy for which the explanation is not immediately known. Intelligent behavior is performed in response to such questions and problems. Thus, society is interested in focusing on human performance under those challenging conditions—dichotomies, dilemmas, paradoxes, ambiguities, and enigmas—that demand strategic reasoning, insightfulness, perseverance, creativity, and craftsmanship to resolve them.

When individuals think of intelligence as something that grows incrementally though experience, intervention, and reflection rather than as a static score, they tend to invest energy to learn something new or to increase their understanding and mastery of tasks. They persist with continued high levels of task-related effort in response to difficulty. Learning goals are associated with the inference that effort and ability are positively related, so that greater efforts create and make evident more ability.

There is body of research dealing with factors that seem to shape these habits—factors that have to do with people's beliefs about the relationship between effort and ability. Children develop cognitive strategies and effort-based beliefs about their intelligence—the habits of mind associated with higher-order learning—when they are continually pressed to raise questions and to accept challenges, to find solutions that are not immediately apparent, to explain concepts, to justify their reasoning, and to seek information. When educators hold children accountable for this kind of intelligent behavior, children take it as a signal that others think they are smart, and they come to accept this judgment. The paradox is that children become smart by being treated as if they already are intelligent (Resnick and Hall 1998).

THE ORGANIZATION OF THIS COLLECTION

Drawing on these contemporary views of intelligences, my energies turned to editing this volume of unique, varied, and informative articles. It became an exercise in analysis, pattern finding, and categorization. My task was to find a satisfying, sensible system for organizing the diverse contents of the volume into a meaningful whole. My self-set goals were to illuminate the issues, intrigue the reader, and make a contribution to the burgeoning literature on intelligence, cognition, and congruent educational practices.

Being a "chronologically gifted" educator, deeply immersed in the past and present jargon of educational discourse, I originally entertained many possible classification systems largely built around current educational rhetoric: school reform, standards-based curriculum, alternative assessment, accelerated learning, and effective instruction. I played with variations on these themes but soon found them to be stilted, hackneyed, and convergent.

I decided that since this was to be a volume on intelligence, it should be presented in an intelligent manner: insightful, cutting-edge, and even risky. It seemed that the categorization system must not only illuminate the themes, it must also be congruent with the topic—an intelligent approach to intelligence!

I asked myself, what are the essential, basic themes that pervade all the articles? Taken as a whole, what do the authors want the reader to know about a modern view of intelligence, and how can this book be organized to communicate the concepts that the authors represent?

Upon reflecting on these questions, I found six messages of intelligence embedded in these articles. They are found in the characteristics of intelligent human beings. These messages are the following:

1. *Think flexibly.* Individuals need to be open to new and divergent ideas, and cast off the shackles of old perceptions. Intelligence is not fixed—rather, it is modifiable. As such, all human beings can become more intelligent over time.
2. *Apply past knowledge and transfer it to new situations.* Educators know a great deal about how meaning is constructed, but often fail to apply it to their students. Educators have an enormous amount of information and theory about brain functioning and environments that maximize human learning, yet they tend to ignore that information when they plan instruction.
3 *Think about your own thinking.* As individuals make decisions about what to teach, how to teach it, and how to assess learning, they should think about how they can monitor their own decision making.
4. *Think and communicate with clarity and precision.* Individuals need to avoid overgeneralizing and be conscious of the deletions and distortions in their language.
5. *Have a questioning attitude and a healthy skepticism.* Intelligent people don't accept everything on face value; they pose powerful questions to clarify issues and generate data, seek proof, and identify assumptions.
6. *Continue learning throughout a lifetime.* Intelligent people are open to new learning. They resist complacency about learning: Everyone who achieves mastery realizes they are merely on the threshold of new learnings.

Building on the belief that intelligence is modifiable, multitudinous, and behavioral, this book is intended to invite readers to experience, practice, and reflect on several of the behaviors believed to be characteristics of "intelligent" human beings (Costa 1991).

The goals of this book, therefore, are threefold: 1) to inform readers of the thinking of outstanding scholars in the field of cognition, education, and intelligence; 2) to elevate, broaden, and inform the deliberation about appropriate curriculum, instruction, and assessment for youth as they confront the complexities of the new millennium; and 3) to practice, reflect on, and enhance six of the behaviors that characterize intelligent human beings—flexibility in thinking, metacognition, striving for accuracy and precision, thinking and communicating with clarity and precision, applying previous knowledge, and continuous learning.

The bottom line is, if we as educators are to promote the growth of intelligence in students, fellow educators, and schools, then we must practice those intelligent behaviors ourselves.

REFERENCES

Costa, A. 1991. The Search for intelligent life. In *The school as a home for the mind.* Arlington Heights, IL: IRI/Skylight Publishing, Inc.

deBono, E. 1991. The CORT thinking program. In *Developing minds: Vol. II. Programs for teaching thinking,* edited by A. Costa. Alexandria, VA: Association for Supervision and Curriculum Development.

Feuerstein, R., Y. Rand, M. B. Hoffman, and R. Miller. 1980. *Instrumental Enrichment: An intervention program for cognitive modifiability.* Baltimore, MD: University Park Press.

Gardner, H. 1983. *Frames of mind: The theory of multiple intelligences.* New York: Basic Books.

Gould, S. J. 1981. *The mismeasure of man.* New York: W. W. Norton

Guilford, J. P., and R. Hoeptner. 1971. *The analysis of intelligence.* New York: McGraw-Hill.

Kotulak, R. 1997. *Inside the brain: Revolutionary discoveries of how the mind works.* Kansas City, MO: Andrew McMeel

Perkins, D. 1995. *Outsmarting IQ: The emerging science of learnable intelligence.* New York: The Free Press

Resnick, L., and M. Hall. 1998. Learning organizations for sustainable education reform. *DAEDALUS: Journal of the American Academy of Arts and Sciences,* Fall: 89–118.

Sternberg R., B. Torff, and E. Grigorenko. 1998, May. Teaching for successful intelligence raises school achievement. *Phi Delta Kappan* 79(9): 667–69

Whimbey, A., and L. S. Whimbey. 1975. *Intelligence can be taught.* New York: Lawrence Erlbaum Associates.

Section 1

Flexibility in Thinking: The Capacity to Shift Perspectives, to Generate Alternate Approaches, and to Change One's Mind

An amazing discovery about the human brain is its plasticity—its ability to "rewire"; to continually change and even repair itself; to become even smarter. Flexible people have the capacity to change their mind as they receive additional data. They engage in multiple and simultaneous outcomes and activities. They draw upon a repertoire of problem-solving strategies and can practice style flexibility, knowing when it is appropriate to be broad and global in their thinking, and when a situation requires detailed precision. They create and seek novel approaches and have a well-developed sense of humor.

Flexible people can approach a problem from a new angle using a novel approach. deBono (1991) refers to this as *lateral thinking.* Flexible people consider alternative points of view or deal with several sources of information simultaneously. Their minds are open to change based on additional information and data or reasoning that contradicts their beliefs. Flexible people know that they have and can develop options and alternatives to consider. They understand not only immediate reactions, but also perceive the bigger purposes that such constraints serve. Flexible thinkers are able to shift, at will, through multiple perceptual positions.

Some people have difficulty considering alternative points of view or dealing with more than one classification system simultaneously. They perceive situations from a very ego-centered point of view: *their* way to solve a problem seems to be the *only* way. Their minds are made up.

The first section of this book opens with three authors who urge us to employ flexibility in thinking as we consider reform in education. Peter Senge draws on vast experiences in helping industries and corporations with the complexities of mindshifts, and makes applications for a similar need for educators. Renate and Geoffrey Caine show how such shifts in perception help individuals see more clearly and unleash newfound power when individuals have the stamina to change their perceptual stance. In the final chapter of this section, I suggest that our traditional curriculum practices are based on an archaic precept and that curriculum will change only when educators are able to shift out of old paradigms.

All the authors invite an openness to new and different perspectives; they ask individuals to see problems from a different point of view and to relinquish old categories, stereotypes, and structures that restrict thinking. They urge educators to promote the intelligent behavior of thinking flexibly about educational practices and purposes.

Systems Change in Education

by Peter Senge

I do not spend my life in schools and school systems and school districts. I do spend a great deal of my time working with businesses. I didn't actually start off in business because I had an inherent interest in it. As a child of the Sixties, I actually had no interest in business whatsoever, and at some level today that's probably still the case in a very particular way. I've grown to have a great deal of interest in the people with whom I've had a chance to work, and I have a great deal of interest in the health of their enterprises. I'm involved in a consortium, a group of organizations that have been working together now for seven or eight years. It probably has some similarities to James Comer's project at Yale in the sense that we came to a belief, maybe about 9 or 10 years ago, that collaboration was absolutely critical. No institution working by itself could ever overcome the extraordinary range of hurdles involved in bringing about significant change. I do care a great deal about those people and those human communities that represent those enterprises, but my interest in business at some level was and still is instrumental.

In our present day society, business is probably the most influential institution. If you want to bring about some sort of fundamental change as an indicator of what's possible, business is a good place to look. That's neither good nor bad; that's not a statement of preference. In some ways I wish that weren't the case. However, I've had enough opportunity in a variety of settings in public education to know that it's a lot harder to bring about the kind of changes that are needed in the institution called public education than, in fact, it is in the institution called business. And it's not easy in business. I've had this notion for a long time that we could build momentum in the world of business, that we could give a kind of credibility to some

---

Adapted from *ENCOUNTER: Education for Meaning and Social Justice*, September 1998, volume 11, no. 3, pp. 60–66.

pretty nutty ideas that might really help in the other institutions of society where change is a little bit more difficult.

In some fundamental way, I believe there is a kind of partnership that's necessary without knowing exactly what the form is, a kind of partnership between the world of business and the world of education. I've seen this develop informally and spontaneously in many settings where, after working 5 or 10 years, a group of people who have really started to develop a fundamentally different way of working together in their business enterprise look around at each other and go "Yeah."

But, in some cases, who really cares? Is the profitability of Shell or Ford 100 years from now really what we care about? Conversely, I don't actually think we have to try to convince people that we all have a responsibility for raising children. I don't think there's any convincing needed whatsoever. I think it's in us, personally, biologically (literally), and in the heritages that represent all of our cultures. I've seen it bubble out of us on countless occasions. When people start to build some real confidence, some real sense that they can shape and alter the nature of the place where they work in a way that represents what they deeply care about, they invariably start to say, "Well, but now what about the kids?" And no one has to tell them to do that. It's not on an intellectual plane like the five disciplines and all that kind of stuff. It's more a sense of, "Boy, there are big forces that are going to have to be mobilized in this world to get us out of the pickles we're in. And maybe they have something to do with this kind of partnership."

. . . raising children . . . it's in us, personally, biologically and in the heritages that represent all of our cultures.

However, I'm not going to focus on five disciplines. They are a set of tools and methods, a set of practices. They're absolutely important. I didn't invent them. They're a summary and synthesis of the work of a lot of people for a lot of years. If I tried to summarize them in this short period of time, it would end up like someone trying to tell you how violins work. You need to pick up a violin and try it sometime. That's the only way to ever understand how a discipline or a tool really works. Moreover, many of the readers of this journal have a fair amount of experience, and I think their experience as practitioners, as implementers, is, in many ways, much more relevant for understanding schools than my experience as a thinker.

The focus here is on what it means when you try to go from one or two people driving their agenda through a school or a school system to actually believing that the only agenda that really matters is the agenda that emerges collectively. When each person gets up in the morning, he/she doesn't think about pursuing somebody else's vision. Hopefully, he/she thinks a little bit about pursuing his/her own vision. It's the only one that really matters for each of us. How do you create a field of harmony amongst the diverse visions that we all represent that can actually align and organize and coordinate a very diverse community? That's what the discipline of building shared vision is all about.

Our schools, our school systems, our corporations, all our institutions are based on the principles of the 16th Century.

In this context, it might be helpful to go back to what's been the cornerstone of my own personal journey in this work for really over 30 years now and consider systems change in education. I'd just like to offer a few comments as someone who's lived with this notion of "system" for a long time, about what it means and what it might mean, and what I would consider some of its of practical implications. The word "system" is a very problematic word. Most all of us have a rich, evoked meaning as soon as we hear it.

For most of us, the kind of things that come to mind when we think of the "system" are "big," "impersonal," "inertia," "external forces." I wouldn't particularly recommend using the word for something you really care about because most people will think of a big, impersonal, set of external forces, constraints, something making one do something or not enabling one to do something.

At this point, however, I'd like to weave a little different picture. There is a revolution that's been occurring for 100 years in our scientific worldview. It started in physics; it carried into biology. My own background is actually in engineering. It's definitely present there. It's gradually working its way through a lot of different branches of science. It's a profound revolution, and it will probably have a huge impact on our societies two to three hundred years from now (if we have societies two to three hundred years from now). That's typically how long it takes for a major revolution in science to work its way into society.

Our schools, our school systems, our corporations, all our institutions are based on the principles of the 16th Century. We have a very Newtonian worldview. And we all learned it in the same place. We learned it in school because school is the carrier of what science says about the way the world works. This wasn't the case 150 years ago. In those earlier schools, people didn't necessarily learn the Newtonian worldview. They learned a lot of different things. They read Ben Franklin's *Poor Richard's Almanac* or learned about the crop rotation or whatever else was relevant. Of course, they learned a little grammar and a little arithmetic and such, but they didn't learn that the world is made up of billiard balls bouncing off of each other. They didn't learn that the nature of science is to figure out all the forces that control things. After all, scientifically, the real effectiveness in any institution is to learn how something works so that you can control it. People who lived on farms didn't think about controlling nature. They thought about working with nature because that's the only sensible mindset that you could have. They didn't think about altering the seasons; they thought about understanding them. But today, it all comes down to understanding so that we can control because that's the Newtonian worldview. Ironically, I always feel like I should apologize to anybody for a word I may use in a kind of derogatory way. I don't mean that as a criticism of Newton, who was actually an extremely religious person. Nonetheless, these things come down through the ages and they have a very particular meaning.

In some sense, science is an agent of culture, and it answers the following question: What's real?

The revolution that's occurring in science today can be described in many different ways, and 100 years from now, somebody will be able to describe it in a way that maybe makes sense. When you're in the middle of these things you never know what they mean, but let me offer you my perspective. In some sense, science is an agent of culture, and it answers the following question: What's real? This, by the way, used to be the primary job of the priesthood but over the last couple hundred years, it's shifted to science, and the question is: "What's reality?" All culture, for as long as there's been culture, always enmeshes its members in these questions: "What's the nature of reality?" "What does it mean to be alive?" "What does it mean to be a human being?" In this modern day and age, we look to science to answer these questions and science has come up with a rather remarkable set of developments in the last 100 years. We no longer see the world as full of billiard balls. We no longer think the most fundamental things are, in fact, things. It appears today that the emerging scientific worldview says something very different than that Newtonian worldview. It says that the fundamental nature of reality is actually "relationship" not "thing." All these things that we are surrounded by and which our culture tells us are solid and hard are, of course, almost completely empty—99% empty space. This thing we call a body is, in fact, a process. It's replacing itself continually. Buckminster Fuller used to be fond of holding up his hand and saying, "What is this"? Everyone answers, "It's a hand." His response was, he says, "Well, that's really interesting, but last night I went to bed with one, and this morning I got a new one. Now, I didn't get a whole new one in one day, but I do get a whole new one over a few years." This is not metaphysics I'm talking. This is physical reality. You know, most of your household dust are our skin cells that die and fall off because they're continually falling off every few minutes.

. . . most of your household dust are our skin cells that die and fall off because they're continually falling off every few minutes.

The revolution in science, in a funny way, is actually about an age-old question that our modern science never dealt with much. What's life? What does it mean to say something is alive? If there's a metaphor or an image for the scientific industrial age of the last 300, 400 years, probably the most compelling metaphor is that of the machine. Our scientific progress, our technological progress has manifested itself in an extraordinary ability to build more and more complex, sophisticated, really quite remarkable machines. The only problem is that when a metaphor becomes deeply rooted in the collective consciousness, we start to see everything like that and before long we see ourselves as machines. We see our organizations as machines. We see kids, although no one would ever want to stand up in public and say it, as machines. I'll come back to this.

So there is the system, a functional mechanism in schools, and we all know the system means *its* rules, *its* regulations, *its* power relationships, *its* organizational charts, *its* requirements for certification, and so on. But behind that is the question of what is a system? Let me consider it from a kid's perspective because I've had just enough experience over the last few years to think if you really want to understand the system, you must understand it from a kid's perspective. The subject of biology, for example, changes incredibly for a kid when it shifts from memorizing isolated facts about cell walls and organelles and protoplasm to understanding how a living cell functions, what it does, how it lives, how it dies, how it interacts with its environment. The cell is the building block of all living systems, and if you put a cell of that tree or my skin under a microscope, very few of us could even tell the difference. But we've been generally studying living phenomena as if they were dead, isolated facts, fragmented bits of information. Do you want to know why no kids or very few kids get excited about biology? That's why.

"Like, my brain popped open again." He rediscovered his music.

Seven or eight years ago, a woman I met was trying to teach English literature in a high school on the south side of Tucson—a very bad socioeconomic area. There were many Hispanic and Native American kids in very tough settings. She had to teach Shakespeare. She, along with her boyfriend who taught science in another school, had developed some really wonderful computer simulation models of how cells worked. They got kids totally engaged in understanding the functioning of a cell and said, "Let's build a simulation model of Shakespeare. Let's do one of Hamlet." Now, here is the bizarre thing. I met a lot of those kids, and those kids absolutely loved it. I think they started to get a feeling that only an actor usually gets. All of a sudden, it came alive. They could ask questions like "What if he hadn't done that? What if he'd done something else? What might happen?" All of a sudden, rather than a static thing, something impossible in which to relate, it suddenly became a living tapestry of people interacting with one another. I'll never forget sitting around with a group of these kids about two years later. Most of them had graduated, and one in particular, Raphael, who would have never graduated, told me about what that experience meant to him. He said, "Like, my brain popped open again." He rediscovered his music. I find these paths of development are more surprising than we expect. From this little computer simulation model of Hamlet, he didn't simply decide he was going to go off to college and major in English literature. He rediscovered his music and his desire to make a career for himself as a musician (which he had given up).

There's something different when we start to study things as if they're alive. When we apply this to schools and school systems, the most useful thing that I have discovered over the last ten years of opportunities working in depth over long periods of time with people in enterprises, is that you have got to look at the system in a very broad way. You need to keep asking, "Why is it this way? And why are the rules set up exactly like that?" Furthermore, you cannot settle for pacifying explanations. "Well, it's because the people who have power want it that way." End of story. That stops all inquiry.

There are many levels to a system and, without doubt, the most important levels are not the rules and regulations; they're not the procedures; they're not all of the manifest or obvious things. They are invariably the thinking that lies behind all those. You want to start to inquire deeply into a system, and start asking questions like, "What are the assumptions that are deep down there that we almost never even talk about?" They represent the thinking that produces the procedures and the rules and reinforces them.

Inquiring into underlying assumptions is tricky. You can ask people, "Well, what do you think about learning?" "What are your key assumptions about learning?" What you'll get is what we read in the textbook and what we learned when we got our Ph.D.'s and all the proper theories. The only way to truly understand the assumptions that are operating in any human system is to watch what people do. You must watch how the system actually functions and then ask what might be the thinking that would lie beneath the surface that would lead people to act that way, to function that way. You will often come up with interpretations that almost are diametrically opposed to what people say. You know that old song (I'm just restating it in a different way here), "I cannot hear your words, your actions speak too loudly." That's how you understand the assumptions. You must look at how the system is functioning and what people are doing.

It may be useful for me to share, from my vantage point, a few assumptions that stand out for me about learning and about schools. I offer this with humility as a starting point for discussion by people far more knowledgeable about such things than I do. Most of what I'm going to say I say from my experience as a parent and not as an educator, but these are very real to me as a parent. I'll start off with the "deficit model."

People don't usually give speeches advocating the deficit model. It's not one of these assumptions we feel comfortable talking about, but all kids experience it. All kids. This experience, if anything, is as powerful for the high achievers as for those who don't achieve highly. Children thinking "I'm not all right" experience the deficit model.

"There is something fundamentally amiss with me." "I don't have what I need to succeed in life." The way I've found it most powerfully communicated by kids is when they say, "They don't *respect* me." That's what the deficit model is experientially.

Nature knows how to develop. Left to nature's own devices, development will occur.

Moreover, there's no space or setting or permission for that conversation to occur. There's a particular diagnosis that people who have studied complex social systems find again and again. It is that systems, human systems, "get stuck." There are certain subjects that are undiscussable and the undiscussability is undiscussable. Kids have nobody to sit down with and talk about the lack of respect they feel. Teachers, of course, will say, "Well, of course, I respect you." And then you could add ". . . and that's why I don't listen to you."

I think our theory of learning is based on the fact that somehow children don't have what they need, aren't formed, aren't developed, aren't whatever. We act as if we, the wonderful intervenors, through the beneficence of our grand souls and our extraordinary knowledge, will do what nature has spent millions of years learning how to do, in place of nature. We seem to believe that if there weren't schools, children wouldn't develop. How long have schools been around? At most, a couple of hundred years. Somehow, it must've been luck with Plato or the Buddha, because there weren't schools. Somehow, it must have been luck that these people developed.

Nature knows how to develop. Left to nature's own devices, development will occur. The real question is if we add anything to the process. Or do we systematically undermine the process?

Going to a very different setting, do you think there isn't an education process in a tribal culture? Is there no education going on? Is there no development occurring? There is a tribal system of education. It occurs around the world. It occurs in indigenous cultures everywhere in slightly different forms and traditions, because obviously culture creates its own unique flavor, but, ultimately, it's exactly the same everywhere. It's universal. It's been developed for at least 200,000 years, and it's been utilized for that long. We pay no attention to it whatsoever. At a certain point in time, a young person wants to learn something and hangs out with the people who seem to know something about it. That's how it works. It's a little oversimplified, but that's basically how it works. There's not a lot of evidence of dilettantism. There's not a lot of evidence that people grow up and never learn anything, or that individuals expect the tribe to take care of them. There is not much evidence of that. They all seem to find their place. They all seem to find what they really want to learn about. They all seem to find their place to contribute.

Present that notion today and, of course, people say "Well, that's ludicrous. Children wouldn't learn on their own." Those very same children who we have to tie to their chairs to learn in school are learning outside of school—learning, continually. They may not learn what we'd like them to learn, but they're learning a great deal. You can't *not* make learning occur. There's nothing you can do to keep learning from occurring. Learning is nature expressing itself in its search for its own development. It cannot *not* occur. But, we sure can make it difficult with the assumption of the deficit model. The child is in some way deficient, and we will fix him/her.

A second assumption about learning: Ask most people in our culture and in the industrial cultures where learning occurs and see where they point. They point to their heads. We think learning somehow is up there. We don't think of it in our bodies. All indigenous cultures (in fact, most Asian cultures to this day even as there are a lot of clashes because industrialization is gradually sweeping across the Asian cultures) will still say that knowledge is in their bodies not in their heads. We may have some ideas up there, but that's different than knowledge. Knowledge is about the capacity to *do* something. You and I, most of us, know how to ride a bicycle, but very few of us actually even know the theories of gyroscopic motion whereby it works. We don't have the ideas, but we know how to ride a bicycle. We know how to walk. We know how to talk. We think that stuff is trivial? By comparison, most of what we learn in school is quite trivial. Learning language is an extraordinarily complex process.

The assumption that learning is in the head is mainly a European tradition that has its roots in the aristocracy versus the common people. You always must remember Michelangelo could not have dinner with his patrons. He could not share a meal with his patrons because his patrons were the aristocracy and they did not work with their hands. The common person was defined as a person who worked with his or her hands. So, in some ways it was natural for the aristocracy to see knowledge as in the head.

This, of course, leads us to extraordinarily limited notions of development. It's tragic because it really is the musical intelligence and the kinesthetic intelligence and the interpersonal or emotional intelligence, as well as the abstract, symbolic reasoning that characterizes development. We all have different propensities. Some of us are brilliant in one of them and good enough in the others. But we have in all of them capacities that we have often lost. How many of us learned in school that we couldn't sing? How many of us learned in school that we couldn't draw or paint? How many of us learned in school that we weren't too good in math or that we really weren't very good in English? That's the deficit model played out in these fragmented worldviews. But the basic assumption about learning here is that learning is in the head, rather than in all of us. I'll never forget a story told by a retired chairman of the physics department at MIT. When he was a young child, his grandmother played the piano. He said his most vivid memories as a child were sitting underneath the piano while his grandmother played. He said he could still remember as a three- or four-year-old sitting under that piano as she played Bach. He explained that as the music washed around him, he became a physicist. Cognitive, in the head? Nonsense!

A third assumption about learning follows directly from the second. The third assumption about learning embedded in our culture and in our schools is, of course, that there are smart kids and dumb kids. It's a corollary to the second, but is relatively new, culturally speaking. It's a clear product of the industrial age. I can give you some food for thought as to why the industrial age would produce this assumption. That there are smart kids and dumb kids is in contrast to the quite universal notion that all children are born with gifts, unique gifts. The healthy functioning of any tribe is defined by its capacity to create an environment for each of those gifts to develop. They don't develop all by themselves. They develop from a lifetime of interactions of a human being with his/her environment. Smart kids and dumb kids is a byproduct of the machine.

This assumption is most clear if we explore it in the context of a few assumptions about school. The assumptions I've been discussing about learning are transcendent but embodied or instantiated in the institution we call school. If you really want to inquire why school works the way it does, you must think about what are our deeper assumptions about learning, the nature of knowledge, the nature of human development, etc., because they then get embodied in this institution we call school.

The first assumption about school, in looking at how it works (not how it's espoused), is the classic industrial age management system where we break up all the jobs into different pieces. We let somebody be a superintendent, a principal, and a teacher and assume that that is the right way to manage it. We do not build partnerships amongst these people. We do not build a sense of collective responsibility amongst people. We build on the sense that if each person is doing his/her job, then the thing ought to work out fine. It's the antithesis of a real team. It would be like someone thinking, if I just rebound, the team will succeed. The team won't meet with success if we believe we are each responsible for only one thing. That's the industrial age management model. Break it up into pieces, create specialists in the pieces, let everybody do their piece, and, by golly, it should work out. The rebounder won't be on a team very long even though he/she might be great at that job because on a successful team everybody must do a little bit of everything. Most importantly, we all have to have a real sense that if we don't function well together, real success will not happen. In schools, the one person that the kids are most aware of is the teacher because they don't think a lot about superintendents. They may think a little bit about principals if they're like me and had to talk to them on a few occasions. They think a lot about teachers. They know exactly what the teacher's job is. The teacher's job, of course, is to make sure the kid learns. In turn, the kid's job is to do everything he/she can to please the teacher—not to learn, but to gain the teacher's approval. That's the flip side of it; that's the kid's job. A kid's job is not learning in this system. The kid's job is pleasing the teacher. It doesn't matter if kids think they're really good at things. If the teacher doesn't think so, they're not. The teacher, not the kid, has the power to define.

One of the things we know is important in our society is lifelong learning. All businesses will tell you that whatever people learn in school, they're likely to keep learning throughout their lives. What do you think happens to lifelong learners whose primary skill is about pleasing a teacher? Do they then go to work and seek to please a boss? Are they very good lifelong learners? Of course not, because one of the cornerstones of a lifelong learner is to have greater and greater capacity for rigorous, objective self-assessment, to know how well he or she is doing. A system of fragmented responsibility directly limits lifelong learning.

There's another related assumption that's embedded in the educational enterprise in the industrial age—that knowledge itself is fragmented. Knowledge is thought to exist in separate little categories. Geography is over here; this is a body of knowledge called geography. Over there we have literature, and over there, we have mathematics. You might, as you go through your daily life sometime, just notice when you encounter a problem that's just mathematics as opposed to a problem that may need and require you to summarize some statistics or one that's just about history or just about geography. Life isn't that way. Life is about all this stuff as it presents itself in the process of living. But that isn't our theory of education. Our theory of education makes one narrower and narrower (until finally, they kick you out of the system and give you a Ph.D., piled high and deep). It produces the cult of expertise. We believe that some experts have got things figured out because they've got more stuff in their pile than anybody else.

A system of fragmented responsibility directly limits lifelong learning.

That's our theory of knowledge in the West. It's deeply fragmented. There is no notion that reality is made up of relationships and that to understand reality in a meaningful way is to understand the interrelatedness of things. Our education system does not allow the idea.

We have a system of education, a school system that's based on what philosophers call naïve realism. In this system, we believe teachers do not teach their views. They do not teach their opinions. They do not teach their interpretation of what happened. They teach what's actually fact. The kids learn that "this" is what happened in history, that history is just as the author said. They don't think that this is what this teacher (or author) has interpreted to have happened, but that things happened just as they were told.

There's a famous Chilean scientist, Umberto Maturana, working in the field of biology (one of the areas of scientific development that is really putting the nail in the coffin of naïve realism, because it's been falling apart for a couple hundred of years), who has developed a pioneering theory about how biological entities actually produce something we call cognition. It has revolutionized the cognitive sciences. He says very bluntly, "All things said are said by somebody." That's all you need to know. "All things said are said by somebody."

No human being ever produces a definitive statement about reality. It's not actually biologically possible. Think about what that would mean in schools.

We all can think of teachers who we knew didn't know the answers, who were, at the same time, so excited about the time they were going to get to spend with us and what we might learn together. We loved them as teachers. We knew they thought a great deal, and we were interested in their experiences and their thoughts even though they didn't give us THE answer. When they told us what happened in history, they said they were giving one view. Our history books still don't point out that Ben Franklin for 30 years was the Ambassador of the Iroquois nation and that most of our ideas about the design of the Constitution came from the Iroquois. That just didn't get into the story. But the good teacher transcends that myth of "I have the answer you need" (as would fit into the deficit theory). I have what you need, it's called *an* answer. This is how the institution embodies that view of learning; the teacher must have answers, not questions, not curiosity or passion.

"All things said are said by somebody."

The last assumption I'd like to share with you is that school is a machine. It is not a living system. Think about a few definitional cornerstones between machines and living systems, and you can see very quickly what I mean.

Does a machine evolve itself or does it just sit there and do what it's designed to do? Does your car grow? Does it evolve? Now someone could say that some of the machines that are being created today might have the ability to actually evolve through the way they're programmed. Be that as it may, machines function in certain ways towards determined ends. A living system is, almost by definition, in change. It never stops changing. Look in the mirror; we never stop changing. It's the nature of a living system. A machine operates according to its design specifications. It can't really operate much differently than the way it was designed to operate.

One of the most obvious machine-like characteristics of all schools is they are designed to run at a certain speed. Every teacher knows what they've got to cover in a semester or a year, and the machine has got to go at that rate. It can't go slower and it can't go much faster. Kids who might want to go faster get lost, but kids who really might want to go slower have no place to go. If you want to look at all the different features of school and just hold up one that everybody can look at and say is crazy, it is this underlying assumption of a set speed. What's so magical about 18 years of age for graduation from school? There's no difference if a kid left school at 15 or 16 or 25. What difference does it make?

A machine has no purpose of its own. It has its designer's purpose.

I spent the weekend with one of the foremost people in the world in cost accounting who invented something called activity-based costing. If there's ever a Nobel Prize given in the field of accounting, he and his colleague undoubtedly will get it. He's revolutionized business. His son, he and his wife live in Sweden. Their son has cerebral palsy, and we spent most of the weekend talking about their struggles in school and all the things they were told their child would never be able to do. But he's done almost every one; it just took a little longer. He finally completed high school at about 22. He's now in college. But the only reason he succeeded is because his mother has devoted her life to battling. A machine runs at a certain speed, and if you don't run at that speed, you don't fit into the machine.

There are a few other characteristics of machines versus living systems but maybe that's enough to make the point. I'll end with one thought. A machine has no purpose of its own. It has its designer's purpose. An important question to ponder (and, again, assumptions have to be inferred, deep assumptions, by looking at how things work, not by what people say) is what is the purpose of this machine, school? I would recommend engaging kids in this conversation because, unfortunately, we adults have been part of the machine for a long time. Ask a six, seven, or eight year old. He or she will probably have very fresh perspectives from their experiences because he or she is coming in from a different world.

A living system creates its own purpose. If I had one kind of wish for all of our institutions, and schools in particular, it is that we wake up and dedicate ourselves simply to allowing them to be what they would naturally become, which is human communities and not machines—living communities where beings continually ask the question why we are here and continually keep rediscovering and rearticulating that purpose.

Unleashing the Power of Perceptual Change

by Geoffrey Caine and Renate Caine

The call for higher standards in schools is unrelenting. The amount of money being spent on, and the amount of attention being devoted to education is unprecedented. And yet, most of the efforts to improve the quality of schooling in the United States and many other countries share a common flaw. They focus on the actions that educators need to take but ignore their attributes as human beings.

Research suggests that some improvements can be made by focusing on skills, curriculum, and student work. However, our research suggests that high-level teaching, the sort of teaching that can significantly increase the capacities and performance of students, is always built on a foundation of personal and professional characteristics and qualities that include assumptions about learning. We call these perceptual orientations. They are ways of viewing the world. And we argue that it is these orientations that make sophisticated education possible.

The nature of these orientations emerged out of our attempts to develop a theory of learning that made sense to educators and that was firmly grounded in the emerging findings from brain research.

BRAIN/MIND LEARNING PRINCIPLES

Although cognitive scientists, social scientists, and others have been working diligently for decades to make sense of learning, their findings tend not to find their way into the work and lives of practitioners. Research journals are not widely read by teachers; their language tends to be abstruse; and they generally focus on small issues that simply do not relate to teachers dealing with classrooms full of living students.

SkyLight Professional Development

We, therefore, have attempted to integrate and synthesize a vast amount of research from different disciplines into a set of twelve general principles of learning. The goal was for the principles to make immediate sense at a surface level and also to function as gateways into the research for those practitioners who might be interested.

They are intended to be system principles. That is, educators need to understand that every student is not a machine with identifiable parts, but a whole person and living system in which every part interacts, but in understandable ways. That is why principle one states "The brain is a living system: Body, mind, and brain form one dynamic unity." The central point is that every event is processed in the brain as a complex experience. Whenever we set out to "teach" kids, they experience a complex event that isn't just registered in the neocortex as information—there are sensory and emotional layers of processing that also result in physiological changes that influence what is ultimately registered and that impact the whole person.

Our brain/mind learning principles are:

- Principle One: The brain is a living system: Body, mind, and brain are one dynamic unity
- Principle Two: The brain/mind is social
- Principle Three: The search for meaning is innate
- Principle Four: The search for meaning occurs through patterning
- Principle Five: Emotions are critical to patterning.
- Principle Six: The brain/mind processes parts and wholes simultaneously
- Principle Seven: Learning involves both focused attention and peripheral perception
- Principle Eight: Learning always involves conscious and unconscious processes
- Principle Nine: We have at least two ways of organizing memory: A spatial memory system and a set of systems for rote learning
- Principle Ten: Learning is developmental
- Principle Eleven: Complex learning is enhanced by challenge and inhibited by threat
- Principle Twelve: Each brain/mind is uniquely organized

How the Principles Work: An Example

Every educator knows that emotions are important in learning. However, for a long time most of the research has been blind as to just how important emotions are. In the heyday of behaviorism, for instance, when the mind was treated as a black box whose contents did not matter, the only emotions that were dealt with were pleasure and pain, addressed in the form of rewards and punishments.

Goleman suggests that success in the real world depends on the capacity of the individual to manage and monitor his or her emotions and to relate to other people.

In the last three decades or so, cognitive science has come to grips with the fact that the mind is real and is important (imagine psychologists not willing to acknowledge this!) and there has been a great deal of work on the nature of concept formation and the construction of knowledge. At the same time, emotions are seen as very important in therapy, for example, but cognition and emotion were dealt with separately. That is why we were told as educators to deal with different "domains" separately: namely the cognitive, affective, and psychomotor domains.

More recently, the notion of emotional intelligence has emerged, the term having been reported by Goleman (1995). This suggests that success in the real world depends on the capacity of the individual to manage and monitor his or her emotions and to relate to other people.

However, other really important research has suggested for many years that there is more. If we look at the work of linguists, particularly those who have been interested in the metaphor, such as Lakoff and Johnson (1980), we find that concepts and feelings actually seem to be intertwined—they are parts of each other. Thus, the word *sweet* may suggest "sweet as honey," and there is clearly an image and a feeling that give the concept substance.

Other work, such as that of the philosopher and psychologist Eugene Gendlin (1962, 1981), suggests that when we have a real insight, we have a total, full experience in which thought, emotion, senses, and the entire body unite. When we understand something so fully, Gendlin calls it a "felt meaning."

The clear implication from Gendlin, Lakoff, and Johnson is that to really understand any concept, we also have to feel it quite deeply:

we need to relate to it in some way. This point has been overlooked by almost all cognitive scientists. They have done much work on cognitive dissonance as a precursor to conceptual change but have done very little work on the emotional aspects of understanding.

Our own solution was to simplify the research and to integrate thought and feeling. Thus we have principles three, four, and five, which simply say as follows:

- Principle Three: The search for meaning is innate
- Principle Four: The search for meaning occurs through patterning
- Principle Five: Emotions are critical to patterning

One of the great sources of confirmation in recent times has come from brain research. As they map neural pathways and explore the chemistry of body and mind, neuroscientists such as Damasio (1994) make statements such as this: "The brain and the body are indissociably integrated by mutually targeted biochemical and neural circuits . . . The organism constituted by the brain-body partnership interacts with the environment as an ensemble, the interaction being of neither the body nor the brain alone" (Damasio 1994, 87–88).

Another neuroscientist, Candace Pert (1997), made a key discovery that supports Damasio. She demonstrated that some of the neurotransmitters (the chemicals that convey information between the synapses that connect neurons in the brain) are also found in the entire immune system. In other words, there are chemical messengers for the emotions that flow throughout the body and every thought, without exception, is influenced by some of these "molecules of emotion."

The practical implication is enormous. If we really want students to master a subject deeply, they must connect with and relate to it, almost as they relate to a friend. This applies to everything from math to economics to art. And that means that schedules, instruction, assessment, and everything else in the school day must be designed with this sort of relationship in mind.

Incidentally, there are some cognitive scientists such as John Bruer (1997, 1999) who argue that brain research has nothing of value for educators at this point in time. They are clearly wrong. The key is to know how to use the brain research by relating it to general principles of human functioning and learning. When we do that, education stands to benefit greatly. However, it is probably educators who have to figure out how to capitalize on the emerging research and to understand that for the time being we need a better grasp of what learning is.

The Real Change—A Perceptual Shift

When we first developed these principles, we found that many educators took the same words and interpreted them very differently. This puzzled us. But as we worked with schools, particularly using our Mindshifts group process (1999), which is a very powerful way of helping educators begin to internalize the principles and make them real, we found that some teachers actually began to look at the world and their students differently. So we researched this difference, and came to a really challenging conclusion: The people who internalized the principles to the point where they became the foundation for their classroom decisions taught differently. From our perspective, they were better at getting students to use more of their brain. Internalizing the principles gave them a "felt meaning" of how students actually learn. Their work in the process groups had given them a clear sense of how they themselves learn and what genuine "whole brain" learning feels like and looks like. This shift in perception resulted in a clear and distinctively altered world view. It is this world view—which we called a perceptual orientation—that makes it possible to make good use of the most powerful and complex teaching strategies.

. . . it is probably educators who have to figure out how to capitalize on the emerging research and to understand that for the time being we need a better grasp of what learning is.

We found that there are four dimensions or qualities that are a critical part of this shift. We observed educators making the following shifts as they moved from one world view to another:

- From the use of *power* and coercion to *empowerment grounded in authenticity*
- From *narrow* to *broad cognitive horizons*
- From *planning for action,* or what to do next, to *self-reference and process*
- From *control* of the learning process to *building relationships that facilitate self-organization*

Cognitive Horizons: An Example

Some people have narrow cognitive horizons. In particular, this means that they see the world as though it is a machine within which everything can be fragmented. With a world view like this, a fragmented curriculum is natural. Each subject seems to be separate. Fifty-five minute blocks of time are fine. Subjects unrelated to actual student experience present no difficulty when notions of an integrated curriculum are presented to people who think like this, they have trouble with it because interdisciplinary teaching and learning literally do not make much sense to them.

One of the facets of what we call broad cognitive horizons is that everything is naturally connected to and a part of everything else. Once teachers can see how subjects relate and interact it becomes easier for them to see how they can "embed" critical curriculum, skills, and facts in student-initiated projects and ideas.

People with broad cognitive horizons understand that, just like in ecosystems, in the real world no subject ever exists alone: Math is a part of science; language is a part of math; history is intimately connected with language; and so on. For these people, the integrated curriculum makes sense at a deep level—they have a felt meaning for it. And that is what it takes to make interdisciplinary teaching work well.

Thus, we have a powerful educational tool—interdisciplinary teaching—but only those with adequate cognitive horizons can make it work.

CONCLUSION

If we want high standards, we must have high standards for staff development. And the best staff development of all works at two levels simultaneously—skill development and personal development. For our students to become all they can be, we must do the same.

The ultimate goal is for educators to step back from "strategies that work" in order to understand how real people and students learn. Once we do that we can begin to revisit all our strategies as we recognize their limitations and potential. The real message is that we all need to be learners, educators and students alike, and that more great strategies alone cannot change education.

REFERENCES

Bruer, J. T. 1997. Education and the brain: A bridge too far. *Educational Researcher* 26(8): 4–16.

Bruer, J. T. 1999, May. In search of . . . brain-based education. *Phi Delta Kappan*, 649–657.

Caine, G., R. N. Caine, and S. Crowell. 1999. *Mindshifts.* 2d ed. Tucson, AZ: Zephyr.

Caine, R. N., and G. Caine. 1997. *Unleashing the power of perceptual change.* Alexandria, VA: Association for Supervision and Curriculum Development.

Damasio, A. R. 1994. *Descartes' error: Emotion, reason and the human brain.* New York: Avon.

Gendlin, E. T. 1962. *Experiencing and the creation of meaning.* Glencoe, CA: The Free Press of Glencoe.

Gendlin, E. T. 1981. *Focusing.* 2d ed. New York: Bantam.

Goleman, D. 1995. *Emotional intelligence: Why it can matter more than IQ.* New York: Bantam.

Lakoff, G., and M. Johnson. 1980. *Metaphors we live by.* Chicago: University of Chicago Press.

Pert, C. B. 1997. *Molecules of emotion.* New York: Scribner.

Changing Curriculum Means Changing Your Mind

by Arthur L. Costa

> Insanity is continuing to do the same thing over and over and expecting different results.
> Albert Einstein

Lord Kelvin, the 19th century British physicist and astronomer said, "When you cannot measure it; when you cannot express it in numbers, your knowledge is of a very meager and unsatisfactory kind."

As we enter the 21st century, this mental set still serves educators as a rationale for justifying curriculum decisions. Much like a dog chasing its tail, the level of adopted curriculum outcomes sets the intent of instruction and the focus of assessment. This cycle seals systems into a mindset that outcomes are significant because they are easily and immediately measured, barring consideration of working for more long-range, enduring, and essential learnings.

Based on this archaic 19th century industrial, reductionist mentality, we have translated our curriculum and assessments into observable, measurable outcomes and performances. We have become fascinated and enamored with

- the amount of time on task
- the number of questions asked at each level of Bloom's Taxonomy (1956)
- gain scores on achievement tests
- class size: numbers of students and ratio of students to adults
- length of time in school, days in attendance, and minutes of instruction
- IQ scores as a basis for grouping

Adapted from *Think Magazine,* October 1998, pp. 14–17.

- percentages of objectives attained
- numbers of competencies needed for promotion or graduation
- school effectiveness based on published test scores
- numbers of As and Bs on report cards (often rewarded with dollars)

As we enter an era in which knowledge doubles in less than five years, and the projection is that by the year 2020 it will double every 73 days, it is no longer feasible to anticipate the future information requirements for an individual. Our increasingly complex world is forcing us to use our brains more. We must think differently and deeply about what learning is and its worth.

> As we let go of the machine models of work, we begin to step back and see ourselves in new ways, to appreciate our wholeness, and to design organizations that honor and make use of the totality of who we are (Wheatley 1992, p. 12).

SHIFTING MENTAL MODELS

The most critical, but least understood, component of school reform is the restructuring of curriculum—it is what drives everything else. We need, in the words of Michael Fullan (1993), to take a "quantum leap" in how we think about and develop curriculum. This article invites a shift in how we think about educational outcomes.

Some educators, legislators, and parents are perceptually bound by outmoded traditions, out-of-date laws, past practices, obsolete policies, and antiquated metaphors. Invested in their present ways of working, they believe that if they can just do what they are presently doing better—give more money to education, hire more teachers, extend the school year, "toughen" teacher certification standards, hold schools more accountable—everything will improve.

For most people, changing mental models implies the unknown—the psychologically unknown risks of a new venture, the physically unknown demands on time and energy, and the intellectually unknown requirement for new skills and knowledge. To adopt a new vision, a shift away from our traditional and obsolescent thinking about learning, teaching, achievement, and talent will be needed. The concepts in this article invite a shift in our present paradigm from quantity to quality. Changing our mental models will require patience, stamina, and courage.

SEVEN CURRICULUM MIND SHIFTS

What follows are descriptions of mind shifts toward a more quantum conception of curriculum.

1. From Transmitting Meaning to Constructing Meaning

Merlin Wittrock (1986) reminds us that the brain's capacity and desire to make or elicit patterns of meaning is one of the keys of brain-based learning. We never really understand something until we can create a model or metaphor derived from our unique personal world. The reality we perceive, feel, see, and hear is influenced by the constructive processes of the brain as well as by the cues that impinge upon it.

Meaning making is not a spectator sport. Knowledge is a constructive process rather than a finding. It is not the content stored in memory but the activity of constructing it that gets stored. Humans don't get ideas; they make ideas.

Humans don't get ideas; they make ideas.

Meaning making is not just an individual operation. The individual interacts with others to construct shared knowledge. There is a cycle of internalization of what is socially constructed as shared meaning, which is then externalized to affect the learner's social participation. Constructivist learning, therefore, is viewed as a reciprocal process in that the individual influences the group and the group influences the individual (Vygotsky 1978).

Our perceptions of learning need to shift from educational outcomes that are primarily an individual's collections of subskills to include successful participation in socially organized activities and the development of students' identities as conscious, flexible, efficacious and interdependent meaning makers. We must let go of having learners acquire *our* meanings and have faith in the processes of individuals' construction of their own and shared meanings through social interaction. That's scary because the individual and the group may *not* construct the meaning we want them to—a real challenge to the basic educational framework with which most schools are comfortable.

2. From Episodic, Compartmentalized Subjects to Transdisciplinary Learning

> . . . there is an underlying unity . . . one that would encompass not just physics and chemistry, but biology, information processing, economics, political science, and every other aspect of human affairs. If this unity were real . . . it would be a way of knowing the world that made little distinction between biological science , physical science—or between either of those sciences and history or philosophy. Once, the whole intellectual fabric was seamless. And maybe it could be that way again. (Cowan, as quoted in Waldrop 1992, p. 67).

Over 350 years ago, Renee Descartes classified knowledge into discrete compartments. He separated algebra from the study of geometry, distinguished meteorology from astronomy, and initiated the concept of hematology.

We are still operating, under this obsolescent rubric, the organization of curriculum into these static compartments while a helpful classification system for allocating time, hiring and training teachers, managing testing, and purchasing textbooks or organizing university departments has probably produced more problems than benefits. Organizing curriculum around the disciplines limits teachers of different departments, grade levels, and disciplines from meeting together, communicating about and finding connections and continuities among students' learnings.

Certain disciplines are perceived to be of more worth than others. Through credit requirements, time allotments, allocation of resources, national, state and local mandates, standards, testing, etc., schools send covert messages to students and the community concerning which subjects are of greater worth. This fractionalization across departments results in incongruent goals among the different people involved.

The disciplines, as we have known them, may no longer exist. With the advent of increased technology and the pursuit of knowledge in all quarters of human endeavor, the separate disciplines are being replaced by human activities that draw upon vast, generalized, and transdisciplinary bodies of knowledge and relationships applied to unique, domain-specific settings. To be an archeologist today, for example, requires employment of radar and distant satellite infrared photography as well as understanding of radioactive isotopes. Professions have combined multiple disciplines into unique and ever-smaller specialties: Space-biology, genetic-technology, neuro-chemistry, astro-hydrology.

What distinguishes the disciplines may be their modes of inquiry. Each content has a logic that is defined by the thinking that produced it: its purposes, problems, information, inferences, concepts, assumptions, implications, points of view, forms of communication, technology and its interrelationships with other disciplines. What makes a discipline a discipline is a disciplined mode of thinking (Paul and Elder 1994). The terms—biology, anthropology, psychology, and cosmology, for example—end in . . . *logy*, which comes from the Greek, meaning logic. Thus, bio-*logy* is the logic of the study of life forms. Psycho-*logy* is the logic of the study of the mind, etc. All areas of study are topics of interest in which something has to be reasoned out. Mathematics means being able to figure out a solution to a problem using mathematical *reasoning*. Any discipline must, therefore, be understood as a mode of figuring out correct or reasonable solutions to a certain range of problems.

The disciplines deter transfer. Knowledge, as traditionally taught and tested in school subjects, often consists of a mass of knowledge-level content that is not understood deeply enough to enable a student to think critically in the subject and to seek and find relationships with other subjects. Immersion in a discipline will not necessarily produce learners who have the ability to transfer the concepts and principles of the discipline into everyday life situations. Students acquire the idea that they learn something for the purpose of passing the test, rather than accumulating wisdom and personal meaning from the content.

The separations of the disciplines produce episodic, compartmentalized and encapsulated thinking in students. When the biology teachers says, "Today we're going to learn to spell some biological terms," students often respond by saying, "Spelling—in biology? No way!" Biology has little meaning for physical education, which has no application to literature and has even less connection to algebra. They may be viewed as a series of subjects to be mastered rather than habituating the search for meaningful relationships and the application of knowledge beyond the context in which it was learned.

Biology has little meaning for physical education, which has no application to literature and has even less connection to algebra.

The disciplines, presented as separate organized bodies of content, may deceive students into thinking they are incapable of constructing meaning. Students frequently have been indirectly taught that they lack the means to create, construct, connect, and classify knowledge. They are taught that organized theories, generalizations, and concepts of a particular discipline of knowledge are the polished products created by expert minds far removed from them. Thus students may think they are incapable of generating such information for themselves. While students are challenged to learn the information, the manner in which such information was created and classified often remains mysterious. All they can hope for is to acquire other peoples' meanings and answers to questions that someone else deems important.

Life in the real-world . . . demands multiple ways to do something well.

We need students to transfer and apply their knowledge from one situation to another, to draw forth from their storehouses of knowledge, and to apply knowledge in new and novel situations. The curriculum should capitalize on the natural interdependency and interrelatedness of knowledge.

We need, therefore, to put together teams of teachers who have been artificially separated by their departments and to redefine their task from teaching their isolated content to instead, develop multiple intellectual capacities of students. Peter Senge (1997) contends that we are all natural systems thinkers and the findings in cognitive research are compatible and supportive of the need to move from individual to collective intelligence, from disciplines to themes, from independence to relationships.

3. From Knowing Right Answers to Knowing How to Behave When Answers Are Not Readily Apparent

Schools tend to teach, assess, and reward convergent thinking and the acquisition of content and with a limited range of acceptable answers. Life in the real-world, however, demands multiple ways to do something well. A fundamental shift is required from valuing right answers as the purpose for learning, to knowing how to behave when we don't know answers—knowing what to do when confronted with those paradoxical, dichotomous, enigmatic, confusing, ambiguous, discrepant, and sometimes overwhelming situations that plague our lives. It requires a shift from valuing knowledge acquisition as an outcome to valuing knowledge production as an outcome. We want students to learn how to develop a critical stance with their work: inquiring, thinking flexibly, learning from another person's perspective. The critical attribute of intelligent human beings is not only having information but knowing how to act on it.

If all people were alike we could have "one size fits all" schools, a common curriculum, and even standardized tests.

By definition, a problem is any stimulus, question, task, phenomenon, or discrepancy, the explanation for which is not immediately known. Thus, we are interested in focusing on student performance under those challenging conditions that demand strategic reasoning, insightfulness, perseverance, creativity, and precision to resolve a complex problem.

As our paradigm shifts, we will need to let go of our obsession with acquiring content knowledge as an end in itself, and make room for viewing content as a vehicle for developing broader, more pervasive and complex goals such as personal efficacy, flexibility, craftsmanship, consciousness, and interdependence (Costa and Garmston 1994).

We must finally admit that process *is* the content. The core of our curriculum must focus on such processes as learning to learn, knowledge production, metacognition, transference of, decision making, creativity, and group problem solving. These *are* the subject matters of instruction. Content, selectively abandoned and judiciously selected because of its fecund contributions to the thinking/learning process, becomes the vehicle to carry the processes of learning. The focus is on learning *from* the objectives instead of learning *of* the objectives (Costa and Liebmann 1997).

4. From Uniformity to Diversity

It is acceptance and trust that make it possible for each bird to sing its own song— confident that it will be heard—even by those who sing with a different voice (Hateley and Schnidt 1995).

Life might seem easier if all members of the learning community thought and acted in a similar fashion. If all people were alike we could have "one size fits all" schools, a common curriculum, and even standardized tests. Human beings, however, are made to be different. Diversity is the basis of biological survival. Each of us has a different genetic structure, unique facial features, a distinguishing thumbprint, a distinctive signature, diverse backgrounds of knowledge, experience, and culture, and a preferred way of gathering, processing, and expressing information and knowledge. We even have a singular frequency in which we vibrate (Leonard 1978). We need to capitalize on these differences to enhance intellectual growth.

Interdependent learning communities are built not by obscuring diversity but by valuing the friction those differences bring and resolving those differences in an atmosphere of trust and reciprocity. Appreciation for diversity can be encouraged by deliberately bringing together people of different political and religious persuasions, cultures, gender, cognitive styles, belief systems, modality preferences and intelligences. In an atmosphere of trust, structuring such diversity within decision-making groups not only enhances the decisions that are made but also stretches members' capacity for flexibility and empathy. Our old perceptions of uniformity need to yield in deference to valuing diversity—the true source of power in today's world.

5. From External Evaluation to Self-Assessment

Evaluation of learning has been viewed as summative measures of how much content a student has retained. It is useful for grading and segregating students into ability groups. It serves real-estate agents in fixing home prices in relationship to published test scores.

Since these new process-oriented goals cannot be assessed using product-oriented assessment techniques, our existing evaluation paradigm must shift as well. Evaluation should be neither summative nor punitive. Rather, assessment is a mechanism for providing ongoing feedback to the learner and to the organization as a necessary part of the spiraling processes of continuous renewal: self-managing, self-monitoring and self-modifying. We must constantly remind ourselves that the ultimate purpose of evaluation is to have students become self-evaluative. If students graduate from our schools still dependent upon others to tell them when they are adequate, good, or excellent, then we've missed the whole point of what self-directed learning is about.

Evaluation, the highest level of Bloom's Taxonomy, means generating, holding in your head, and applying a set of internal and external criteria. For too long, adults alone have been practicing that skill. We need to shift that responsibility to students—to help them develop the capacity for self-analysis, self-referencing, and self-modification. We should make student self-evaluation as significant an influence as external evaluations (Costa and Kallick 1995).

6. From Episodic to Continual Learning

Tolstoy said, "The only thing that we can know is that we know nothing and that is the highest flight of human wisdom."

A great paradox about humans is that we confront learning opportunities with fear rather than mystery and wonder. We seem to feel better when we know rather than when we learn. We defend our biases, beliefs, and storehouses of knowledge rather than inviting the unknown, the creative, and the inspirational. Being certain and closed gives us comfort while being doubtful and open gives us fear.

A great paradox about humans is that we confront learning opportunities with fear rather than mystery and wonder.

From an early age, employing a curriculum of fragmentation, competition, and reactiveness, we are trained to believe that deep learning means figuring out the truth rather than developing capacities for effective and thoughtful action. We are taught to value certainty rather than doubt, to give answers rather than to inquire, to know which choice is correct rather than to explore alternatives.

Our wish is for creative students who are eager to learn. That includes the humility of knowing that we don't know, which is the highest form of thinking we will ever learn. Paradoxically, unless you start off with humility you will never get anywhere, so as the first step you have to have already what will eventually be the crowning glory of all learning: to know—and admit—that you don't know.

7. From Motivation to Liberation

> Children come fully equipped with an insatiable drive to explore and experiment. Unfortunately the primary institutions of our society are oriented predominantly toward controlling rather than learning, rewarding individuals for performing for others rather than cultivating their natural curiosity and impulse to learn (Senge 1990, p. 7)

Human beings are active, dynamic, self-organizing systems with an integration of mind, body, and spirit. According to Wheatley and Kellner-Rogers, "Life's natural tendency is to organize. Life organizes into greater levels of complexity to support more diversity and greater sustainability" (1996, p. 30).

One of the purest examples of a self-organizing learning system that organizes into greater levels of complexity is the young child. Infants and toddlers are in a constant state of exploring everything they can lay their hands, eyes, and lips on. They live in a state of continuous discovery: dismayed by anomaly, attracted to novelty, compelled to mastery, intrigued by mystery, curious about discrepancy. They derive personal and concrete feedback from their tactile/kinesthetic adventures. Their brains are actually being transformed with each new experience.

If we accept that there currently is a shift away from the industrial model of society to a learning society, then our understanding of the focus of education also needs to shift.

As children mature, the constraints of safety, family expectancies, cultural mores, and public decency demand that the child's natural tendencies of exploration be curbed. This provides both tensions and additional learnings as children become acculturated. Unfortunately, training in mental and emotional passivity starts with the first days of school. Traditional school learning may cause students to perceive that the purpose of acquiring knowledge is for passing tests on the content rather than accumulating wisdom and personal meaning from the content. Students learn to read someone else's static accounts of history, study abstract theories of science, and comprehend complex ideas unrelated to their own life experiences and personal aspirations. They perceive learning to be a game of mental gymnastics with little or no relevant application beyond the school to everyday living, further inquiry, or knowledge production.

Thus children, whose natural tendency is to create personal meaning, are gradually habituated to think they are incapable of generating such information for themselves and that they lack the means to create and construct meaning on their own. All they can hope for is to acquire other peoples' meanings and answers to questions someone else deems important. Eventually students become convinced that knowledge is accumulated bits of information and that learning has little to do with their capacity for effective action, their sense of self, and how they exist in their world.

We must vow to serve and maintain this natural tendency of humans to inquire, experience, pattern, integrate, and seek additional opportunities to serve the human propensity for learning. A goal of education, therefore, should be to recapture and sustain the natural self-organizing learning tendencies inherent in all human beings: curiosity and wonderment, mystery and adventure, humor and playfulness, connection and finding, inventiveness and creativity, continual inquiry and insatiable learning.

IN SUMMARY

If we accept that there currently is a shift away from the industrial model of society to a learning society, then our understanding of the focus of education also needs to shift. This change will require a movement away from a measurable, content-driven curriculum to a curriculum that provides individuals with the dispositions necessary to engage in lifelong learning. Simultaneously, the vision of the educator needs to shift from the information provider to one of a catalyst, model, coach, innovator, researcher, and collaborator with the learner throughout the learning process.

Of all forms of mental activity, the most difficult to induce is the art of handling the same bundle of data as before, by placing them in a new system of relations with one another by giving them a different framework, all of which virtually means putting on a different kind of thinking cap for the moment. It is easy to teach anybody a new fact . . . but it needs light from heaven above to enable a teacher to break the old framework in which the student is accustomed to seeing (Koestler 1972).

There is a necessary disruption when we shift mental models. If there is not, we are probably not shifting; we may be following new recipes but we will end up with the same stew! Growth and change is found in "disequilibrium," not balance. Out of chaos, order is built, learning takes place, understandings are forged, and gradually, organizations function more consistently as their vision is clarified, as their mission is forged, and their goals operationalized.

Mind shifts do not come easily, as they require letting go of old habits, old beliefs and old traditions. But in the words of Sylvia Robinson,"Some people think you are strong when you hold on. Others think it is when you let go." How strong are we?

REFERENCES

Bloom, B., and D. R. Krathwohl. 1956. *Taxonomy of educational objectives. Handbook I. Cognitive domain.* New York: David McKay.

Chopra, D. 1993. *Ageless body, Timeless mind.* New York: Harmony Books.

Costa, A., and B. Garmston. 1994. *Cognitive coaching: A foundation for renaissance schools.* Norwood, MA: Christopher-Gordon.

Costa, A., and B. Kallick. 1995. *Assessment in the learning organization: Shifting the paradigm.* Alexandria, VA: Association for Supervision and Curriculum Development.

Costa, A., and R. Liebmann. 1997. *Envisioning process as content.* Thousand Oaks, CA: Corwin Press.

Fullan, M. 1993. *Change forces.* New York: Falmer.

Hateley B. and W. Schnidt. 1995. *A peacock in the land of penguins: A tale of diversity and discovery.* San Francisco: Berrett-Koehler.

Koestler, A. 1972. *The roots of coincidence.* New York: Vintage.

Leonard, G. 1978. *The silent pulse: A Search for the perfect rhythm that exists in each of us.* New York: Bantam Books.

Paul, R., and L. Elder. 1994. All content has logic: That logic is given by a disciplined mode of thinking: Part I. *Teaching thinking and problem solving* 16(5): 1–4. Newsletter of the Research for Better Schools, Philadelphia, PA.

Senge, P. 1990. *The fifth discipline.* New York, NY: Doubleday.

Senge, P. 1997. Forward in Costa, A., and R. Liebmann. (Eds.), *Envisioning process as content.* Thousand Oaks, CA: Corwin Press.

Vygotsky, L. 1978. *Society of mind.* Cambridge, MA: Harvard University Press.

Waldrop, M. M. 1992. *Complexity: The emerging science at the edge of order and chaos.* New York: Touchstone.

Wheatley, M. J. 1992. *Leadership and the new science.* San Francisco: Berrett-Kohler.

Wheatley, M. J., and M. Kellner-Rogers. 1996. *A simpler way.* San Francisco, CA: Berrett-Kohler.

Wittrock, M. 1986. *Handbook of research on teaching.* 3rd ed. New York: Macmillan.

Section 2

Applying Past Knowledge to New Situations: The Capacity to Draw Forth Prior Knowledge and Transfer It to New Situations

Intelligent human beings learn from experience. When confronted with new and perplexing problems they often draw forth experience from their past. They can be heard to say, "This reminds me of . . ." or "This is just like the time when I . . . ." They explain what they are doing in terms of analogies with or references to previous experiences. They call upon their store of knowledge and experience as sources of data to support, theories to explain, or processes to solve each new challenge. Furthermore, they are able to abstract meaning from one experience, carry it forth, and apply it in a new and novel situation.

Some people are not so inclined. They have what psychologists refer to as an "episodic grasp of reality" (Feuerstein 1980). That is, each event in life is a separate and discrete event with no connections to what may have come before and with no relation to what follows.

Furthermore, their learning is so encapsulated that they seem unable to draw forth from one event and apply it in another context.

Similarly in education, educators sometimes approach change in an episodic way. The learning community's vision of desired educational outcomes may become temporarily blurred or obscured by fads, bandwagons, other educational "panaceas," and by pressures from public and vocal special-interest groups. Educational innovations are often viewed as mere "tinkerings" with the instructional program. They are so frequent and limited in impact that educators sometimes frustratingly feel, "this, too, shall pass." Instead of applying what they know about effective instruction, learning, school organization, assessment, and curriculum, educators succumb to current and sometimes politically expedient mandates. While educators need to consider other perspectives, it takes persistence to hold these distractions in abeyance and maintain a focus on the development of intelligences as enduring and essential educational outcomes.

In the second section of this collection, educators are invited to reflect on and apply the intelligent behavior of relating their vast accumulation of educational knowledge to the conduct of the educational enterprise. The first chapter, by Meir Ben-Hur, presents the case for this intelligent behavior: learning and transfer. Educators sometimes forget that the ultimate intent of education is for students to apply learnings beyond the context in which they were learned—in life, in careers, in homes, and in society.

Pat Wolfe and Ron Brandt invite us to draw on our expanding knowledge about brain functioning and apply it to curriculum and instruction.

Robert Sylwester reminds us of what many educators have long held dear—that the arts are basic to all forms of human learning. This is sometimes forgotten when educators are admonished to be accountable, to prove effectiveness by demonstrating increases in test scores, and when told that the arts are a frill.

These authors all remind educators that knowledge is most useful when applied to learnings that students can use in their everyday life, and discuss how educators can draw on their own learnings to meet this purpose.

Learning and Transfer—A Tautology

by Meir Ben-Hur

I recall an experience I had with Linda, a sixth grade student who could compute

$$1/2 + 1/3 + 1/6 = \frac{3+2+1}{6} = 6/6 = 1$$

But when I asked her to explain the following chart,

she named the largest piece of the pie as the "largest third" and the smallest piece as the "smallest third." Her math grade suggested that she is a good learner. What did she learn about fractions? Where is the transfer? Is there learning without transfer?

Teachers struggle with these questions on a daily basis, and they're desperately looking for answers. Teachers want to know how to prepare students to apply learned concepts, skills, and attitudes across time, space, contexts, and contents—in essence, the transfer of learning. This is indeed one of the fundamental issues concerning not only education but various social functions performed at clinics, offices, lecture halls, religious institutions, prisons, laboratories, training simulators, and other settings. Education, training, psychotherapy, even persuasion, are only worthwhile practices when we accept the assumption that learning transfers. Yet, this assumption is subject to a century-old debate and countless research studies.

For thousands of years, educators believed that training in Latin or geometry would show advantages in other fields not previously studied. At the beginning of the twentieth century, this idea was flatly rejected by Thorndike. He argued that teaching Latin or geometry was wasteful because it does not facilitate learners' performance in such mundane subjects as shopwork or bookkeeping. His research concluded that transfer exists only where the learning experiences share "identical elements" with their applications (Thorndike 1906, 246).

Thorndike's work influenced educational practices and supported arguments that counter the old Aristotelian tradition. Such, for example, is the nature of some current opposition to the various new standards in education. Opponents hold that since they do not believe transfer is possible, it is not necessary for all students to learn concepts that are not useful in ordinary life, such as advanced mathematical concepts, and thus advocate a more general, or "watered-down," curriculum for most students.[1]

Immanuel Kant suggested that the mind is an active organ that transforms experiences into a system of thought that, in turn, affects new experiences.

The cognitive revolution of the twentieth century added an important dimension to the debate over the transfer of learning. A growing body of theory and related research has altered the positivistic orientation to the treatment of the construct to a relativistic one—not whether transfer is possible or not, but how or what are the conditions that permit learned experiences to transfer?

LEARNING AS RECONSTRUCTION

Over a century ago, Immanuel Kant (1724–1804) suggested that the mind is an active organ that transforms experiences into a system of thought that, in turn, affects new experiences. This proposition has been one of the pillars of modern psychology.[2] Cognitive development has come to be viewed as a mastery of some hierarchy of skills; education is considered as a field concerned with cognitive development. If we equate learning with experiences that transform systems of thought and promote their development, then we must identify the transfer of learning in the way systems of thought form new experiences. If we accept this conceptual framework, we embrace constructivism.

Constructivism influenced the most prevalent contemporary philosophy of cognitive psychology and education. The origin of this as an educational philosophy can be traced to Jean Piaget's early work during the 1930s and 1940s. Research in this tradition analyzes learning as a process of cognitive reconstruction. It shows that when challenged by incongruent experiences, biologically and experientially mature humans may naturally construct new systems of thought to replace their former ones, that is, new skills, concepts, meanings, attitudes, and dispositions, etc. It confirms that when new systems of thought are crystallized, they replace old ones, determine a person's cognitive performance, and form the basis for future reconstruction. According to this philosophy, educators should seek the most efficient means by which to develop students' appropriate systems of thought, crystallize those systems, and render them flexible enough for adaptation in variable conditions and for future learning.

Theories often evolve from empirical work.

In order to truly understand learning and transfer, it seems that a theory that explains the interrelationship between the two is needed. However, there has been little research that links transfer with learning as it is viewed by constructivists and, for the most part, research on transfer has been independent of research on learning. Nonetheless, existing research is important to defending or refuting current theories of learning and theories of transfer.

MOVING TOWARD A UNIFIED THEORY OF TRANSFER AND LEARNING

Theories often evolve from empirical work. This may well describe the evolution of a unified theory on learning and transfer.

A significant amount of empirical studies have been conducted on transfer. Researchers distinguish between two types of transfer of learning: lateral and vertical (Gagne 1968). They generally define lateral transfer as transfer of skills or concepts across situations, such as in the case of numerical and graphical presentations of fractions similar to those Linda was struggling with, and vertical transfer as transfer between lower-level and higher-level concepts or skills, as in the case of a deeper understanding of fractions in terms of the relative nature of part and whole and their relationships. Some researchers suggest that transfer usually is an interaction of the two types.

Despite Thorndike's conclusion that transfer is dependent on situations that share *identical elements,* researchers have documented cases where lateral transfer occurred as learners recognized the existence of a *relationship* between a learned experience and a new one despite the lack of identical elements (Nisbett, Fong, Lehman, and Cheng 1988).

Vertical transfer represents the construction of concepts and deeper understandings that hold together different applications. Three types of research on vertical transfer are compatible to the constructivist notion of a hierarchy of skills or concepts. One type studies the differences between experts and novices (e.g., Kay and Black 1985; Silver 1979). The results confirm that experts have a deeper (or more abstract) representation of problems, processes, and solutions than those held by novices. The second type shows that developmental hierarchies of skills and concepts indeed exist (e.g., Ferrara et al. 1986). A third type, with mixed results, examines whether learning general or abstract, rules or concepts, such as in statistics or logic, is sufficient for transfer in various contents and contexts (e.g., Lehman and Nisbett 1990; Jackson and Griggs 1988). Although some studies show transfer in such cases, most are disappointing.

Recent research is more eclectic. For example, psychologists concerned with motor development have shown that growth requires both lateral and vertical transfer. Thelen (Thelen and Smith 1994) showed that walking depends on walking-specific and nonwalking-specific skills. She showed that the nonwalking-specific skills must transfer laterally to the walking situation at the same time that the vertical transfer is evident from lower-level to higher-level skills that are walking specific.

Studies differ in their definition of "learning" and in their determination of what constitutes an evidence of transfer. Nonetheless, researchers seem to agree that transfer is not an automatic byproduct of human experiences. Taken as a whole, research supports the idea that at least one condition for transfer beyond similar situations depends on the successful reconstruction of concepts or skills—transfer depends on the quality of the learning experience.

MEDIATED LEARNING EXPERIENCES AND TRANSFER

The concept of mediated learning may be found in different forms in the works of philosophers, psychologists, educators, sociologists, anthropologists, and linguists over the past several decades. In fact, not by much of a stretch of one's imagination, references to this idea may be found in the Old Testament and even, perhaps, in more ancient documents on social issues. It is the sophistication and depth by which this concept has been elaborated upon by the works of Russian social psychologist Lev Vygotsky and Israeli psychologist Reuven Feuerstein that deserve careful analysis.

Early constructivists held that mediated learning does little to help the reconstruction of systems of thought (schemata). They believed that reconstruction is a product of self-discovery (Inhelder and Piaget 1958). This argument was rejected by Vygotsky and, independently, by one of Piaget's own students, Feuerstein. Vygotsky (1978) claimed that every level of human development is a product of learning that starts as an interpsychological (between people) process and continues as an intrapsychological (within the individual) process. Feuerstein similarly argued that the most significant factor in cognitive development, especially early cognitive development, is mediated learning. Both believed that mediated learning fosters the construction of concepts and skills. Furthermore, they both considered the *ability* to construct and reconstruct concepts and skills itself a product of prior mediated learning. In Feuerstein's view, structural flexibility and modifiability are products of mediated learning experiences (MLEs).

Feuerstein similarly argued that the most significant factor in cognitive development, especially early cognitive development, is mediated learning.

Unlike the unfocused learning that may be produced by a person's direct exposure to stimuli (objects, events, data, reading materials, and other sources of information), MLEs are systematic and intentional mediated learning experiences in which a mediator facilitates the reconstruction of the cognitive system. The orientation and direction of the reconstruction are not implicit in the stimuli; rather, they are the sole contribution of the mediator (Feuerstein and Feuerstein 1991). Mediators facilitate the development of ideas, of meanings, of higher levels of understanding. They help the learner move beyond the concrete. Analysis of the concept of mediation suggests important principles for the "teaching for transfer."

THE PRINCIPLES OF THE TEACHING FOR TRANSFER—OR MEDIATION

If the ultimate goal of education is to achieve transfer of learning, then there is no need to consider transfer as an independent construct. Education then is indeed qualified only to the extent that it achieves cognitive reconstruction, or "cultivation" of specific behaviors/understanding of specific concepts, and is quantified in terms of the degree of their crystallization, their stability, and their permanence. This idea is central to Feuerstein's didactic.[3] Teachers who act as mediators *intend* to structurally change, cultivate, and crystallize specific student cognitive behaviors or concepts; they target student cognitive behaviors and/or concepts whose values *transcend* the specific time, place, context, and content they use in teaching; and they form learning experiences that are embued with *meaning*.[4] These ideas often are well received by teachers. However, I have observed that even informed teachers form learning experiences that often stop short of producing complete reconstruction and transfer. I will devote the balance of this discussion to the process that fosters complete cognitive reconstruction.

My model is based on five principles of mediation practices that foster transfer.

- First, learning is accomplished only when a skill, or concept, is crystallized. Therefore, learning must include sufficient *practice.*
- Second, teachers must use a variety of contents and contexts as a vehicle for *decontextualization* of skills or concepts.
- Third, the development of students' deeper understanding *(meaning)* should be facilitated by teacher-led reflective discussions following the learners' experiences.
- Fourth, teachers should lead students in connecting new concepts or skills with students' past experiences *(recontex-tualization).*
- Finally, teachers should encourage students to *realize* situations where their newly acquires skills or concepts will be useful and apply them.

1. Practice

The term *cognitive schema,* or *cognitive structure,* was defined by Piaget in terms of habituated and crystallized cognitive behaviors. New behaviors or concepts that have not been crystallized or habituated were recognized by Vygotsky as belonging to what he called the Zone of Proximal Development. Such behaviors are not consistent and are lost if not reinforced. Crystallized cognitive behaviors are consistent and resistant to change.

The establishment of new cognitive habits or new concepts, and, more so, the correction of inappropriate cognitive behaviors or mis-

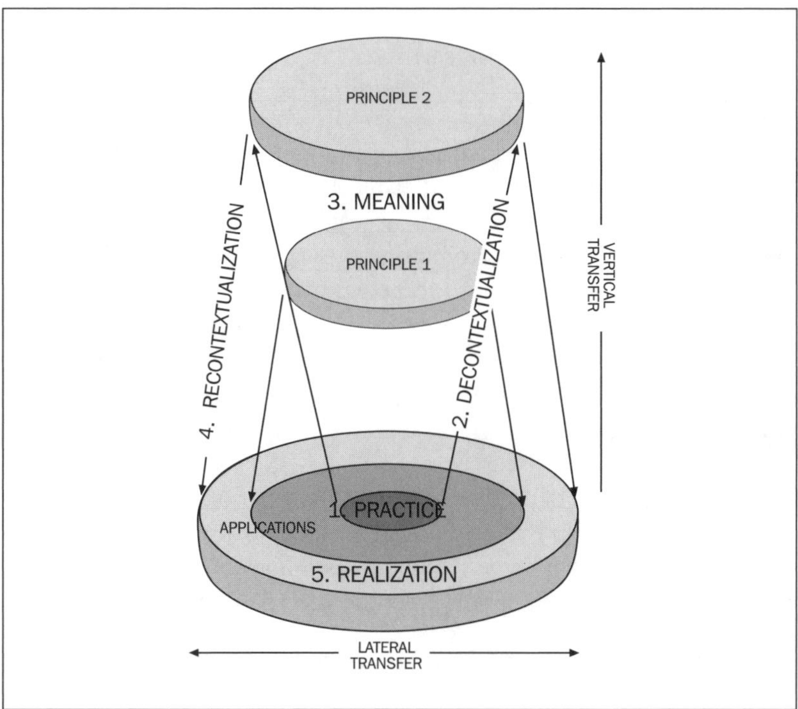

Figure 1

conceptions, requires sufficient practice, namely, a systematic exercise that involves repetitive application. Sufficient practice maximizes the efficiency of the schema in terms of its mobility and the ease by which it is applied. It is a function of the amount and nature of the repetition.

Amount of Repetition

Practice is time consuming. Therefore, it often is the first sacrificed by teachers who feel they are "running out" of time to "accomplish" the expected curricular standards. Teachers often stop the practice as soon as they judge that a "reasonable" number of (or perhaps certain individual) students reach the mastery level. They often assign this part of the learning process as homework that not all students complete or do appropriately (Hunter 1982).

Successful programs such as Feuerstein's Instrumental Enrichment (FIE) stress and demonstrate to teachers and students the return on investment of practice. They show that abilities develop as a curved rather than a linear progression to alleviate their anxiety about the initial slow pace of learning.

Nature of Repetition

Practice often is associated with laborious and tedious processes. Therefore, most students and many teachers resist it.

Since standardized achievement tests and other measures increasingly are used as indicators of teacher accountability, the practice teachers choose often produces "rigid" habits that do not permit generalization. They drill students on specific testlike items that predictively will appear on tests rather than promote the deeper understanding of concepts. Consequently, test results are misleading and student learning is limited.

Optimally, practice can be challenging (not too easy or too difficult), with exercises of gradually increasing levels of complexity and novelty that maintain the level of learners' excitation. It should provide experiences with many various and dissimilar contents while maintaining the focus on the application of the same desired concept or skill.

2. Decontextualization—Distance from a Concrete Learning Context

Ask chess players why they choose a certain move when they play chess and they will show you that this move is guided by a principle they developed about playing chess. Ask a teacher why she consistently acts in a particular way when she teaches and she will show you she is guided by her own principles about good teaching. Such principles may be referred to as metacognitive functions (Brown et al. 1983). As new concepts or new skills develop, learners simultaneously develop principles that support them and relate them to universal applications. For example, as we learn to drive, our principles determine how we use our skills of driving in different conditions. Often, the quality of such principles determine the flexibility by which crystallized behaviors or concepts are applied. The development of metacognition constitutes an important part of the learning process.

By their very nature, metacognitive functions must be free of the context of the learning experience itself. In fact, their quality is largely determined by their distance from the concrete experience that constituted their learning. For example, consider a primary grade student who learned how to solve addition problems only by using Equalize

The Equalize patterns combine features of comparing and change in order to teach primary grade students how to solve addition and subtraction word problems in mathematics like:

Problem 1:
Jim had 4 cookies. Al had 7 cookies. How many cookies would Al have to eat to have as many as Jim?

Problem 2:
Sally had 8 rings. Jan had 5 rings. How many more would Jan have to get to have as many as Sally?

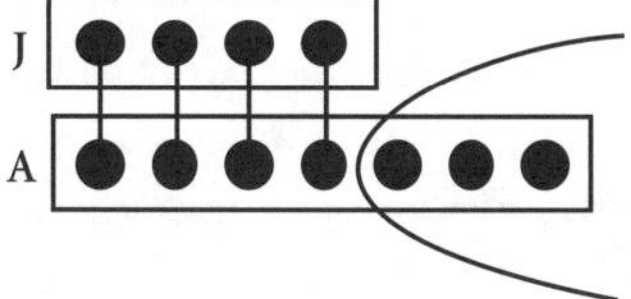

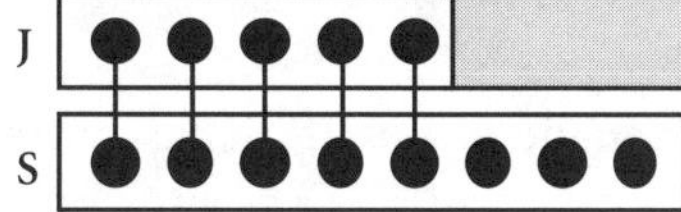

Adapted from "Instructional Representations Based on Research about Understanding," by J. G. Greeno. In *Cognitive and Mathematics Education,* edited by A. H. Schoenfeld. Hillsdale, NJ: Lawrence Erlbaum Associates, 1987.

Figure 2

patterns (see figure 2). This student knows how to solve addition and subtraction problems using Equalize patterns on problems about children eating cookies. This learning does not ensure that the student will be able to use this procedure with other problems.

If students are expected to develop the concept of addition and subtraction, these operations first must be decontextualized in the students' minds from a specific instance of their application in this learning experience. This is true not only in terms of the cognitive nature of the learned skill or concept but also in terms of the motivation of using such skills or concepts.

Feuerstein explained that the automatization of a schema is achieved when its motive is learner intrinsic, that is, when it is connected with "an internal need system which has become detached from and independent of the extrinsic need that initially produced [the learning]" (Feuerstein et al. 1979, 273). The motives that facilitate the learning experiences are associated with the learning situations and contents. They either are linked to social rewards (nontask-related rewards) or to the nature of the specific task but not to the transcending value of the learning. If the transcending value of the new skill or concept is to be motivating, it first must be recognized by the learner. The process that leads to such recognition by the learner is called decontextualization.

There are at least two conditions for the successful decontextualization of learning experiences. First, learners must experience variable applications for their new skills or concepts. For example, a primary grade student needs to practice not only the Equalize patterns system with a variety of problems but also needs to practice other systems of representation for addition and subtraction. For example, they could use different kinds of manipulatives as well as student-made products. Second, they must recognize the relationships that exist among the various representations and identify their similarities in the new terms of addition and subtraction.

A reflective process that follows a practical experience can lead to the induction and conception of metacognitive functions. This process can be facilitated by carefully designed and teacher-led classroom discussions with the intended goal of decontextualization. Discussions that facilitate this process deal with such learning activities as planning, monitoring, comparing, contrasting, classifying, summarizing, evaluating experiences, and reviewing student errors. Reviewing student errors is of special importance.

Student errors are important sources of information for both teachers and students. All too familiar are trial-and-error behaviors. In many cases, these behaviors reflect a lack of student insight and the fragile state of newly developed constructs. The consideration of errors is not only important to the evaluation of a new skill or concept but also to the development of the related metacognitive structure. Since students make errors because former cognitive structures have not been fully modified, errors provide important contexts for mediated learning. Mediators encourage students to evaluate their work and explain it, compare their work to other students', identify and explain the differences and the processes that produced them. Analyzing student errors can guide the process of decontextualization. However, decontextualization does not automatically result in the development of deep meaning.

3. Development of Meaning (Concept, or Principle)

When verbalized, meaningful principles start with words such as *always* or *never* and do not disclose the specific nature of the experiences (content or context) from which they were generated. For example, after several learning experiences, Linda should understand that all 1/a's *always* represent equal parts of the same whole. This "principle" does not disclose the nature of the tasks that originated its conception.

Learners must develop meaning that holds their learning experiences together. When individuals develop principles that are general and meaningful, they are more apt to apply their new related skills or concepts to a wide variety of situations. However, the role of teachers in the students' education of such principles is often subject to a debate among educators. Some experts believe that teachers should explicitly teach principles and others think that students should discover principles on their own.

The idea that abstract, superordinate concepts or principles, hold our experiences together is generally accepted. In fact, this notion is the incentive for the five-billion-dollar industry of educational consulting in the United States. This industry sells powerful behavioral *principles* that promise to improve human output. The results are not always as powerful as the principles themselves.

Consider, for example, the Shewhart Cycle Problem-Solving Process that is used for an employee training program on problem solving (Michel 1992).

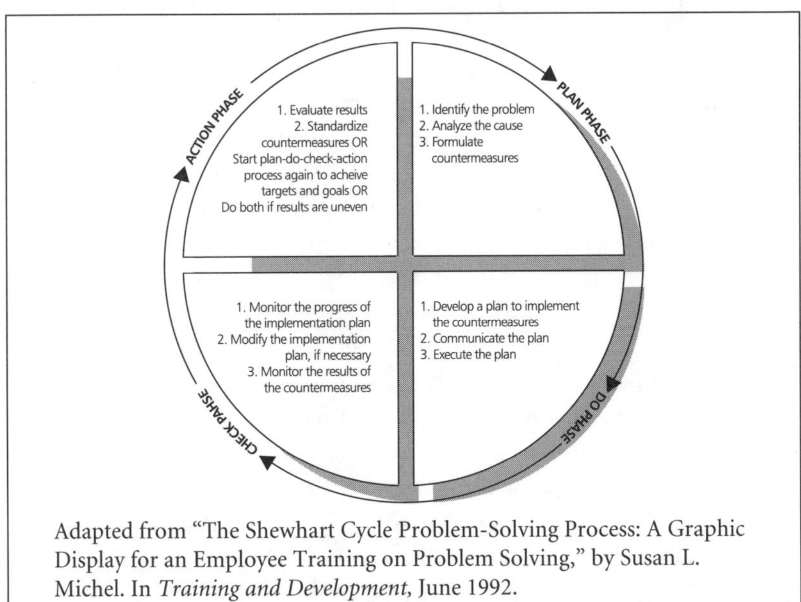

Adapted from "The Shewhart Cycle Problem-Solving Process: A Graphic Display for an Employee Training on Problem Solving," by Susan L. Michel. In *Training and Development,* June 1992.

Figure 3

This model of behavioral principles is undoubtedly valid. Consultants need to do only a little to convince their clients of its validity. Yet, the results generally are poor. Participants learn about the principles but don't apply them in actual situations (Beer et al. 1993). It is clear that meaning must develop as part of guided learning experiences and can not simply be "taught."

It is clear that meaning must develop as part of guided learning experiences and can not simply be "taught."

Traditional constructivism describes appropriate teacher actions in rather passive terms: respecting ideas, accepting ideas, encouraging ideas, promoting collaboration among students, and asking open-ended questions. Recently, some constructivists suggest a more directive didactic as "shap[ing] students' reasoning toward the accepted [science] view through carefully 'scaffolding' their questions," (Driver and Oldham 1986, 113). In contrast to traditional construc-tivism that holds that learning is entirely child-intrinsically driven, Feuerstein's theory of mediated learning requires that teachers interpose themselves between the child and his or her experiences. It argues that to a large extent the diversity in student performance reflects the different needs for mediated learning. For many students, meaningful learning and the development of new concepts can not happen without mediation.

Teachers contribute to meaningful learning by asking questions that otherwise would not be raised in the learners' minds. They ask students to look back when they are looking forward, they ask students to anticipate when they are fixated with a past or present experience, they ask students to compare an experience with other experiences when they may be content with an episode, they ask students to compare their experiences to their friends' when they are satisfied with their own. They ask students to label their experiences and define their learning outcomes when the students think they have already accomplished their learning task. They ask students to give examples to situations where what was learned can be applied when students are ready to move on "to the next chapter." Teachers can help students verbalize meaningful principles as they develop them.

Meaningful principles are far reaching. While every learning experience should produce meaningful principle(s), with more variable experiences the principles reach higher and embrace a wider set of possible applications. Consider, for example, the evolution of

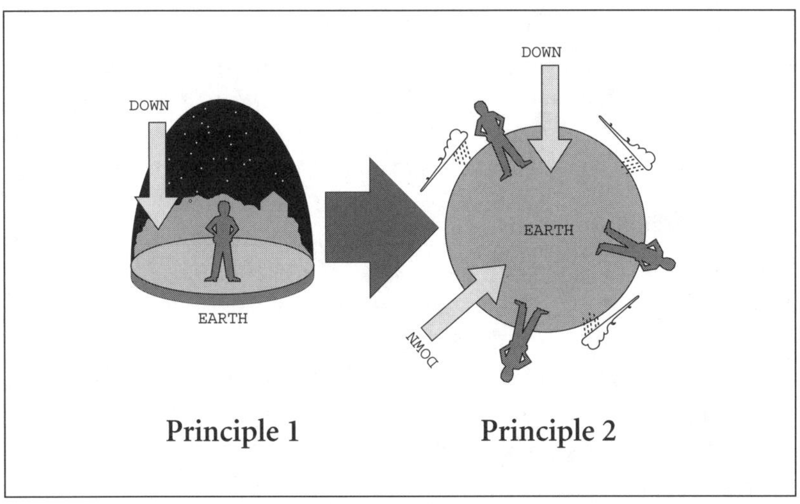

children's notion of Earth's shape and the direction of "down" from the flat Earth and the "absolute down" (principle 1) to the spherical Earth and gravity (principle 2) (Nussbaum 1985; Baxter 1989). This deeper understanding of Earth and gravity reflects a lateral movement.

The meaningfulness of principles may actually be defined in terms of their distance from the actual instances that constituted the original learning task (see figure 1). It does take a longer time and more reflection to achieve higher levels of generalization with all students and it does extend the journey of Socratic questioning beyond what most of us travel.

4. Recontextualization

When we move away from the product-oriented approach to teaching, we consider learning as a process just as crossing a river is a process. When crossing a river, one has to first detach from the bank to travel over the river. Then one travels over the river and lands on the other bank. When learning, one has to first detach from a specific experience and construct a different, higher understanding of it and thereby reach a new application for it.

Recontextualization is the assignment of new meaning to objects, events, or feelings from past or concurrent experiences that previously were unrelated. Recontextualization is a mental act.

The idea that meaning is not implicit in the world of objects, events, and feelings themselves but is only the creation of the mind is quite obvious. However, as teachers, we often realize that meaningful new principles don't necessarily "travel" well into the past experiences of our children. There is a simple explanation. Students need to unlearn past connections in order to allow new concepts to reconnect their past experiences. For example, Linda must first understand that not all numbers represent discrete entities before she can learn fractions.

Teachers must understand that students need time to think and that examples not found by students do not help them form new connections. Wait time is indeed critical.

Experiences are stored in memory in clusters of categories and subcategories, concepts and prototypes. If the mind creates new categories and subcategories, new concepts and new prototypes, then it needs to reprocess and reorganize past experiences. Students' memories are not readily organized to efficiently access situations they have experienced as instances of a newly acquired concept, skill, disposition, belief, or feeling. Their memory has to unlearn past connections first. How can teachers facilitate this process?

Asking students to find examples for a new principle starts a process. However, teachers often do not wait long enough for the completion of the process before they despair and give their own examples or accept poor examples. Teachers must understand that students need time to think and that examples not found by students do not help them form new connections. Wait time is indeed critical. Furthermore, teachers' examples often simply serve as new prototypes and pull the discussion away from the higher grounds of the principle itself. Teachers could facilitate the students' search for examples in a different way.

To use an analogy, consider the case of reorganizing a computer filing system. In reorganizing a computer filing system, it appears that the most efficient process to follow is to systematically take every existing file and distribute its contents in accordance with the new categories. Similarly, teachers can help students reorganize their memory systems by guiding them in the search for examples for a new principle or concept in specific areas rather than having them wonder at large. For example, if the principle learned is phrased as "All 1/3's of the same whole are *always* the same proportion," then Linda's teacher can ask her to think about examples in which the whole consists of discrete elements (e.g., number of cookies, number of foods), examples of the whole as a complete entity (e.g., pie, cake), then of a whole as part of a complete entity (e.g., a half of a watermelon). Then she can ask her to find examples in geography, or science, rather than asking for examples in general.

Finding particular applications for a meaningful principle should not be considered an end in itself. It could provide the means by which learners test the principle they constructed or by which they gain a deeper insight into their learning that allows them to reformulate the principle itself. Teachers should make sure that students are critical about examples, that students examine the relevance of each example or its incongruity with the principle. In this sense, the value of a principle is also determined by the variety of its applications—teachers should encourage students to find different examples. The re-evocation and connecting of present and prior knowledge have to happen in the learner's mind.

Finding particular applications for a meaningful principle should not be considered an end in itself.

Recontextualization of a principle is generally limited to past and concurrent experiences. Realization of a principle is the linking of a principle to future applications.

5. Realization

Realization involves the enaction of a newly learned skill, concept, disposition, or feeling in new contents and/or contexts. In general, educators have considered realization passively as something that will happen automatically and independently of the teacher. They considered it significant only in terms of monitoring and evaluating learning. Research shows that realization requires consistency of teachers' expectations, support, and even coaching.

Consider, for example, the case of fourteen-year-old Chad. I first was introduced to him as a behavior-problem student who was failing school. I was pleasantly surprised to find a very intelligent youngster who expressed a renewed high motivation to succeed academically. But I was even more surprised at his answer (as much as he was at my question) when I asked him why he thought a logical person such as himself was failing school. His answer was simply that academic success has nothing to do with being logical. To him, learning is a mundane, reproductory process (i.e., "cloning" the teacher).

Consider, for example, what would be needed to make the academic learning logical and creative: Consistency in teacher expectations of intelligent student performance; an environment that reinforces or certainly does not penalize such intelligent performance; a system of values and standards that support learning; an environment that fosters the student application of new learning. When I spoke to Chad's teachers, they each had a different opinion of his abilities. Chad had a different opinion of his own abilities, different preferences for his teachers, and his performance was inconsistent, even within a subject area. Chad was apparently a victim of severe discontinuity and inconsistency in his school environment.

The supportive school environment is such that teachers share their teaching goals and assessment with other teachers and parents who interact with the same students. In such an environment, a student who learned a new concept in Class A will be provided an opportunity to apply it in Class B. In fact, students would be *accountable* for the realization of their learning across different academic areas. Or simply put, schooling must continuously coach the realization of students learning (Fullan 1993).

We are still struggling with continuity even within academic areas. Remember Linda, the sixth-grade student who could compute fractions? Linda only learned the power of following a procedure and she will follow it rigorously whenever she sees numerical fraction problems. Yet, she never learned the meaning of fractions.

SUMMARY

Teaching for transfer is a tautology. According to the constructivist theories, meaningful learning always transfers. If transfer is not evident, one must examine the state of the learning process and consider it incomplete. A unified theory of transfer and learning proposes that learning consists of practice, decontextualization, formulation of principles, recontextualization, and realization. Every step of this process must be facilitated and coached by teachers and ultimately be accomplished by the learners. Teaching in this context can be defined as mediation of learning. It is characterized as an intentional teacher action to change students in accordance with goals that transcend the immediate contents and seeks meaningful learning.

NOTES

1 See, for example, Michael Smith's argument for decreasing mathematics education for most students in his article "Why Is Pythagoras Following Me?" *Phi Delta Kappan,* February 1989, pp. 446–454.

2 This is true perhaps with the exception of "behaviorism," which excludes any discussion of the "mind."

3 Interested readers can find a good discussion on mediation in *Mediated learning experience: Theoretical, psychological and learning implications,* edited by R. Feuerstein, P. S. Klein, and A. J. Tannenbaum. London: Freund Publishing House, 1991.

4 For a discussion on the implication of this model to teachers, see my article "Mediation of Cognitive Competencies for Students" in *Phi Delta Kappan,* May 1998, pp. 661–666.

REFERENCES

Baxter, J. 1989. Children's understanding of familiar astronomical events. *International Journal of Science Education* 11: 502–513.

Beer, M., et al. 1993. Why change programs don't produce change. In *The learning imperative: Managing people for continuous innovations,* edited by R. Haas and R. Howard. Cambridge, MA: Harvard Business Review.

Brown, A. L., J. Bransford, R. Ferrara, and J. Campione. 1983. Learning, remembering and understanding. In *Handbook of Child Psychology* 3, edited by P. H. Mussen. New York: Wiley.

Driver, R., and V. Oldham. 1986. A constructivist approach to curriculum development in science. *Studies in Science Education* 13: 105–122.

Ferrara, R. A., A. L. Brown, and J. C. Campione. 1986. Children's learning and transfer of inductive reasoning rules: Studies of proximal development. *Child Development* 57: 1087–1099.

Feuerstein, R., et al. 1979. *Instrumental Enrichment.* Baltimore, MD: University Park Press.

Feuerstein R., and S. Feuerstein. 1991. Mediated learning experience: A theoretical review. In *Mediated learning experience: Theoretical, psychological and learning implications,* edited by R. Feuerstein, P. S. Klein, and A. J. Tannenbaum. London: Freund Publishing House.

Fullan, M. 1993. *Change forces.* New York: Falmer.

Gagne, R. M. 1968. Learning hierarchies. *Educational Psychologist* 6: 1–9.

Greeno, J. G. 1987. Instructional representations based on research about understanding. In *Cognitive science and mathematics education,* edited by A. H. Schoenfeld. Hillsdale, NJ: Lawrence Erlbaum Associates.

Hunter, M. 1982. *Teaching for transfer.* El Segundo, CA: TIP Publications.

Inhelder, B., and J. Piaget. 1958. *The growth of logical thinking from childhood to adolescence.* New York: Basic Books.

Jackson, S. L., and R. R. Griggs. 1988. Education and the selection task. *Bulletin of the Psychometric Society* 26: 327–330.

Kay, D. S., and J. B. Black. 1985. The evolution of knowledge representation with increasing expertise in using systems. Paper presented at the Seventh Annual Conference of the Cognitive Science Society in Boston, Massachusetts.

Lehman , D. R., and R. E. Nisbett. 1990. A longitudinal study of the effects of undergraduate training on reasoning. *Developmental Psychology* 26(6): 952–960.

Lehman, D. R., R. O. Lempert, and R. E. Nisbett. 1988. The effects of graduate training on reasoning: Formal discipline and thinking about everyday-life events. *American Psychologist* 43: 431–442.

Michel, Susan L. 1992, June. The Shewhart Cycle Problem-Solving Process: A graphic display for an employee training on problem solving. *Training and Development.*

Nisbett, R. E., G. T. Fong, D. R. Lehman, and P. W. Cheng. 1988. Teaching reasoning. *Science* 238: 625–631.

Nussbaum, J. 1985. The Earth as a cosmic body. In *Children's ideas in science,* edited by R. Diver, E. Guesne, and A. Tiberghien. Bristol, PA: Open University Press.

Silver, E. A. 1979. Student perceptions on relatedness among mathematics verbal problems. *Journal for Research in Mathematics Education* 10(3): 195–210.

helen, E., and K. E. Adolph. 1992. Arnold L. Gesell: The paradox of nature and nurture. *Developmental Psychology* 28(3): 368–380.

Thelen, E., et al. 1993. The transition to reaching: Mapping intention and intrinsic dynamics. *Child Development.* 64(4): 1058–1098.

Thelen, E., and L. B. Smith. 1994. *A dynamic systems approach to the development of cognition and action.* Cambridge, MA: MIT Press.

Thorndike, E. 1903. *Educational psychology.* New York: Lemke and Buechner.

Thorndike, E. 1906. *Principles of teaching.* New York: Seiler.

Vygotsky, L. S. 1978. *Mind and society: The development of higher psychological processes,* edited by M. Cole, V. John-Steiner, S. Scribner, and E. Souberman. Cambridge, MA: Harvard University Press.

Vygotsky, L. S. 1986. *Thought and language* (Rev. ed.). Cambridge, MA: MIT Press.

What Do We Know from Brain Research?

by Pat Wolfe and Ron Brandt

In July 1989, following a congressional resolution, President Bush officially proclaimed the 1990s the "Decade of the Brain." And indeed in the past nine years, we have seen an unprecedented explosion of information on how the human brain works. Thousands of research projects, books, magazine cover stories, and television specials regale us with new facts and figures, colorful PET scans, and at times, suspiciously simple ways to improve our memories, prevent Alzheimer's, and make our babies geniuses.

Our knowledge of brain functioning has been revolutionized. And many of the new findings have changed medical practice. We have a much better understanding of mental illnesses and the drugs that ameliorate them. Treatment for tumors, seizures, and other brain diseases and disorders has become much more successful.

But what about the educational applications of these new findings? Have we learned enough to incorporate neuroscientific findings into our schools? Is it possible that the Decade of the Brain will usher in the Decade of Education?

INTERPRETING BRAIN RESEARCH FOR CLASSROOM PRACTICE

Brain science is a burgeoning new field, and we have learned more about the brain in the past 5 years than in the past 100 years. Nearly 90 percent of all the neuroscientists who have ever lived are alive today. Nearly every major university now has interdisciplinary brain research teams.

But almost all scientists are wary of offering prescriptions for using their research in schools. Joseph LeDoux from New York University and author of *The Emotional Brain* (1996) says, "There are no quick fixes. These ideas are very easy to sell to the public, but it's too easy to take them beyond their actual basis in science," Susan Fitzpatrick, a neuroscientist at the McDonnell Foundation, says scientists don't have a lot to tell educators at this point. She warns,

> Anything that people would say right now has a good chance of not being true two years from now because the understanding is so rudimentary and people are looking at things at such a simplistic level. (1995, p. 24)

Researchers especially caution educators to resist the temptation to adopt policies on the basis of a single study or to use the neuroscience as a promotional tool for a pet program. Much work needs to be done before the results of scientific studies can be taken into the classroom. The reluctance of scientists to sanction a quick marriage between neuroscience and education makes sense. Brain research does not—and may never—tell us specifically what we should do in a classroom. At this point it does not "prove" that a particular strategy will increase student understanding. That is not currently the purpose of neuroscience research. Its purpose is to learn how the brain functions. Neuroscience is a field of study separate from the field of education, and it is unrealistic to expect brain research to lead directly to pedagogy. So how do we use the current findings?

We need to critically read and analyze the research in order to separate the wheat from the chaff. If educators do not develop a functional understanding of the brain and its processes, we will be vulnerable to pseudoscientific fads, inappropriate generalizations, and dubious programs.

Then, with our knowledge of educational practice, we must determine if and how brain research informs that practice. Educators have a vast background of knowledge about teaching and learning. This knowledge has been gained from educational research, cognitive science, and long experience. Given this knowledge base, educators are in the best position to know how the research does—or does not—supplement, explain, or validate current practices.

Although we must be cautious about many neuroscientific findings, a few are well established. Some validate what good educators have always done. Others are causing us to take a closer look at educational practice.

FINDING ONE

> The brain changes physiologically as a result of experience. The environment in which a brain operates determines to a large degree the functioning ability of that brain.

Researchers agree that at birth, humans do not yet possess a fully operational brain. The brain that eventually takes shape is the result of interaction between the individual's genetic inheritance and everything he or she experiences. Ronald Kotulak, in his book *Inside the Brain* (1996), uses the metaphor of a banquet to explain the relationship between genes and the environment.

> The brain gobbles up the external environment through its sensory system and then reassembles the digested world in the form of trillions of connections which are constantly growing or dying, becoming stronger or weaker depending on the richness of the banquet. (p. 4)

The environment affects how genes work, and genes determine how the environment is interpreted. This is a relatively new understanding. It wasn't too many years ago that scientists thought the brain was immutable or fixed at birth. Scientists had known for some time that with a few specialized exceptions, a child's brain at birth has all the brain cells or neurons that it will ever have. Unlike tissue in most other organs, neurons do not regenerate, so researchers assumed that the brain you had at birth was the brain you were stuck with for life.

However, Marian Diamond and her colleagues at the University of California at Berkeley pioneered research in the mid-1960s showing that brain structures are modified by the environment (Diamond and Hopson 1998). Her research established the concept of neural plasticity—the brain's amazing ability to constantly change its structure and function in response to external experiences. A further finding that should please us all is that dendrites, the connections between brain cells, can grow at any age. Researchers have found this to be true in humans as well as in animals. Contrary to folk wisdom, a healthy older person is not necessarily the victim of progressive nerve cell loss, diminishing memory, and cognitive abilities.

So our environment, including the classroom environment, is not a neutral place. We educators are either growing dendrites or letting them wither and die. The trick is to determine what constitutes an enriched environment. A few facts about the brain's natural proclivities will assist us in making these determinations.

1. The brain has not evolved to its present condition by taking in meaningless data; an enriched environment gives students the opportunity to make sense out of what they are learning, what some call the opportunity to "make meaning."

2. The brain develops in an integrated fashion over time. Babies don't talk one week, tie their shoes the next, and then work on their emotional development. An enriched environment addresses multiple aspects of development simultaneously.

3. The brain is essentially curious—it must be to survive. It constantly seeks connections between the new and the known. Learning is a process of active construction by the learner, and an enriched environment gives students the opportunity to relate what they are learning to what they already know. As noted educator Phil Schlechty says, "Students must do the work of learning."

4. The brain is innately social and collaborative. Although the processing takes place in our students' individual brains, their learning is enhanced when the environment provides them with the opportunity to discuss their thinking out loud, to bounce their ideas off their peers, and to produce collaborative work.

FINDING TWO

IQ is not fixed at birth.

This second finding is closely linked to the first. Craig Ramey, a University of Alabama psychologist, took on the daunting task of showing that what Diamond did with rats, he could do with children. His striking research (Ramey and Ramey 1996) proved that an intervention program for impoverished children could prevent children from having low IQs and mental retardation.

Ramey has directed studies of early educational intervention involving thousands of children at dozens of research centers. The best programs, which started with children as young as six weeks and mostly younger than four months, showed that they could raise the infants' scores on intelligence tests by 15 to 30 percent. It is important to note that although IQ tests may be useful artifacts, intelligence is probably much more multifaceted. Every brain differs, and the subtle range of organizational, physiological, and chemical variations ensures a remarkably wide spectrum of cognitive, behavioral, and emotional capabilities.

FINDING THREE

> Some abilities are acquired more easily during certain sensitive periods, or "windows of opportunity."

At birth, a child's cerebral cortex has all the neurons that it will ever have. In fact, in utero, the brain produces an overabundance of neurons, nearly twice as many as it will need. Beginning at about 28 weeks of prenatal development, a massive pruning of neurons begins, resulting in the loss of one-third to one-half of these elements. (So we lose up to half of our brain cells before we're born.) While the brain is pruning away excess neurons, a tremendous increase in dendrites adds substantially to the surface area available for synapses, the functional connection among cells. At the fastest rate, connections are built at the incredible speed of 3 billion a second. During the period from birth to age 10, the number of synaptic connections continues to rise rapidly, then begins to drop and continues to decline slowly into adult life.

Much credit for these insights into the developing brain must be given to Harry Chugani and Michael Phelps at the UCLA School of Medicine. Phelps co-invented the imaging technique called Positron Emission Tomography (PET), which visually depicts the brain's energy use. Using PET scans, Chugani has averaged the energy use of brains at various ages. His findings suggest that a child's peak learning years occur just as all those synapses are forming (1996). Chugani states that not only does the child's brain overdevelop during the early years, but that during these years, it also has a remarkable ability to adapt and reorganize. It appears to develop some capacities with more ease at this time than in the years after puberty. These stages once called "critical periods" are more accurately described as "sensitive periods" or "windows of opportunity."

Probably the prime example of a window is vision. Lack of visual stimulation at birth, such as that which occurs with blindness or cataracts, causes the brain cells designed to interpret vision to atrophy or be diverted to other tasks. If sight is not restored by age 3, the child will be forever blind. Similarly, the critical period for learning spoken language is totally lost by about age 10. When a child is born deaf, the 50,000 neural pathways that would normally activate the auditory cells remain silent, and the sound of the human voice, essential for learning language, can't get through. Finally, as the child grows older, the cells atrophy and the ability to learn spoken language is lost.

Not all windows close as tightly as those for vision and language development. Although learning a second language also depends on the stimulation of the neurons for the sounds of that language, an adult certainly can learn a second language and learn to speak it quite well. However, it is much more different to learn a foreign language after age 10 or so, and the language will probably be spoken with an accent. We might say that learning a second language is not a window that slams shut—it just becomes harder to open.

The implications of the findings regarding early visual, auditory, motor, cognitive, and emotional development are enormous. Indeed, in many places work has already begun to enrich prenatal and early childhood environments. One example is the application of the research with premature infants. Premature babies who are regularly touched in their incubators gain weight at twice the rate of those who are not touched. Preemies whose parents visit them regularly vocalize twice as much in the third week as babies who are visited infrequently or not at all.

The research findings on early development are in stark contrast with the current situation in society.

- An estimated 12 percent of infants born in this country suffer significant reduction of their cognitive ability as a result of preterm birth; maternal smoking, alcohol use, or drug use in pregnancy; maternal and infant malnutrition; and postbirth lead poising or child abuse (Newman and Buka 1997). Many of these factors could be eliminated with education programs for parents (or future parents). Twenty-five percent of all pregnant women receive no prenatal care.
- The early years, which are the most crucial for learning, receive the least emphasis in federal, state, and local programs. We spend at least seven times more on the elderly than we do on children from birth to age 5.
- About half of all children in the United State are in full-time day care within the first year. Yet many day care centers not only are underfunded, but they are also staffed by untrained, low-paid workers and have too high an adult/child ratio. (Thirty-eight states do not require family child care providers to have any training prior to serving children.)
- Our present system generally waits until children fall behind in school, then places them in special education programs. With intense early intervention, we could reverse or prevent some adverse effects. It is possible that the billions of dollars spent on special education services might be better spent on early intervention.

FINDING FOUR

Learning is strongly influenced by emotion.

The role of emotion in learning has received a good deal of press in the past few years. Daniel Goleman's *Emotional Intelligence* (1995) and Joseph LeDoux's *The Emotional Brain* (1996) have been instrumental in increasing our understanding of emotion.

Emotion plays a dual role in human learning. First, it plays a positive role in that the stronger the emotion connected with an experience, the stronger the memory of that experience. Chemicals in the brain send a message to the rest of the brain: "This information is important. Remember it." Thus, when we are able to add emotional input into learning experiences to make them more meaningful and exciting, the brain deems the information more important and retention is increased.

In contrast, LeDoux has pointed out that if the emotion is too strong (for example, the situation is perceived by the learner to be threatening), then learning is decreased. Whether you call this "downshifting" or decreasing the efficiency of the rational thinking cortex of the brain, it is a concept with many implications for teaching and learning.

EXPECT MORE FINDINGS

On the horizon are many more studies that may have implications for the education of the human brain from birth through old age. Current research areas include these:

- The role of nutrition in brain functioning
- How brain chemicals affect mood, personality, and behavior
- The connection between the mind/brain and the body

Rather than passively wait for research findings that might be useful, educators should help direct the search to better understand how the brain learns. James McGaugh of the University of California at Irvine has suggested that we educators need to be more proactive and tell the scientists, "Here's what we need to know. How can you help us?"

Should the Decade of the Brain lead to an enlightened Decade of Education? Eventually, yes. Along with cognitive research and the knowledge base we already have, findings from the neurosciences can provide us with important insights into how children learn.

They can direct us as we seek to enrich the school experience for all children—the gifted, the creative, the learning disabled, the dyslexic, the average students, and all the children whose capabilities are not captured by IQ or other conventional measures. We can help parents and other caregivers understand the efforts of maternal nutrition, prenatal drug and alcohol use, the role of early interaction, enriched environments. Brain research can also offer valuable guidance to policymakers and school administrators as they strive to focus their priorities.

Does what we are learning about the brain matter? It must, because our children matter.

REFERENCES

Chugani, H. T. 1996. *Fundamental maturation of the brain.* Paper presented at the Third Annual Brain Symposium. Berkeley, California.

Diamond, M., and J. Hopson. 1998. *Magic trees of the mind: How to nurture your child's intelligence, creativity, and healthy emotions from birth through adolescence.* New York: Penguin Putnam.

Fitzpatrick, S. 1995, November. Smart brains: Neuroscientists explain the mystery of what makes us human. *American School Board Journal.*

Goleman, D. 1995. *Emotional intelligence: Why it can matter more than IQ.* New York: Bantam.

Kotulak, R. 1996. *Inside the brain: Revolutionary discoveries of how the mind works.* Kansas City, MO: Andrews & McMeely.

LeDoux, J. 1996. *The emotional brain: The mysterious underpinnings of emotional life.* New York: Simon & Schuster.

Newman, L., and S. L. Buka. 1997. *Every child a learner: Reducing risks of learning impairment during pregnancy and infancy.* Denver, CO: Education Commission of the States.

Ramey, C. T., and S. L. Ramey. 1996. *At risk does not mean doomed.* National Health/Education Consortium Occasional Paper #4. Paper presented at the meeting of the American Association of Science, February 1996.

Art for the Brain's Sake

by Robert Sylwester

George Bernard Shaw suggested that we use a mirror to see our face and the arts to see our soul. Although our physical survival doesn't seem to depend on this aesthetic search for our soul, the visual, aural, and movement arts have long been prominent in human life. Because our visual, auditory, and motor systems are essential to cognition, it's probable that the arts emerged to help develop and maintain them.

Because the arts can be expensive, their presence throughout human history reflects their importance. Creating the long strings of beads discovered in ancient sites required many hours of personal effort (Allman 1996) and buying today's equally nonfunctional string of pearls takes the income from many working hours. The energy and cost are similarly high for the choreography and improvisation of *dance*—from square dancing to ballet, figure skating to hockey, couple dancing to tennis. The visual, aural, and movement arts are expensive, and we pay with little complaint.

What is odd, then, are moves to reduce or eliminate funding for school arts programs (and in this discussion, I'm including physical education and sports within the broad category of the arts). Why would a culture that values aesthetics and peak performance in the arts cut educational programs that prepare the next generation of artists and athletes?

Part of the explanation may lie in the current push for increased school efficiency and economy. Good arts programs are not *efficient.* They're difficult to evaluate in an era concerned with measurable standards. Educators have therefore had to continually justify arts programs, but not algebra or spelling. This justification tends to focus heavily on public performance (concerts, plays, sports, and art

From *Educational Leadership,* November 1998, vol. 56, no. 3, pp. 31–35.

shows) as if that's all that the arts are about. Further, it has led to dubious cause-and-effect claims that the arts improve scores in other curricular areas. It's a real stretch to imagine that the arts emerged aeons ago to enhance spelling and algebra. The arts, language, and mathematics have important biological values in themselves, beyond their marvelous interactive properties. Must math also then enhance music to remain in the curriculum?

. . . the arts (along with such functions as language and math) play an important role in brain development and maintenance . . .

Evidence from the brain sciences and evolutionary psychology increasingly suggests that the arts (along with such functions as language and math) play an important role in brain development and maintenance—so it's a serious matter for schools to deny children direct curricular access to the arts.

The arts are highly integrative, involving many elements of human life. Let's focus on two key elements: (1) the heightened motor skills that we call performance, and (2) the heightened appreciation of our sensory-motor capabilities that we call aesthetics. Humans have a seemingly innate desire to go beyond the mundane, and to do it with style and grace. The discussion below focuses on four emerging themes that help provide biological support for school arts programs that build a basic background in the arts for all students (such as movement skills in physical education and singing in music) and beginning specialization for those whose interests and abilities warrant it (such as in sports and orchestra).

MOVEMENT IS CENTRAL TO LIFE AND TO THE ARTS

Why do we have a brain? Plants seem to do fine without one; many trees far outlive us. We have a brain because we have muscle systems that allow us to move toward opportunities and away from danger. Plants must take whatever comes along, including predators that nibble leaves and commit other indignities. So why would an immobile tree even want a sensory system that could recognize an approaching logger when it is incapable of fleeing the impending assault?

Or consider the sea squirt, which initially swims about until it permanently attaches to a rock or coral. It then begins the rest of its immobile life by eating its now superfluous brain.

Because we humans are mobile throughout life, we need an intelligent cognitive system that can transform sensory input and imagination into appropriate motor output—to decide whether to move or to stay. Mobility is central to much that's human—whether the movement of information is physical or mental. We can move and talk. Trees can't. Misguided teachers who constantly tell their students to sit down and be quiet imply a preference for working with a grove of trees, not a classroom of students.

Although a cognitive decision to move may involve billions of neurons, only about a half-million motor neurons activate the muscle groups that make up almost half our body's weight. Our jointed motor system, with its complex brain-muscle connections, provides our brain with a remarkably effective external mechanism for action. It comprises the toe/foot/leg system that's about half our body's length, the finger/hand/arm system that extends our reach about two feet beyond our body, a flexible neck that increases the geographic range of our head's sensory receptors, and a remarkable mouth that begins digestion and also communicates through both sound and expressive facial movements.

Our sensitive sensory system and finely controlled movements are also central to the visual, aural, and movement arts, whether it's the fine-motor control of a painter, the practiced pizzicato of a violinist, or the choreographed pick-and-roll of an NBA team.

Consider the cultural significance of virtuosity in our three bottom-to-top motor systems (the movers, the handlers, and the talkers): the legs of skaters, runners, and dancers; the expressive hands of pianists, artists, and mimes; the mouth of speakers, singers, and horn players. Our culture values them all because they so celebrate what are otherwise simple, ordinary movements. How can one promote a curriculum that reduces the acceptable movement of this magnificent appendage system to one hand laboriously writing words on a playing field the size of a sheet of typing paper? It's bizarre.

Some argue that schools aren't in the business of developing such skills at the virtuoso level, that basic motor skills should suffice. OK, but I wonder why these same people relentlessly press for (1) higher performance standards in curricular areas whose skill component is being displaced by computer technology and (2) the simultaneous reduction of programs that move students from basic to advanced levels in arts areas that are so central to the human spirit.

SOPHISTICATED MOVEMENTS MUST BE LEARNED

Developing smoothly controlled muscular systems is a priority of childhood and adolescence. Suckling is almost the first mobile act of an infant, followed by the brain-outward maturation of the arm and leg systems—eating before grasping before walking. Because mobility is a central human characteristic, these innate systems must develop early at the survival level without formal instruction or even mimicry (blind children master walking without ever having observed it). This development includes specific, currently ill-understood periods during which various specialized brain systems develop (such as walking at about age 1, talking at about age 2).

Children denied the opportunity to develop a survival skill that they would normally master with ease during its *window of opportunity* may not recover from the deprivation. A good example is the tragic case of Genie. By the time she was discovered at 13, her disturbed parents had almost totally deprived her of normal language development. Competent therapists who tried to undo the damage were only marginally successful (Rymer, 1993).

Our brain's language and music systems both must be developmentally stimulated—and especially those subsystems that regulate highly controlled motor activity.

Most folks realize that the neural systems that process language must be stimulated through conversation to master the local language, and we correctly insist that schools focus on the key elements. Within the same student brain, however, is another set of neural systems that processes musical forms distinct from language. Song uses such elements as tone, melody, harmony, and rhythm to insert important emotional overtones into a now slowed-down verbal message. Our brain's language and music systems both must be developmentally stimulated—and especially those subsystems that regulate highly controlled motor activity (such as speaking, singing, writing, and playing musical instruments).

Both language and music permeate our environment. How can anyone justify a curriculum that seeks to develop language but not musical capabilities? Is spelling really *biologically* more important than melody, when both express culturally significant sequential information? Are our innate music networks something like unwanted tonsils or appendix tissue to be removed rather than to be understood and enhanced? How can anyone have such a limited view of our brain and the curriculum? Recall the plight of Genie. How many musically limited students are now emerging from school, having had practically no competent professional development of their innate musical ability—or for that matter, of their spatial processing centers that are so central to the visual and movement arts?

We're born into a complex world with an immature brain that is one-third its adult size. Because we can live in a wide variety of environments, our sensory-motor development beyond our innate survival needs tends to focus on the specific environmental demands that each brain confronts.

Highly specialized and coordinated movement patterns, such as those used in calligraphy, violin playing, and tap dancing, must thus be taught, and mastery is typically difficult. The importance of the early acquisition of such skills was demonstrated in a recent study of right-handed violinists (Elbert, Pantex, Wienbruch, Rockstroh, & Taub, 1995). Separate, specific brain areas control right-hand and left-hand finger movements. Violinists who began lessons before the age of 12 developed important differences in the size and complexity of these motor areas, which didn't develop in nonviolinists (who had little need for left-hand digital dexterity) or even in good violinists who began later.

Michael Jordan, a basketball superstar, is another interesting example (Klawans, 1996). At 31, he decided to switch to baseball. With all his athletic ability and resolve, he didn't do nearly as well as he had hoped. Throwing a basketball through a hoop requires sensory-motor skills different from those needed to hit a baseball approaching at 90 miles an hour. Even major-league pitchers are not recycled into hitters when their pitching abilities wane.

Survival-level cognitive and motor skills are universal and innate. Early instruction and effort can get us beyond mere survival levels into the normal limits of human capability. Virtuoso-level abilities are highly specific and require the commitment of early and extensive training. Many young people exhibit this skill-specific commitment when they continually practice specialized skills. Call it play if you will, but Jean Piaget suggested that play is the serious business of childhood.

SMOOTH MOVEMENTS ENHANCE SELF-CONCEPT

Scientists have recently been exploring fluctuations in the levels of the neurotransmitter serotonin. Serotonin inhibits quick motor responses and thereby enhances relaxation and the calm assurance that leads to smoothly controlled and coordinated movements. Because effective movement is so central to human life, it's not surprising that serotonin fluctuations help regulate our level of self-esteem and our position in movement-related social hierarchies. Our own awareness of our increased motor skills and the positive feedback of others play key roles. Most people periodically experience bursts of self-esteem—if only after making a neat turn on the dance floor.

Our culture spends heavily to develop and appreciate virtuosity in aesthetic movement patterns—sports, concerts, theater, dance.

Elevated serotonin levels are associated with high self-esteem and social status, and reduced serotonin levels, with low self-esteem and social status. In motor terms, low serotonin levels cause the irritability that leads to impulsive, uncontrolled, reckless, aggressive, violent, and suicidal behavior (Sylwester, 1997).

This knowledge about serotonin suggests that good school arts and physical education programs can play an important role in developing the fine-motor control that allows youngsters to discover how remarkable the human body is—whether it's drawing a picture with tightly controlled movements or dancing with abandon. Human mobility isn't just about getting from here to there. It's doing it with style and grace. The arts are often the celebration of the ordinary, but we tend to celebrate artists, musicians, dancers, and athletes whose movement patterns are extraordinary.

VIRTUOSO MOVEMENTS ARE TRANSCENDENT

Our culture spends heavily to develop and appreciate virtuosity in aesthetic movement patterns—sports, concerts, theater, dance. Scientists now know that the initial instruction for many such abilities must begin early, and we can argue that it shouldn't depend entirely on parental ability to finance private lessons if our entire culture benefits from the abilities.

But we can run only so fast and jump only so high. Some people devote years of their youth trying to jump an inch higher than anyone else has ever jumped. Others are content to use a ladder. Technologies are thus another way to go beyond normal human limitations—whether it's using a calculator to compute, a phone book to extend memory, a drum to increase the sound of chest beating, or skates to create an art form out of slipping on ice.

Some people move artistically and others just watch other people move. People who don't sing attend concerts; people who don't play attend sporting events; people who don't paint purchase paintings. One marvelous aspect of the arts is that they cognitively stimulate both those who do them and those who observe others do them. The arts are a total win-win situation. The doers and the observers both discover something about the further reaches of being human. Art appreciation (or aesthetics) is thus an important element of an arts education.

The arts may provide another important cognitive service, however. We have multiple neural systems to process emotion and intelligence, and some may infrequently activate in real life. The arts (and probably our dreams) help maintain the strength of such systems by activating them in stimulating *pretend* situations during periods when real life doesn't challenge them. Use it or lose it is a cognitive reality for neural systems tuned to the challenges of the immediate environment.

For example, fear is a key alerting emotion (with a distinct neural system) that may infrequently activate in real life. But the arts frequently activate it. Is the universal childhood attraction to fearful fairy tales and other scary stories and games related to an unconscious need to develop our fear-system responses in playful non-threatening situations so that the system will function effectively in real-life threatening situations? Consider other basic emotions: anticipation, surprise, joy, sadness, acceptance, disgust, anger. The arts embrace them all—whether it's the joyful emotional release of a clown's comedy, the disgust of war elicited by Picasso's *Guernica*, the exciting anticipation of the unknown ending of a close sporting event, or the sudden alertness brought about by the crescendo bars of Haydn's *Surprise Symphony*.

The situation is similar with our multiple intelligences systems. The arts develop and rehearse many of these—a pianist simultaneously activates bodily-kinesthetic, musical, and intrapersonal systems; children playing a team game simultaneously activate just about all systems. Or consider the task that young children face when learning the completely arbitrary 26-letter sequence of the English alphabet. Most of us have trouble remembering the 10-digit sequence of an area code and phone number. Children use a simple melody to easily master an abstract 26-unit sequence, ending the song with a request that the adults be impressed. We truly are. Try it without musical support.

Emotion drives attention and attention drives learning, problem solving, behavior, and just about everything else.

Emotion is an unconscious body and brain system that alerts us to dangers and opportunities. It activates our powerful, multifaceted attention system in order to organize the myriad conscious and unconscious rational systems that our brain uses to solve the current challenge. Emotion and attention thus become the pathways into all rational cognitive behavior. Consider the cognitive plight of those with disorders of their emotion and attention pathways—ADHD, anxiety, autism, bipolar disorder, dyslexia, mental retardation, obsessive-compulsive disorder, schizophrenia.

Emotion and attention are thus critically important brain systems that must be nurtured beyond their innate initial survival levels into the limits of human capability. They're the unconscious doorway into a cortical room abuzz with conscious conversation and problem solving. Unfortunately, schools currently tend to value the conscious conversation and solutions, not the unconscious doorway to the solutions (Goleman, 1995). We can access our rational/logical thoughts through easily measured language, but our unconscious emotion/attention only through difficult-to-measure, nonverbal body states and feelings—our conscious awareness of unconscious emotions (LeDoux, 1996).

Emotion and attention (which are central to all activity in the arts) often lead us to important rational behaviors that wouldn't have emerged if we hadn't walked through that arts-enhanced doorway. Emotion drives attention and attention drives learning, problem solving, behavior, and just about everything else.

THE ARTS ARE A WISE EDUCATIONAL INVESTMENT

It's probably appropriate that emotion, attention, and their arts-handmaiden don't lend themselves to the easily measurable efficiency of rational thought. One can argue for the biological value of an alerting/focusing system that can rapidly size up and respond to the flow of things, untrammeled by conscious factual detail, verbal categorization, and precise evaluation. The regrets that follow precipitous decisions are preferable to death from delay. This may be why emotionally improvised movements are such a stimulating element of the arts—whether it's the broken field run of a football halfback, the intricate interplay of a jazz trio, or the flow of an abstract painting.

Emotion, attention, and the arts aren't about the security of a correct answer, but rather about a jack-of-all-trades emotional brain that has quick, multiple, inventive solutions to most problems. Even when a part of the response pattern is set, improvisation can occur within the response. Ten pianists playing the same sonata will play it 10 different ways.

To argue for the importance of emotion and attention in cognition doesn't suggest that reason and logic are unimportant. Reason and logic consciously move us toward an intelligent, learned response that's typically our first choice when we confront the problem again. Our brain thus developed two separate but integrated systems, and the transcendent movement patterns that characterize the arts often provide the integration between emotion/attention and reason/logic. Only the mindless would suggest that education can function with one system but not with the other. Only the unimaginative would suggest that both systems must be judged by the same criteria of economy, efficiency, and objective measurability.

This discussion of the arts began with the importance of *motion,* and it ends with the importance of *emotion.* Both are central to the arts and to life. They're two inseparable sides of a very valuable biological coin that each generation must invest in its young. School arts programs are a worthy investment of that coin.

REFERENCES

Allman, W. (1996, May 20). The dawn of creativity. *U.S. News and World Report,* 53–58.

Elbert, T., Pantex, C., Wienbruch, C., Rockstroh, B., & Taub, E. (1995). Increased cortical representations of the fingers of the left hand in string players. *Science, 270,* 305–306.

Goleman, D. (1995). *Emotional intelligence: Why it can matter more than I.Q.* New York: Basic Books.

Klawans, H. L. (1996). *Why Michael couldn't hit: And other tales of the neurology of sports.* New York: Freeman.

LeDoux, J. (1996). *The emotional brain: The mysterious underpinnings of emotional life.* New York: Simon & Schuster.

Rymer, R. (1993). *Genie: An abused child's flight from silence.* New York: HarperCollins.

Sylwester, R. (1997). The neurobiology of self-esteem and aggression. *Educational Leadership, 54*(5), 75–79.

Section 3

Metacognition: The Human Capacity to Be Aware of and Reflect on Our Own Thinking

When the mind is thinking it is talking to itself—Plato

Metacognition occurs in the neocortex and is the ability individuals have to know what they know and what they don't know. It is one's ability to plan a strategy for producing the information that is needed, to be conscious of one's own steps and strategies during the act of problem solving, and to reflect on and evaluate the productiveness of one's thinking. The major components of metacognition are developing a plan of action, maintaining that plan over a period of time, and then reflecting back on and evaluating the plan upon its completion. Planning a strategy before embarking on a course of action assists individuals in consciously keeping track of the steps in a sequence of planned behavior for the duration of the activity. It facilitates making temporal and comparative judgments, assessing readiness for more or different activities, and monitoring interpretations, perceptions, decisions, and behaviors.

Intelligent people plan for, reflect on, and evaluate the quality of their own thinking skills and strategies. Metacognition means becoming increasingly aware of one's actions and the effect of those actions on others and on the environment; forming internal questions as one searches for information and meaning; developing mental maps or plans of action; mentally rehearsing prior to performance; monitoring plans as they are employed; being conscious of the need for midcourse correction if the plan is not meeting expectations; reflecting on the plan upon completion for the purpose of self-evaluation; and editing mental pictures for improved performance.

In section three, the authors examine the metacognitive processes of decision making and greater awareness of one's own in-the-moment-thinking about educational practices.

Using the metaphor of a computer's working memory, Robin Fogarty's chapter presents its case by suggesting that what individuals pay attention to is a conscious choice; what they decide to internalize is determined by what they feel is relevant—their emotional attachments, interests, and needs.

Robert Sternberg examines the metacognitive process by suggesting that creativity is a conscious decision. He believes that if individuals choose to be creative, they must take part in a complex set of decisions if their creativity is to reach fruition.

Pat Wolfe defines the teaching act as a series of decisions that teachers make and discusses how research in the neurosciences support those thoughtful processes that teachers engage in before, during, and after instruction.

Donna Ogle invites educators to draw on their understanding of Howard Gardner's theories of multiple intelligences and apply them to effective reading instruction. She provides a host of teaching practices that are applicable in a wide range of classroom settings.

These authors all discuss using metacognition to make teaching practices and student learning more effective, reflective, and self-evaluative.

Memory, the Thing I Forget With

by Robin Fogarty

I once laughed at the line, "Memory, the thing I forget with," but I have repeated it many times in my talks on cognitive behavior. In fact, I use the ambiguity of the statement to make a point about the memory system. Memory is the thing I forget with because the brain is designed that way. In an intricate and complex system, the brain is programmed to let go of information that is not needed (Sylwester 1995). If, however, the brain is emotionally hooked (Goleman 1995) into paying attention to some incoming input, the converse is also true. While the brain drops out the information judged to be unimportant, it in turn, hangs onto or keeps other information. In this second scenario, the brain is alerted to take notice and the memory mechanism goes into high gear (Sousa 1995). Therefore, paradoxically, memory is the thing I forget with . . . and the thing I remember with. If that incoming data gets my attention, if it is instantaneously coded as important, it literally, as my friend, Michael would say, "Gets on my screen" (Fogarty 1998).

A closer look at this concept of memory leads naturally to the idea of learning. In fact, with the emergence of advanced technologies for brain-imaging techniques, scientists are now able to visually track the memory process and they're better able to understand the role of memory in how people actually learn. Interestingly, while memory and learning are inextricably linked in the literature and in our dialogue about how one learns, recent findings on the memory system shed new light on the complexity of the process (Sylwester 1995). These reports suggest strongly that memory is stored all over the brain, which suggests that learning seems to be less localized than originally thought (Sylwester 1995). This evolving thinking on the memory/learning system is so critical, Sylwester predicts that future

---

brain research will focus on the role of emotions, attention and memory as we pursue our understanding of how people learn.

Let's explore more deeply the various phases of the memory/ learning process and, following Michael's metaphor, let's examine how the brain decides whether or not I can say, "It's on my screen"; it's in my memory bank; it's in my learning repertoire. Let's unravel the paradox of memory as a function of forgetting, as well as a function of remembering.

If it gets my brain's attention, "It's on my screen," and, I can start to do something with it.

According to Wolfe (1994), there are a number of phenomena that impact on memory: *sensory input, attention, meaning and relevance. Sensory memory* results when sights, sounds, tastes, smells, and touches are noticed by the brain. If there is no notice taken, no attention to the incoming data, the information never gets into the brain in the first place. Therefore, sometimes it's not a matter of forgetting something, but rather a matter of never noticing it in the first place.

IT'S ON MY SCREEN

Attention, then comes into play. It is the key to memory and learning (Sylwester 1995), and attention can be an elusive thing. So, how do we get the brain to attend to the sensory input in ways that alert the memory system? It seems that the answer here lies in the realm of the emotional intelligence system (Goleman 1995). It seems that without an emotional hook, some emotional connection to the incoming sensory input, there is no attention to the information and thus no memory of it. In other words, sensory input must have an emotional tie-in to get my brains attention. If it gets my brain's attention, "It's on my screen," and, I can start to do something with it.

An example of this concept of an emotional hook to the sensory input is when someone is introduced to me, and a moment later, I have to say, "What was your name, again?" The initial introduction, for some reason, does not alert my emotional brain to pay attention, so my brain simply decides that the information is not important enough to notice. I am probably busy thinking about other things . . . probably what genius response I am going to make to this person. However, when I realize it's time to address this person, the emotion of anticipation takes over and I say, "What was your name, again? Now, my brain is consciously on alert for the incoming input. I am attentive and awaiting the information for coding and placement in my memory. That's when I can say, "It's on my screen."

IT'S ON MY DESKTOP

Once the information is on my screen, I am able to start processing it in my quest to make sense of it. The brain searches for ways to connect this to something it already knows (Caine and Caine 1991), to tie it to some prior knowledge or past experience that has *meaning* for me. This is how the memory/learning system begins to put this idea into short-term memory. For example, as the person talks with me and suddenly gets my attention with a reference to Santa Fe, I immediately begin to create mental images of the scene, based on previous pictures in my mind of similar scenes that are in my memory bank. While the pictures may not actually be similar, they are in my mind because it's the only reference I have. It fits my schemata. But, more importantly, I recognize that at this moment, "It's on my desktop," because I have it in working memory. I'm doing something with the information. I'm beginning to make sense of it and crystallize it in my mind.

"It's on my desktop," because I have it in working memory. I'm doing something with the information.

IT'S ON MY MENU

It is beginning to have relevance for me because it's connecting to me personally and it's evoking emotional tie-ins. *Relevance* is another key to unlocking the mysterious marvel called memory. When my brain senses something has relevance, I have reason to want to hold onto to it. If my mind thinks I need the data, it pays attention, processes, rehearses and stores the information. Once stored, of course, the expectation is that it can be readily retrieved.

To continue the computer screen metaphor a bit further, first, "It's on my screen", because I am emotionally hooked to pay attention. Then, "It's on my desktop", as meaning becomes more clear and my mental connections take hold. In my pragmatic brain, I look for relevance and reason to continue to keep this information. Once I know that it is useful, that it's likely that it can be used in the future, "It's on my menu." It's there in working memory for quick reference when needed. In the case of the new acquaintance hooked into my short-term memory with the reference to Santa Fe, I have now connected this person to some of my experiences there and therefore the meeting has meaning.

IT'S ON MY HARD DRIVE

Later, as I mention the person in a letter to a friend in Santa Fe, the memory has transcended into a personally relevant episode. I can say, at this point, "It's on my hard drive," because it's been placed into long-term memory for storage. It is now believed that memory is stored in multiple modes and the same memory chunk can be cued in a number of different ways. For example, this memory may be retrieved through the idea of Santa Fe, the friend who introduced us, or even the friend I have written to. In addition, it may be revisited through a visually similar face, or similarly sounding name or even through the sense of smell as I notice the fragrance of the cologne the person had been wearing.

"It's on my hard drive," because it's been placed into long-term memory for storage.

With this recursive process called memory/learning more fully exposed, the initial dilemma of memory as the thing I forget with or memory, the thing I remember and learn with, seems even more genuine. If my brain is to retain the information, it seems that it must be emotionally linked to the incoming sensory input. Otherwise, the data never actually gets on my screen Therefore, it's not as much about forgetting, as it is about whether or not my brain decided to hit the save key. Once that miraculous memory cycle is ignited, through sensory input, attention, meaning and relevance, you can be sure, something's going to be on my screen!

REFERENCES

Baron, J. B., and R. J. Sternberg. (Eds.). 1987. *Teaching thinking skills: theory and practice.* New York: W. H. Freeman and Company.

Barrett, S. L. 1992. *It's all in your head: A guide to understanding your brain and boosting your brain power.* Minneapolis, MN: Free Spirit Publishing Inc.

Bloom, F. E., and A. Lazerson. 1988. *Brain, mind, and behavior.* 2nd ed.. New York: w. H. Freeman and Company.

Brandt, R. (Moderator.). 1997. *How should educators use the new knowledge from the brain research?* ASCD 52nd Annual Conference. Alexandria, VA: Association for Supervision and Curriculum Development.

Caine, R. N., G. Caine, and S. Cromwell. 1994. *Mindshifts: A brain-based process for restructuring schools and renewing education.* Tucson, AZ: Zephyr Press.

Caine, R. N., and G. Caine. 1997. *Education on the edge of possibility.* Alexandria, VA: Association for Supervision and Curriculum Development.

——. 1991. *Making connections: Teaching and the human brain.* Alexandria, VA: Association for Supervision and Curriculum Development.

Calvin, W. H. 1996. *How brains think: Evolving intelligence, then and now.* New York: Basic books.

Damasio, A. R. 1994. *Emotion, reason, and the human brain.* New York: Avon Books.

Fogarty, R. 1997. *Problem-based learning and other curriculum models for the multiple intelligence classroom.* Arlington Heights, IL: IRI/SkyLight Training and Publishing, Inc.

Goleman, D. 1997. Emotional intelligence: A new model for curriculum development. ASCD 52nd Annual Conference. Alexandria, VA: Association for Supervision and Curriculum Development.

Hart, L. A. 1983. *Human brain, human learning: Books for educators.* Kent, WA.

Healy, J. M. 1990. *Endangered minds.* New York: Touchstone.

——. 1987. *Your child's growing mind: A guide to learning and brain development from birth to adolescence.* New York: A Main Street Book Doubleday.

Hermann, N. 1988. *The creative brain.* Lake Lure, NC: The Ned Hermann Group.

Howard, P. J. 1994. *The owner's manual for the brain: Everyday applications from the mind-brain research.* Austin, TX: A Bard Productions Book.

Jensen, E. 1995. *The learning brain.* Del Mar, CA: Turning Point.

——. 1997. *Brain compatible strategies: Hundreds of easy-to-use brain-compatible activities that boost attention, motivation, learning and achievement.* Del Mar, CA: Turning Point Publishing.

——. 1997. *Links between diversity training and brain research.* ASCD 52nd Annual Conference Audiotape. Alexandria, VA: Association for Supervision and Curriculum Development.

——. 1996. *Brain research/learning.* National Conference of Texas. Austin, TX: Reliable Communications.

——. 1996. *Completing the puzzle: A brain-based approach to learning.* Del Mar, CA: Turning Point Publishing.

——. 1988. *SuperTeaching: Master strategies for building student success.* Del Mar, CA: Turning Point for Teachers.

Kotulak, R. 1996. *Inside the brain.* Kansas City, MO: Andrews and McMeel A University Press Syndicate Company.

Margulies, N. 1997. *Inside Brian's brain: Interactive comics, Volume 3.* Tucson, AZ: Zephyr Press.

Parker, S. 1995. *Brain surgery for beginners and other major operations for minors: A scalpel-free guide to your insides.* Brookfield, CT: The Millbrook Press.

Perkins, D. 1992. *Smart schools: From training memories to educating minds.* New York: The Free press.

Potter, B., and S. Orfali. 1993. *Brain boosters: Foods and drugs that make you smarter.* Berkeley, CA.

Rico, G. 1991. *Pain and possibility: Writing your way through personal crisis.* New York: G. P. Putnam's Sons.

Sousa, D. A. 1995. *How the brain learns.* Reston, VA: National Association of Secondary School Principals.

Sperry, R. W. 1968. Hemisphere disconnection and unity conscious awareness. *American Psychologist* 23(10): 723-733.

Sternberg, R. J. 1986. *Intelligence applied: Understanding and increasing your intellectual skills.* New York: Harcourt Brace Javanovitch Publishers.

Sternberg, R. J., and C. A. Berg. 1992. *Intellectual development.* New York: Cambridge University Press.

Sylwester, R. 1996. *A celebration of neurons: A conversation about the educational applications of recent cognitive science developments.* Alexandria, VA: Association for Supervision and Curriculum Development.

——. 1995. *A celebration of neurons: An educator's guide to the brain.* Alexandria, VA: Association for Supervision and Curriculum Development.

Tierno, S. F. 1996. *Brain b.i.t.s: Brain connections to bilingual integrated thinking and thematic strategies.* Danbury, CT: Creative Thinkers, Inc.

——. 1994. *A staff developer's guide to the brain.* Audiotapes 1 and 2. Ft. Royal, VA: National Cassette Services, Inc.

Wolfe, P. 1996. *Live seminars on tape: Translating brain research into the classroom.*

Creativity Is a Decision

by Robert J. Sternberg

A politician and his wife decide to eat dinner in a fancy French restaurant in Washington, DC. The waiter approaches their table and asks the wife what she would like as an appetizer. "The paté de foie gras," she tells the waiter. "And the main course?" the waiter asks. "The filet mignon," responds the politician's wife. "And the vegetable?" asks the waiter. "He'll have the same," responds the politician's wife.

This story demonstrates that creativity is not an attribute limited to the "greats"—the Darwins, the Picassos, the Hemingways. Rather, it is something anyone can use. It also shows that creativity is a decision. The politician's wife decided, through her cutting remark, for creativity.

People who decide to be creative are like good investors: They decide to buy low and sell high in the world of ideas. In this article, I first describe this idea of creativity as a decision, which is formalized as an investment theory of creativity. Then, I describe the abilities that are necessary for successful creativity. Finally, I describe 12 techniques individuals can use in their teaching to foster creativity in their students and themselves.

THE INVESTMENT THEORY OF CREATIVITY

The investment theory of creativity (Sternberg and Lubart 1995a, 1995b) asserts that creative thinkers are like good investors: they buy low and sell high. Whereas investors do so in the world of finance, creative people do so in the world of ideas. Creative people generate ideas that are like undervalued stocks (stocks with a low price-to-earnings ratio), and both the stocks and the ideas are generally rejected by the public. When creative ideas are proposed, they often are viewed as bizarre, useless, and even foolish, and are summarily re-

---

jected. The person proposing them often is regarded with suspicion and perhaps even with disdain and derision.

Creative ideas are both novel and valuable. But, they are often rejected because the creative innovator stands up to vested interests and defies the crowd. The crowd does not maliciously or willfully reject creative notions. Rather, it does not realize, and often does not want to realize, that the proposed idea represents a valid and advanced way of thinking. Society generally perceives opposition to the status quo as annoying, offensive, and reason enough to ignore innovative ideas.

Evidence abounds that creative ideas are often rejected (Sternberg and Lubart 1995a). Initial reviews of major works of literature and art are often negative. Toni Morrison's *Tar Baby* received negative reviews when it was first published, as did Sylvia Plath's *The Bell Jar.* The first exhibition in Munich of the work of Norwegian painter Edvard Munch opened and closed the same day because of the strong negative response from the critics. Some of the greatest scientific papers have been rejected not just by one, but by several journals before being published. For example, John Garcia, a distinguished biopsychologist, was immediately denounced when he first proposed that a form of learning called classical conditioning could be produced in a single trial of learning (Garcia and Koelling 1966).

Creativity is as much a decision about and an attitude toward life as it is a matter of ability.

From the investment view, then, the creative person buys low by presenting a unique idea and then attempting to convince other people of its value. After convincing others that the idea is valuable, which increases the perceived value of the investment, the creative person sells high by leaving the idea to others and moving on to another idea. People typically want others to love their ideas, but immediate universal applause for an idea usually indicates that it is not particularly creative.

Creativity is as much a decision about and an attitude toward life as it is a matter of ability. Creativity is often obvious in young children, but it is harder to find in older children and adults because their creative potential has been suppressed by a society that encourages intellectual conformity.

BALANCING SYNTHETIC, ANALYTIC, AND PRACTICAL ABILITIES

Creative work requires applying and balancing three abilities—synthetic, analytic, and practical—that all can be developed (Sternberg 1985; Sternberg and Lubart 1995a; Sternberg and O'Hara 1999; Sternberg and Williams 1996).

Creative work requires applying and balancing three abilities—synthetic, analytic, and practical—that all can be developed

Synthetic ability is what we typically think of as creativity. It is the ability to generate novel and interesting ideas. Often the person others call creative is a particularly good synthetic thinker who makes connections between things that other people do not recognize spontaneously.

Analytic ability is typically considered to be critical thinking ability. A person with this skill analyzes and evaluates ideas. Everyone, even the most creative person, has better and worse ideas. Without well-developed analytic ability, the creative thinker is as likely to pursue bad ideas as to pursue good ones. The creative individual uses analytic ability to work out the implications of a creative idea and to test it.

Practical ability is the ability to translate theory into practice and abstract ideas into practical accomplishments. An implication of the investment theory of creativity is that good ideas do not sell themselves. The creative person uses practical ability to convince other people that an idea is valuable. For example, every organization has a set of ideas that dictate how things, or at least some things, should be done. When an individual proposes a new procedure, he or she must sell it by convincing others that it is better than the old one. Practical ability is also used to recognize ideas that have a potential audience.

Creativity requires these three abilities. The person who is only synthetic may come up with innovative ideas, but cannot recognize or sell them. The person who is only analytic may be an excellent critic of other people's ideas, but is not likely to generate creative ideas. The person who is only practical may be an excellent salesperson, but is as likely to promote ideas or products of little or no value as to promote genuinely creative ideas.

Teachers can encourage and develop creativity by teaching students to find a balance among synthetic, analytic, and practical thinking. A creative attitude is at least as important as are creative thinking skills (Schank 1988). The majority of teachers want to encourage creativity in their students, but they are not sure how to do so. Teachers can use the following 12 strategies to develop creativity in themselves, their students, and others around them. Although the strategies are presented in terms of teachers and students, these strategies apply equally to administrators working with teachers, parents working with children, or people trying to develop their own creativity.

TWELVE WAYS TO DECIDE FOR CREATIVITY

1. Redefine Problems

Redefining a problem means taking a problem and turning it on its head. Many times in life individuals have a problem and they just don't see how to solve it. They are stuck in a box. Redefining a problem essentially means extricating oneself from the box. This process is the synthetic part of creative thinking.

Redefining a problem essentially means extricating oneself from the box. This process is the synthetic part of creative thinking.

A good example of redefining a problem is summed up in the story of an executive at one of the biggest automobile companies in the Detroit area. The executive held a high-level position, and he loved his job and the money he made on the job. However, he despised the person he worked for, and because of this, he decided to find a new job. He went to a headhunter, who assured him that a new job could be easily arranged. After this meeting the executive went home and talked to his wife, who was teaching a unit on redefining problems as part of a course she was teaching on Intelligence Applied (Sternberg and Grigorenko, in press). The executive realized that he could apply what his wife was teaching to his own problem. He returned to the headhunter and gave the headhunter his boss's name. The headhunter found a new job for the executive's boss, which the boss—having no idea of what was going on—accepted. The executive then got his boss's job. The executive decided for creativity by redefining a problem.

There are many ways teachers can encourage students to define and redefine problems for themselves, rather than—as is so often the case—the teacher doing it for them. Teachers can promote creative performance by encouraging their students to define and redefine *their own* problems and projects. Teachers can encourage creative thinking by having students choose their own topics for papers or presentations, choose their own ways of solving problems, and sometimes having them choose again if they discover that their selection was a mistake. Teachers should also allow their students to pick their own topics, subject to the teacher's approval, on at least one paper or presentation each term. Approval ensures that the topic is relevant to the lesson and has a chance of leading to a successful project.

Creative people question assumptions and eventually lead others to do the same. Questioning assumptions is part of the analytical thinking involved in creativity.

A successful project (1) is appropriate to the course's goals, (2) illustrates a student's mastery of at least some of what has been taught, and (3) has the possibility of earning a good grade. If a topic is so far from the learning goals that teachers feel compelled to lower the grade, they should ask the student to choose another topic.

Teachers cannot always offer students choices, but giving choices is the only way for students to learn how to choose. A real choice is not deciding between drawing a cat or a dog, nor is it picking one state in the United States to present at a project fair. Giving students latitude in making choices helps them to develop taste and good judgment, both of which are essential elements of creativity.

At some point everyone makes a mistake in choosing a project or in the method they select to complete it. Teachers should remember that an important part of creativity is the analytic part—learning to recognize a mistake—and give students the chance and the opportunity to redefine their choices.

2. Question and Analyze Assumptions

Everyone has assumptions. Often one does not know he or she has these assumptions because they are widely shared. Creative people question assumptions and eventually lead others to do the same. Questioning assumptions is part of the analytical thinking involved in creativity. When Copernicus suggested that Earth revolves around the sun, the suggestion was viewed as preposterous because everyone could see that the sun revolves around Earth. Galileo's ideas, including the relative rates of falling objects, caused Galileo to be banned as a heretic. When an employee questions the way his boss manages the business, the boss does not smile. The employee is questioning assumptions that the boss and others simply accept—assumptions that they do not wish to open up to questions.

Sometimes it is not until many years later that society realizes the limitations or errors of their assumptions and the value of the creative person's thoughts. The impetus of those who question assumptions allows for cultural, technological, and other forms of advancement.

Teachers can be role models for questioning assumptions by showing students that what they assume they know, they really do not know. Of course, students shouldn't question every assumption. There are times to question and try to reshape the environment, and there are times to adapt to it. Some creative people question so many things so often that others stop taking them seriously. Everyone must learn which assumptions are worth questioning and which battles are worth fighting. Sometimes it's better for individuals to leave the inconsequential assumptions alone so that they have an audience when they find something worth the effort.

Teachers can teach this talent by making questioning a part of the daily classroom exchange. It is more important for students to learn what questions to ask—and how to ask them—than to learn the answers. Teachers can help students evaluate their questions by discouraging the idea that they ask questions and students simply answer them. Teachers need to avoid perpetuating the belief that their role is to teach students the facts, and instead help students understand that what matters is the students' ability to use facts. This can help students learn how to formulate good questions and how to answer questions.

Society tends to make a pedagogical mistake by emphasizing the answering and not the asking of questions. The good student is perceived as the one who rapidly furnishes the right answers. The expert in a field thus becomes the extension of the expert student—the one who knows and can recite a lot of information. As John Dewey (1933) recognized, how one thinks is often more important than what one thinks. Schools need to teach students how to ask the right questions (questions that are good, thought-provoking, and interesting) and lessen the emphasis on rote learning.

3. Do Not Assume That Creative Ideas Sell Themselves: Sell Them

Everyone would like to assume that their wonderful, creative ideas will sell themselves. But as Galileo, Edvard Munch, Toni Morrison, Sylvia Plath, and millions of others have discovered, they do not. On the contrary, creative ideas are usually viewed with suspicion and distrust. Moreover, those who propose such ideas may be viewed with suspicion and distrust as well. Because people are comfortable with the ways they already think, and because they probably have a vested interest in their existing way of thinking, it can be extremely difficult to dislodge them from their current way of thinking.

Thus, students need to learn how to persuade other people of the value of their ideas. This selling is part of the practical aspect of creative thinking. If students do a science project, it is a good idea for them present it and demonstrate why it makes an important contribution. If they create a piece of artwork, they should be prepared to describe why they think it has value. If they develop a plan for a new form of government, they should explain why it is better than the existing form of government. At times, teachers may find themselves having to justify their ideas about teaching to their principal. They should prepare their students for the same kind of experience.

Students need to learn how to persuade other people of the value of their ideas. This selling is part of the practical aspect of creative thinking.

4. Encourage Idea Generation

Creative people demonstrate a "legislative" style of thinking: They like to generate ideas (Sternberg 1997b). The environment for generating ideas can be constructively critical, but it must not be harshly or destructively critical. Students need to acknowledge that some ideas are better than others. Teachers and students should collaborate to identify and encourage any creative aspects of ideas that are presented. When suggested ideas don't seem to have much value, teachers should not just criticize. Rather, they should suggest new approaches, preferably ones that incorporate at least some aspects of the previous ideas that seemed in themselves not to have much value. Students should be praised for generating ideas, regardless of whether some are silly or unrelated, while being encouraged to identify and develop their best ideas into high-quality projects.

5. Recognize That Knowledge Is a Double-Edged Sword and Act Accordingly

Some years ago, I was visiting a very famous psychologist who lives abroad. As part of the tour he had planned for me, he invited me to visit the local zoo. We went past the cages of the primates, who were, at the time, engaged in what euphemistically could be called "strange and unnatural sexual behavior." I, of course, averted my eyes. However, my host did not do the same. After observing the primates for a short amount of time, I was astounded to hear him analyze the sexual behavior of the primates in terms of his theory of intelligence. I realized at that time, as I have many times since, how knowledge and expertise can be a double-edged sword.

On the one hand, one cannot be creative without knowledge. Quite simply, one cannot go beyond the existing state of knowledge if one does not know what that state is. Many students have ideas that are creative with respect to themselves, but not with respect to the field because others have had the same ideas before. Those with a greater knowledge base can be creative in ways that those who are still learning about the basics of the field cannot be.

At the same time, those who have an expert level of knowledge can experience tunnel vision, narrow thinking, and entrenchment. Experts can become so stuck in a way of thinking that they become unable to extricate themselves from it. Such narrowing does not just happen to others. It happens to everyone, myself included. For example, at one point in my career, every theory I proposed seemed to have three parts. (Of course, there were *three* good reasons for this . . . .) At that point, I was "stuck on threes." Learning must be a lifelong process, not one that terminates when a person achieves some measure of recognition. When a person believes that he or she knows everything there is to know, he or she is unlikely to ever show truly meaningful creativity again.

The upshot of this is that I tell my students that the teaching-learning process is a two-way process. I have as much to learn from my students as they have to learn from me. I have knowledge they do not have, but they have flexibility I do not have—precisely because they do not know as much as I do. By learning from, as well as teaching to one's students, one opens up channels for creativity that otherwise would remain closed.

6. Encourage Students to Identify and Surmount Obstacles

Buying low and selling high means defying the crowd. And people who defy the crowd—people who think creatively—almost inevitably encounter resistance. The question is not whether one will encounter obstacles; that obstacles will be encountered is a fact. The question is whether the creative thinker has the fortitude to persevere. I have often wondered why so many people start off their careers doing creative work and then vanish from the radar screen. I think I know at least one reason why: Sooner or later, they decide that being creative is not worth the resistance and punishment. The truly creative thinkers pay the short-term price because they recognize that they can make a difference in the long term. But often it is a long while before the value of creative ideas is recognized and appreciated.

It is a long while before the value of creative ideas is recognized and appreciated.

One example of having to wait for ideas to be recognized occurred in my own experience. When I was very young, I became interested in intelligence and intelligence testing as a result of poor scores on intelligence tests. As a seventh grader of the age of 13, I decided it would be interesting to do a science project on intelligence testing. I found the Stanford-Binet Intelligence Scales in the adult section of the local library and started giving the test to friends. Unfortunately, one of my friends tattled to his mother, who reported me to the school authorities. The head school psychologist threatened to burn the book that contained the test if I ever brought it into school again. He suggested I find another interest. Had I done so, I never would have done all the work I have done on intelligence, which has meant a great deal to my life, and, I hope, something to the world. His opinion presented a major obstacle to me, especially as an early adolescent. However, because I surmounted that obstacle, I have been able to do research on intelligence, which has been very fulfilling for me.

Teachers can prepare students for these types of experiences by describing obstacles that they, their friends, and well-known figures in society have faced while trying to be creative; otherwise, students may think that they are the only ones confronted by obstacles. Teachers should include stories about people who weren't supportive, about bad grades for unwelcome ideas, and about frosty receptions to what they may have thought were their best ideas. To help students deal with obstacles, teachers can remind them of the many creative people whose ideas were initially shunned and help them to develop an inner sense of awe of the creative act. Suggesting that students reduce their concern over what others think is also valuable. However, it is often difficult for students to lessen their dependence on the opinions of their peers.

When students attempt to surmount an obstacle, they should be praised for the effort, whether or not they were entirely successful. Teachers can point out aspects of the student's attack that were successful and why, and suggest other ways to confront similar obstacles. Having the class brainstorm about ways to confront a given obstacle can get them thinking about the many strategies people can use to confront problems. Some obstacles are within oneself, such as performance anxiety. Other obstacles are external, such as others' bad opinions of one's actions. Whether internal or external, obstacles must be overcome.

7. Encourage Sensible Risk-Taking

When creative people defy the crowd by buying low and selling high, they take risks in much the same way as do people who invest. Some such investments simply may not pan out. Moreover, defying the crowd means risking the crowd's wrath. But there are levels of sensibility to keep in mind when defying the crowd. Creative people take sensible risks and produce ideas that others ultimately admire and respect as trendsetting. In taking these risks, creative people sometimes make mistakes, fail, and fall flat on their faces.

Whether internal or external, obstacles must be overcome.

I emphasize the importance of sensible risk-taking because I am not talking about risking life and limb for creativity. To help students learn to take sensible risks, teachers can encourage them to take some intellectual risks with courses, activities, and teachers—to develop a sense of how to assess risks.

Nearly every major discovery or invention entailed some risk. When a movie theater was the only place to see a movie, someone created the idea of the home video machine. Skeptics questioned if anyone would want to see videos on a small screen. Another initially risky idea was the home computer. Many wondered if anyone would have enough use for a home computer to justify the cost. These ideas were once risks that are now ingrained in our society.

I took a risk as an assistant professor when I decided to study intelligence, as the field of intelligence has low prestige within academic psychology. When I was being considered for tenure, it came to my attention that my university was receiving letters that questioned why it would want to give tenure to someone in such a marginal and unprestigious field. I sought advice from a senior professor, Wendell Garner, telling him that perhaps I had made a mistake in labeling my work as being about intelligence. Indeed, I could have done essentially the same work but labeled it as being in the field of "thinking" or of "problem solving"—fields with more prestige. His advice was that I had come to Yale wanting to make a difference in the field of intelligence. I had made a difference, but now I was afraid it might cost me my job. I was right: I had taken a risk. But he maintained that there was only one thing I could do—exactly what I was doing. If this field meant so much to me, then I needed to pursue it, just as I was doing, even if it meant losing my job. I am still at the university, but other risks I have taken have not turned out as well. When taking risks, one must realize that some of them just will not work, and that is the cost of doing creative work.

When taking risks, one must realize that some of them just will not work, and that is the cost of doing creative work.

Few children are willing to take risks in school, because they learn that taking risks can be costly. Perfect test scores and papers receive praise and open up future possibilities. Failure to attain a certain academic standard is perceived as deriving from a lack of ability and motivation and may lead to scorn and lessened opportunities. Why risk taking hard courses or saying things that teachers may not like when that may lead to low grades or even failure? Teachers may inadvertently advocate students to only learn to "play it safe" when they give assignments without choices and allow only particular answers to questions. Thus, teachers need not only to encourage sensible risk-taking, but also to reward it.

8. Encourage Tolerance of Ambiguity

People like things to be in black and white. People like to think that a country is good or bad (ally or enemy) or that a given idea in education works or does not work. The problem is that there are a lot of grays in creative work. Artists working on new paintings and writers working on new books often report feeling scattered and unsure in their thoughts. They often need to figure out whether they are even on the right track. Scientists often are not sure whether the theory they have developed is exactly correct. These creative thinkers need to tolerate the ambiguity and uncertainty until they get the idea just right.

A creative idea tends to come in bits and pieces and develops over time. However, the period in which the idea is developing tends to be uncomfortable. Without time or the ability to tolerate ambiguity, many may jump to a less than optimal solution. When a student has almost the right topic for a paper or almost the right science project, it's tempting for teachers to accept the near-miss. To help students become creative, teachers need to encourage them to accept and extend the period in which their ideas do not quite converge. Students need to be taught that uncertainty and discomfort are a part of living a creative life. Ultimately, they will benefit from their tolerance of ambiguity by coming up with better ideas.

9. Help Students Build Self-Efficacy

Many people often reach a point where they feel as if no one believes in them. I reach this point frequently, feeling that no one values or even appreciates what I am doing. Because creative work often doesn't get a warm reception, it is extremely important that the creative people believe in the value of what they are doing. This is not to say that individuals should believe that every idea they have is a good idea. Rather, individuals need to believe that, ultimately, they have the ability to make a difference.

All students have the capacity to be creators and to experience the joy associated with making something new, but first they must be given a strong base for creativity.

The main limitation on what students can do is what they think they can do. All students have the capacity to be creators and to experience the joy associated with making something new, but first they must be given a strong base for creativity. Sometimes teachers and parents unintentionally limit what students can do by sending messages that express or imply limits on students' potential accomplishments. Instead, these adults need to help students believe in their own ability to be creative.

I have found that probably the best predictor of success among my students is not their ability, but their belief in their ability to succeed. If students are encouraged to succeed and to believe in their own ability to succeed, they very likely will find the success that otherwise would elude them.

10. Help Students Find What They Love to Do

Teachers must help students find what excites them to unleash their students' best creative performances. Teachers need to remember that this may not be what really excites them. People who truly excel creatively in a pursuit, whether vocational or avocational, almost always genuinely love what they do. Certainly, the most creative people are intrinsically motivated in their work (Amabile 1996). Less creative people often pick a career for the money or prestige and are bored with or loathe their career. Most often, these people do not do work that makes a difference in their field.

Helping students find what they really love to do is often hard and frustrating work. Yet, sharing the frustration with them now is better than leaving them to face it alone later. To help students uncover their true interests, teachers can ask them to demonstrate a special talent or ability for the class, and explain that it doesn't matter what they do (within reason), only that they love the activity.

In working with my students, I try to help them find what interests *them*, whether or not it particularly interests me. Often, their enthusiasm is infectious, and I find myself drawn into new areas of pursuit simply because I allow myself to follow my students rather than always expecting them to follow me.

I often meet students who are pursuing a certain field not because it is what they want to do, but because it is what their parents or other authority figures expect them to do. I always feel sorry for such students, because I know that although they may do good work in that field, they almost certainly will not do great work. It is hard for people to do great work in a field that simply does not interest them.

Of course, taking this attitude is easier said than done. When my son was young, I was heartened that he wanted to play the piano. I play the piano, and was glad that he wanted to play the piano too. But then he stopped practicing and ultimately quit, and I felt badly. A short time thereafter he informed me that he had decided that he wanted to play the trumpet. I reacted very negatively, pointing out to him that he had already quit the piano and probably would quit the trumpet too.

I then found myself wondering why I had been so harsh. How could I have said such a thing? But then I quickly understood it. If someone else's child wanted to play the trumpet, that was fine. But I couldn't imagine any Sternberg child playing the trumpet. It did not fit my ideal image of a Sternberg child. I realized I was being narrow-minded and doing exactly the opposite of what I had told everyone else to do. It's one thing to talk the talk, another to walk the walk. I backpedaled, and Seth started playing the trumpet.

Eventually, he did, in fact, quit the trumpet. Finding the right thing is frustrating work! But Seth eventually did find the right thing. Today he is a college student and already has started two businesses. I don't always like businesses. But businesses and my son are the right thing—absolutely. He is doing what is right for him. Whether it is right for me doesn't matter.

11. Teach Students the Importance of Delaying Gratification

Part of being creative means being able to work on a project or task for a long time without immediate or interim rewards. Students must learn that rewards are not always immediate and that there are benefits to delaying gratification. The fact of the matter is that, in the short term, people are often ignored when they do creative work or even punished for doing it.

Part of being creative means being able to work on a project or task for a long time without immediate or interim rewards.

Many people believe that they should reward children immediately for good performance, and that children should expect rewards. This style of teaching and parenting emphasizes the here and now and often comes at the expense of what is best in the long term.

An important lesson in life—and one that is intimately related to developing the discipline to do creative work—is to learn to wait for rewards. The greatest rewards are often those that are delayed. Teachers can give their students examples of delayed gratification in their lives and in the lives of creative individuals and help them apply these examples to their own lives.

I can relate to the concept of delayed gratification, as one of the greatest rewards of my own life has yet to come. Some years ago I contracted with a publisher to develop a test of intelligence based on my theory of intelligence (Sternberg 1985). Things were going well until the president of the company left and a new president took over. Shortly after that, my project was canceled. The company's perception was that there was not enough of a potential market for a test of intelligence based on my theory of analytical, creative, and practical abilities. My perception was that the company and some of its market was stuck in the past, endlessly replicating the construction and use of the kinds of tests that have been constructed and used since the turn of the century. From my point of view, it is hard to find an industry less creative than the testing industry, at least given the rate of innovation they have shown to date.

Whoever may have been right, a colleague and I ultimately decided that if we wanted to make this test work, we would have to publish it ourselves, not through a conventional publisher. Some years later, we are still working to find a way that the test can be used by others. It is a difficult exercise in delay of gratification. But I try to practice what I preach, and so I wait for the day when the test will see the light of day and make a difference to children's lives.

Children develop creativity not when they are told to, but when they are shown how.

As demonstrated by this example, hard work often does not bring immediate rewards. Children do not immediately become expert baseball players, dancers, musicians, or sculptors. And the reward of becoming an expert can seem very far away. Children often succumb to the temptations of the moment, such as watching television or playing video games. The people who make the most of their abilities are those who wait for a reward and recognize that few serious challenges can be met in a moment. Ninth-grade students may not see the benefits of hard work, but the advantages of a solid academic performance will be obvious when they apply to college.

The short-term focus of most school assignments does little to teach children the value of delaying gratification. Projects are clearly superior in meeting this goal, but it is difficult for teachers to assign home projects if they are not confident of parental involvement and support. By working on a task for many weeks or months, students learn the value of making incremental efforts for long-term gains.

12. Provide an Environment That Fosters Creativity

There are many ways teachers can provide an environment that fosters creativity (Sternberg and Williams 1996). The most powerful way for teachers to develop creativity in students is to *role model creativity*. Children develop creativity not when they are told to, but when they are shown how.

The teachers most people probably remember from their school days are not those who crammed the most content into their lectures. The teachers most people remember are those teachers whose thoughts and actions served as a role model. Most likely they balanced teaching content with teaching students how to think with and about that content. For example, I will never forget the teacher who started off my seventh-grade social studies class by asking whether students knew what social studies was. Of course, everyone nodded his or her head. The class then spent three sessions trying to figure out just what it was.

Occasionally, I will teach a workshop on developing creativity and someone will ask exactly what he or she should do to develop creativity. Bad start. A person cannot be a role model for creativity unless he or she thinks and teaches creatively him- or herself. Teachers need to think carefully about their values, goals, and ideas about creativity and show them in their actions.

Teachers also can stimulate creativity by helping students *to cross-fertilize in their thinking* to think across subjects and disciplines. The traditional school environment often has separate classrooms and classmates for different subjects and seems to influence students into thinking that learning occurs in discrete boxes—the math box, the social studies box, and the science box. However, creative ideas and insights often result from integrating material across subject areas, not from memorizing and reciting material.

Teaching students to cross-fertilize draws on their skills, interests, and abilities, regardless of the subject. If students are having trouble understanding math, teachers might ask them to draft test questions related to their special interests. For example, teachers might ask the baseball fan to devise geometry problems based on a game. The context may spur creative ideas because the student finds the topic (baseball) enjoyable and it may counteract some of the anxiety caused by geometry. Cross-fertilization motivates students who aren't interested in subjects taught in the abstract.

One way teachers can enact cross-fertilization in the classroom is to ask students to identify their best and worst academic areas. Students can then be asked to come up with project ideas in their weak area based on ideas borrowed from one of their strongest areas. For example, teachers can explain to students that they can apply their interest in science to social studies by analyzing the scientific aspects of trends in national politics.

Teachers also need to *allow students the time to think creatively.* This society is a society in a hurry. People eat fast food, rush from one place to another, and value quickness. Indeed, one way to say someone is smart is to say that the person is *quick* (Sternberg 1985), a clear indication of our emphasis on time. This is also indicated by the format of the standardized tests used—lots of multiple-choice problems squeezed into a brief time slot.

Most creative insights do not happen in a rush (Gruber and Davis 1988). People need time to understand a problem and to toss it around. If students are asked to think creatively, they need time to do it well. If teachers stuff questions into their tests or give their students more homework than they can complete, they are not allowing them time to think creatively.

Teachers also should *instruct and assess for creativity.* If teachers give only multiple-choice tests, students quickly learn the type of thinking that teachers value, no matter what they say. If teachers want to encourage creativity, they need to include at least some opportunities for creative thought in assignments and tests. Questions that require factual recall, analytic thinking, *and* creative thinking should be asked. For example, students might be asked to learn about a law, analyze the law, and then think about how the law might be improved.

Teachers also need *to reward creativity.* It is not enough to talk about the value of creativity. Students are used to authority figures who say one thing and do another. They are exquisitely sensitive to what teachers value when it comes to the bottom line—namely, the grade or evaluation.

Creative efforts also should be rewarded. For example, teachers can assign a project and remind students that they are looking for them to demonstrate their knowledge, analytical and writing skills, and creativity. Teachers should let students know that creativity does not depend on the teacher's agreement with what students write, but rather with ideas they express that represent a synthesis between existing ideas and their own thoughts. Teachers need to care only that the ideas are creative from the student's perspective, not necessarily creative with regard to the state-of-the-art findings in the field. Students may generate an idea that someone else has already had, but if the idea is an original to the student, the student has been creative.

Some teachers complain that they cannot apply as much objectivity to grading creative responses as they can to multiple-choice or short-answer responses. They are correct in that there is some sacrifice of objectivity. However, research shows that evaluators are remarkably consistent in their assessments of creativity (Amabile 1996; Sternberg and Lubart 1995a). If the goal of assessment is to instruct students, then it is better to ask for creative work and evaluate it with somewhat less objectivity than to evaluate students exclusively on uncreative work. Teachers should let students know that there is no completely objective way to evaluate creativity.

Teachers also need *to allow mistakes.* Buying low and selling high carries a risk. Many ideas are unpopular simply because they are not good. People often think a certain way because that way works better than other ways. But once in a while, a great thinker comes along—a Freud, a Piaget, a Chomsky, or an Einstein—and shows us a new way to think. These thinkers made contributions because they allowed themselves and their collaborators to take risks and make mistakes.

Although being successful often involves making mistakes along the way, schools are often unforgiving of mistakes.

Many of Freud's and Piaget's ideas turned out to be wrong. Freud confused Victorian issues regarding sexuality with universal conflicts and Piaget misjudged the ages at which children could perform certain cognitive feats. Their ideas were great not because they lasted forever, but rather because they became the basis for other ideas. Freud's and Piaget's mistakes allowed others to profit from their ideas.

Although being successful often involves making mistakes along the way, schools are often unforgiving of mistakes. Errors on schoolwork are often marked with a large and pronounced X. When a student responds to a question with an incorrect answer, some teachers pounce on the student for not having read or understood the material, which results in classmates snickering. In hundreds of ways and in thousands of instances over the course of a school career, children learn that it is not all right to make mistakes. The result is that they become afraid to risk the independent and the sometimes flawed thinking that leads to creativity.

When students make mistakes, teachers should ask them to analyze and discuss these mistakes. Often, mistakes or weak ideas contain the germ of correct answers or good ideas. In Japan, teachers spend entire class periods asking children to analyze the mistakes in their mathematical thinking. For the teacher who wants to make a difference, exploring mistakes can be a learning and growing opportunity.

Another aspect of teaching students to be creative is teaching them *to take responsibility for both successes and failures.* Teaching students how to take responsibility means teaching students to (1) understand their creative process, (2) criticize themselves, and (3) take pride in their best creative work. Unfortunately, many teachers and parents look for—or allow students to look for—an outside enemy responsible for failures.

It sounds trite to say that teachers should teach students to take responsibility for themselves, but sometimes there is a gap between what people know and how they translate thought into action. In practice, people differ widely in the extent to which they take responsibility for the causes and consequences of their actions. Creative people need to take responsibility for themselves and for their ideas.

Teachers also can work *to encourage creative collaboration.* Creative performance often is viewed as a solitary occupation. We may picture the writer writing alone in a studio, the artist painting in a solitary loft, or the musician practicing endlessly in a small music room. In reality, people often work in groups. Collaboration can spur creativity. Teachers can encourage students to learn by example by collaborating with creative people.

Students also need to learn how *to imagine things from other viewpoints.* An essential aspect of working with other people and getting the most out of collaborative creative activity is to imagine oneself in other people's shoes. Individuals can broaden their perspective by learning to see the world from different points of view. Teachers should encourage their students to see the importance of understanding, respecting, and responding to other people's points of view. This is important, as many bright and potentially creative children never achieve success because they do not develop practical intelligence (Sternberg 1985, 1997a). They may do well in school and on tests, but they may never learn how to get along with others or to see things and themselves as others see them.

Teachers also need to help students recognize person-environment fit. What is judged as creative is an interaction between a person and the environment (Csikszentmihalyi 1988; Gardner 1993; Sternberg 1999; Sternberg and Lubart 1995a). The very same product that is rewarded as creative in one time or place may be scorned in another.

In the movie *The Dead Poets' Society,* a teacher who the audience might well judge to be creative is viewed as incompetent by the school's administration. Similar experiences occur many times a day in many settings. There is no absolute standard for what constitutes creative work. The same product or idea may be valued or devalued in different environments. The lesson is that individuals need to find a setting in which their creative talents and unique contributions are rewarded, or they need to modify their environment.

The important thing to remember is that the development of creativity is a lifelong process, not one that ends with any particular high school or university degree.

I once had a student who I gave consummately bad advice concerning environment. She had two job offers. One was from an institution that was very prestigious, but not a good fit to the kind of work she valued. The other institution was a bit less prestigious, but was a much better fit to her values. I advised her to take the job in the more prestigious institution, telling her that if she did not accept the job there, she would always wonder what would have happened if she did. Bad advice: She went there and never fit in well. Eventually she left, and now she is at an institution that values the kind of work she does. Now I always advise students to go for the best fit.

By building a constant appreciation of the importance of person-environment fit, teachers prepare their students for choosing environments that are conducive to their creative success. Encourage students to examine environments to help them learn to select and match environments with their skills.

CONCLUSION

In this essay, I have described 12 relatively simple things any teacher can do to foster creativity in students or in him- or herself. But the important thing to remember is that the development of creativity is a lifelong process, not one that ends with any particular high school or university degree. Once a person has a major creative idea, it is easy for that individual to spend the rest of his or her career following up on it. It is frightening for that person to contemplate that the next idea may not be as good as the last one, or that success may disappear with the next idea. This fear often results in people becoming complacent and the creativity process being halted.

Sometimes, as experts, people become complacent and stop growing. Teachers and administrators are susceptible to becoming victims of their own expertise—to becoming entrenched in ways of thinking that worked in the past, but not necessarily in the future (Frensch and Sternberg 1989). Being creative means that people need to step outside the boxes that they—and others—have created for themselves, and continue to do so throughout their entire life.

Author's Note: For many of its concepts this article draws on Sternberg and Lubart (1995a, 1995b) and on Sternberg and Williams (1996). I am grateful to Todd Lubart and Wendy Williams for their collaborations on creativity. The research leading up to this article was supported in part by a grant from the U.S. Office of Educational Research and Improvement, U.S. Department of Education (Grant R206R950001). The findings and opinions expressed in this article do not necessarily reflect the positions or policies of the U.S. Government.

REFERENCES

Amabile, T. M. 1983. *The social psychology of creativity.* New York: Springer-Verlag.

Amabile, T .M. 1996. *Creativity in context.* Boulder, CO: Westview.

Csikszentmihalyi, M. 1988. Society, culture, and person: A systems view of creativity. In *The nature of creativity,* edited by R. J. Sternberg. New York: Cambridge University Press.

Dewey, J. 1933. *How we think: A restatement of the relation of reflective thinking to the educative process.* Boston, MA: Heath.

Frensch, P. A., and R. J. Sternberg. 1989. Expertise and intelligent thinking: When is it worse to know better? In *Advances in the psychology of human intelligence,* Vol. 5, edited by R. J. Sternberg. Hillsdale, NJ: Lawrence Erlbaum.

Garcia, J., and R. A. Koelling. 1966. The relation of cue to consequence in avoidance learning. *Psychonomic Science* 4: 123–124.

Gardner, H. 1993. *Creating minds.* New York: Basic Books.

Gruber, H. E., and S. N. Davis. 1988. Inching our way up Mount Olympus: The evolving-systems approach to creative thinking. In *The nature of creativity,* edited by R. J. Sternberg. New York: Cambridge University Press.

Schank, R. C. 1988. *The creative attitude: Learning to ask and answer the right questions.* New York: Macmillan.

Sternberg, R. J. 1999. A propulsion model of types of creative contributions. *Review of General Psychology* 3: 83–100.

Sternberg, R. J. 1997a. *Successful intelligence.* New York: Plume.

Sternberg, R. J. 1997b. *Thinking styles.* New York: Cambridge University Press.

Sternberg, R. J. 1985. *Beyond IQ: A triarchic theory of human intelligence.* New York: Cambridge University Press.

Sternberg, R. J., and L. O'Hara. 1999. Creativity and intelligence. In *Handbook of creativity*, edited by R. J. Sternberg. New York: Cambridge University Press.

Sternberg, R. J., and E. L. Grigorenko. in press. *Intelligence applied*, 2d ed. New York: Oxford University Press.

Sternberg, R. J., and T. I. Lubart. 1995a. *Defying the crowd: Cultivating creativity in a culture of conformity.* New York: Free Press.

Sternberg, R. J., and T. I. Lubart. 1995b. Ten tips toward creativity in the workplace. In *Creative action in organizations: Ivory tower visions and real world voices*, edited by C. M. Ford and D. A. Goia. Newbury Park, CA: Sage Publications.

Sternberg, R. J., and W. M. Williams. 1996. *How to develop student creativity.* Alexandria, VA: Association for Supervision and Curriculum Development.

Revisiting Effective Teaching

by Pat Wolfe

Those of us who have worked in schools for a while have watched a lot of programs, theories, and innovations come and go. Many experienced teachers, frustrated with the pendulum swings, have adopted a wait and see, or "this too will pass," attitude. But I wonder whether too often we have eliminated very effective practices in favor of the newer innovations on the block.

Participants in my workshops frequently reinforce this thought as they point out or ask about the connection between Madeline Hunter's Elements of Effective Instruction (1982) and current brain research. I can frequently point out how neuroscience research has validated one or another of the practices Hunter espoused. And it's not just Hunter's work that participants ask about, but that of John Dewey and Alfred North Whitehead in the early 1930s; Jerome Bruner's writings in the 1960s; and the findings from Jere Brophy, Barak Rosenshine, and others whose work we studied under the heading of Effective Teaching research. These studies focused on what teachers did that resulted in increased student learning. We seldom hear much about these findings anymore, but are they really outdated or have we been too quick to look for something new? Is it possible that the effective teaching strategies of 20 years ago are still relevant today and that we can look to current cognitive and neuroscience research to help us understand why they are?

SETTING THE STAGE FOR LEARNING

Let me begin with a relatively simple and familiar example from Hunter's work. Hunter talked about the importance of an anticipatory set, a way of helping students attend to the relevant data of the upcoming instruction. She admonished us to ask focusing questions,

---

From "Revisiting Effective Teaching," by Pat Wolfe. First printed in *Educational Leadership,* November 1998, pp. 61–64.

have students recall previous information, state the objective, or otherwise assist students in focusing on information that they would need to be successful. This emphasis on setting the stage for learning fits precisely with the research on the attentional mechanisms of the brain.

The only way to get information into the brain is through our senses. At any one moment, our sensory receptors (the retina of the eye, the tympanic membrane in the ear, and so on) are simultaneously bombarded with an enormous amount of data. If we were able to pay conscious attention to all this sensory information, we would go stark, raving mad. To keep us sane, our brain immediately starts sifting and sorting through all the sensory input and gets rid of irrelevant material. This initial processing step is unconscious and appears to be accomplished by the brain as it searches through previously stored information and looks for relevant hooks for the new information. There is actually no such thing as a student who is not paying attention. The student's brain is always paying attention to something, although it may not focus on relevant information or on what the teacher intends.

There is actually no such thing as a student who is not paying attention.

For example, if I begin describing a train trip and tell you how many people entrained or detrained at each stop, your brain may search for and retrieve information about previous trips taken. If your brain picks up on the numbers, you may begin mentally to add and subtract the number of people on the train. When I reach the end of the story and ask how many times the train stopped, you probably won't have a clue because your brain had attended to the wrong information. The brain constantly searches through existing neural networks to find a way to make sense of incoming data. An anticipatory set increases the possibility that the brain will search through the right networks and attend to the information that is relevant for a particular topic or issue.

THE LEARNING ENVIRONMENT

The effective-teaching research resulted in a great deal of information about the effects of the learning environment on student achievement. Hunter helped clarify our understanding of the effects of the environment as she discussed levels of difficulty and levels of concern. I don't see many articles in current educational journals or teachers' magazines that use the phrase "level of concern," but I do see a lot written about how a classroom needs a learning atmosphere that is high in challenge but low in threat. Is there a big difference? I don't think so.

Hunter told us that if a task is either too difficult or too easy, we will have little motivation to continue. She also pointed out that a level of concern (or stress) either too high to too low will interfere with efficient learning. Sounds pretty simple, doesn't it? But is it true? Does current research help us understand why stress or level of concern enhances or inhibits learning?

Emotion is a double-edged sword. The brain is hardwired for survival.

Again, let's consider the pathways that information takes as it enters the brain. As part of the initial sorting and sifting process, the brain sends information coming in through the senses to several organs deep within its center. One of these is a small, almond-shaped structure named the amygdala.

The amygdala could be called the psychological sentinel of the brain. Part of its role is to check out information for its emotional content. Is this information potentially threatening or aversive or is it something I like? Should I run away from it or run toward it? If the brain determines that the information is threatening, it immediately sends chemical messages throughout the body to prepare the organs to adjust their activity level to match the demands of the situation.

Most of us are familiar with this reaction, commonly called the fight or flight response. The heart beats faster, lung capacity increases, palms become sweaty, and so on. But in addition to these familiar responses, other less noticeable reactions occur. The immune and digestive systems are suspended; blood-clotting factors increase; and the conscious, rational, thinking part of the brain—the cortex—becomes much less efficient, in a sense "downshifting."

If you've ever been insulted and couldn't think of a response until the next day, you've experienced downshifting. Similarly, downshifting occurs when you forget what you studied for an important test, when you cannot remember what you were going to say as you stand in front of an audience to give a speech, or when you are so angry that you engage in irrational behavior. Anything that an individual brain perceives to be threatening can slow the creative, rational processing of information.

Emotion is a double-edged sword. The brain is hardwired for survival. If the event or information has little or no value, the brain has a tendency to drop it. If the emotional content is too high, downshifting can occur, and the conscious, rational processing becomes less efficient. I think these reactions are exactly what Hunter was describing when she talked about level of concern. Every teacher has seen examples of these behaviors. What research is contributing is an understanding of when they occur. This understanding can help us select appropriate strategies for dealing with them.

TASK ANALYSIS AND MEMORY RESEARCH

One of Hunter's Elements of Instruction that teachers often found difficult was task analysis. Basically, the idea is that the teacher breaks a task (such as identifying the main idea in a story, solving an equation, or shooting a basket) into its essential components to have guidelines for planning instruction. This process increases the possibility of addressing all necessary elements to complete a task successfully. In practice, however, teachers found task analysis arduous and often were not able to complete an analysis. Again, research from the neurosciences helps us understand why task analysis is so necessary, yet so difficult to accomplish.

The brain stores different types of memory in different ways. Most neuroscientists distinguish between two major types of memory, declarative (explicit) and procedural (implicit). Declarative memory consists of semantic information (facts, places, names) and episodic information (episodes of one's life). Both types of declarative memory can be "declared," or stated, and are believed to be stored in the outer layer of the brain, the cortex. To declare information, we must retrieve it and bring it into consciousness.

Procedural memory consists of information or procedures that we have learned at the automatic level, that we most often gain access to without conscious attention. For example, most of us have experienced driving a car over a familiar route, arriving at our destination, and having no conscious recollection of driving there. The processes involved in driving—especially on that route—have become totally automatic. Other examples of procedural memory include remembering how to walk, write, tie a shoelace, decode words, or pass a football. I suspect that many procedures used by teachers in classrooms are also carried out automatically.

Neuroscientists believe that the physiological process underlying procedural memory is one in which brain cells (neurons) that "fire together, wire together." In other words, circuits or networks of neurons that are used over and over get accustomed to firing together and eventually become hardwired and fire automatically. It is interesting to note that Madeline Hunter used the phrase "Practice doesn't make perfect; it makes permanent." If we practice something incorrectly, our neurons don't know the difference and make the permanent connections incorrectly—as anyone knows who has attempted to master a task without expert assistance or coaching.

"Practice doesn't make perfect; it makes permanent."

Why would the brain's design allow us to perform certain tasks automatically? The reason is probably connected to survival, giving us the ability during danger to run without having to think consciously about which muscles to move. Procedural memory appears to involve structures deep within the brain—mainly the hippocampus and cerebellum—that allow us to perform procedures without using the limited conscious-processing space.

Whatever the origin, being able to get some of the basics of a skill at the automatic level is necessary for us to move to higher levels of functioning. (Comprehending what you are reading now would be nearly impossible—or at least laboriously slow and inefficient—if your decoding skills were not automatic.) I recall reading an article in this magazine *[Educational Leadership]* many years ago in which Benjamin Bloom discussed how individuals become experts in various fields. He labeled procedural memory "automaticity" and stated that it is the "hands and feet of genius."

On the surface, procedural memory appears to be the marvel of the brain—until we try to change an automatic procedure or to teach it to someone else. Witness our difficulty in teaching children how to decode. The process is automatic to us, and it is extremely difficult to explain the processes that we use to do it. The same is true of any skill or procedure that we have developed to this level, such as swinging a golf club, regrouping in subtraction, or performing an experiment in chemistry.

Although Madeline Hunter didn't have access to the information on the physiological underpinnings of procedural memory, she knew that teaching would be more effective and efficient if we could somehow "watch" ourselves complete an automatic task, delineate all the component parts of the task, and use that analysis to guide students through the "massed" and "distributed" practice necessary to form those permanent neural connections that are the foundation of procedural memory.

THE IMPORTANCE OF PRIOR LEARNING

The link of prior knowledge to learning was emphasized often in the effective-teaching research; few of us would argue with its importance. Here again, new research increases our understanding of why prior knowledge plays such a crucial role. Information, neuroscience research explains, is not stored in a specific location in the brain. Rather, it is stored in various locations—in the visual, auditory, and motor cortices—and is joined in circuits or networks of neurons. It appears that each time we recall an event or a previous experience, we literally reconstruct it by using the same circuit or circuits we used to store it. (The more modalities we use to store the information or experience, the more pathways we have available to access it.)

The more modalities we use to store the information or experience, the more pathways we have available to access it.)

When we experience something new, the brain looks for an existing circuit or network into which the new information will fit. For example, a young child who has learned that a small furry animal is called a dog may, when seeing a cat for the first time, call it a dog. The child's brain searched through its neural networks to find a place to fit this new animal and selected the closest match. Likewise, if I am reading an article on applying quantum physics to managing an educational system, I will be hampered in my understanding if I lack previously stored information on physics. My brain can find nowhere in its previously constructed networks to fit the new idea.

REAFFIRMING HUNTER

Teachers who have been exposed to no more of Hunter's work than the infamous "lesson design" and who view her work as simply a method of direct instruction may be surprised to learn that she was appalled at this application of her work. She emphasized over and over that teaching is decision making and that the more we know about the science of teaching, the better we can artistically apply that knowledge.

It appears to me that the study of brain research validates her position. Brain research is not a program to be implemented in schools; neuroscience does not prove that any particular strategy of method works. Rather, the research is adding to our knowledge base, helping us better understand how the brain learns—or doesn't learn—and why. We are beginning to gain a scientific understanding of the learning process, and from that understanding, we can make better decisions about how to structure learning environments and instructional practices.

Teaching is still decision making, as Hunter admonished us. Behavioral psychology was the foundation for the effective-teaching research and for Hunter's work. We did not have the tools to look inside the brain while it learns and had to rely on the observation of student behaviors to validate or reject our theories of learning. The absolute explosion of information from current research in the neurosciences is changing that scenario, but it does not necessarily indicate a rejection of the information that preceded it. What we have is a synthesis of psychology and biology that is giving us a new vocabulary and an ability to be more articulate when we talk about learning.

It is not surprising that the research coming from neuroscience parallels many of the earlier findings. Much of the effective-teaching research was based on observing teachers who obtained good results in student learning. While working with and monitoring their students day after day, effective teachers have always been on the front line of "research" about teaching and learning. On the basis of their observations and reflections, they have developed a wisdom of practice that warrants our respect. Theodore Marchese (1998) comments that many of the findings seem to confirm what we've already known, or at least theorized. "I'd be suspicious of any neuroscientific theory of teaching," he says, "that was much at variance with what best teachers already knew and did."

It's time, I think, for all of us to step back before we embrace the newest thing coming down the pike. We need to give teachers time to reflect on their practice, to engage in substantive dialogue with others (including the researchers) about what they are accomplishing and why, and to assist teachers in carefully studying new research and innovations to determine whether they validate their practice, require them to rethink their practice, or both.

REFERENCES

Hunter, M. 1982. *Mastery teaching.* El Segundo, CA: TIP Publications.

Marchese, T. 1998. *The adult learner.* Seattle, WA: New Horizons. Available online at www.newhorizons.org/lrnbus_marchese.html.

Multiple Intelligences and Reading Instruction

by Donna Ogle

Howard Gardner's work in learning (1993) and his argument for multiple intelligences require that educators think more deeply about both the nature of intelligence and the learning opportunities and activities they provide students. Educators now know that "intelligences" is a broad concept, and they must not think unidimensionally about ability even if they would like to. For many, that is the real challenge Gardner poses. As teachers, many find it much easier to develop set routines and build instruction that fits their own habits and preferences rather than prepare instructional activities that meet the range of intelligences of their students. I know that I am guilty of not stretching students to use their logical/mathematical and musical abilities since I am not comfortable in these areas. How many students have I failed to reach by not scaffolding from their preferred modes of learning and not including a wider range of activities and choices?

Those, such as myself, who teach reading and language development are generally most comfortable with language-rich instruction. Our preferences are to use language and verbal activities, so we naturally depend on talk to develop concepts and engage students in thinking. We may rely on small discussion groups or whole class teacher-led discussions both before and after reading. Writing activities are also common in literacy classrooms. We like to have students keep personal journals and encourage written response to reading. Most of us are less comfortable with dramatic and bodily responses to reading and the inclusion of musical or mathematical activities.

Gardner reminds educators that almost any topic of importance can be taught in more than one way, and that educators can develop students' reading and language abilities in a variety of ways. Therefore, I have used his challenge to think about how teachers can involve more of the intelligences students possess as they teach reading. In this article I will share some activities that tap different intelligences, and I will use an example from my own teaching about Harriet Tubman to illustrate how these can be interwoven.

The more society learns about learning, the more it must respect the enormous complexity of the brain.

I share this information realizing that much of what Gardner and others suggest about multiple intelligences and the variety of ways individuals can learn has roots in earlier theory and research. Bruner's work (1986) in cognition and genius has been enlightening. Piaget's work (1959) in thinking and the importance of novelty or cognitive dissonance as a starting place for learning have guided much of my own theory and practice (Ogle 1989). More recently, Sadoski and Paivio's work (1995) has challenged Anderson's schema theory (1984) by demonstrating that readers code information both verbally and visually. The more society learns about learning, the more it must respect the enormous complexity of the brain. For example, the fact that even odors can stimulate long-forgotten challenges some theories. Society is only just beginning to understand the ways human brains attend to, take in, process, and store information.

For me, what is most important now is recognizing that human brains have much more potential for learning than teachers have been able to incorporate in instructional programs. Concepts can be learned most deeply when a variety of receptors in the brain are stimulated—by using language, image, sound, and movement. Teachers also know that students have different strengths in how they learn and in their forms of "intelligence." The more teachers can stimulate learning through a variety of activities and experiences, the more likely they are to reach students in meaningful and productive ways.

As teachers try to use the frame of multiple intelligences to think of their language arts instruction, they also need to keep in mind the differences in using multiple modes for both receptive and expressive activities. For example, a teacher who wants to do more with visual learning needs to think about stimulating her students' receptive abilities with visual input as well as providing opportunities for them to create their own visual images as a result of engagement with texts. Students need to learn to "read" the visual creations of others and to express their own ideas in visual forms. Young children may have strong visual abilities, but unless teachers show students how to use them for and with reading, these students may not tap into their personal resources when they approach print.

HARRIET TUBMAN WITH MULTIPLE INTELLIGENCES IN MIND

A recent experience I had while teaching a group of fifth graders about Harriet Tubman provides an example of using a variety of ways to engage students' intelligences during a reading activity. The teachers in the school in this example have many low-level readers, and I encouraged them to create reading experiences that involved students' intelligences by using more of their brainpower. Rather than just reading a story or poem, I tried to model active engagement with ideas and feelings and emphasize rereading for fluency. I also suggested that activating both emotional intelligence (Goleman 1994) and interpersonal intelligence are motivators for many students that help them stay focused and increase their perseverance. Therefore, I included partner and whole group activities.

Students need to learn to "read" the visual creations of others and to express their own ideas in visual forms.

I chose a poem about Harriet Tubman since the students were reading about America in the 1800s in their social studies program. I began by asking the students what they knew about Harriet Tubman. The information they shared was very factual—she led slaves to freedom, she was a slave herself, and so on. I hoped to move them into a deeper appreciation of her contribution by engaging them in more than the textbook summary. I next showed the students Jacob Lawrence's book *Harriet and the Promised Land,* which contains his strong primary-colored paintings and a poem about Harriet. I read the text orally as I showed the paintings page by page. We discussed what the students saw and felt on our second "reading" of the pictures.

Then, I explained that we would do a choral reading and pantomime of this text and if the students wanted we could share our interpretation with the other fifth grade classes in the school. Students could select to be either readers or dramatic personas and were to work with a partner. I had already copied the text of the poem and divided it into "stanzas" of about four lines each, which were to be read orally. The partners that chose to be readers had the task of practicing their stanza and determining just how they wanted to read it together to make an interesting interpretation of the ideas presented.

The students who selected to pantomime were to take one of the stanzas and create a pantomime that would include at least two movements depicting the content of that part of the poem.

Each pair of partners had time to plan its own part, and then we put it all together. On one side of the room the choral readers gathered; on the other side, the pantomimers. It took a few practice runs before the two groups were coordinated, but the results were impressive. The students felt the power of Harriet's acts of bravery and vision. They expressed her feelings with their bodies.

After experiencing the art and the poem that made up the book in these active, personal, and interpersonal ways, the students developed a much deeper, more emotional, and real sense of just who Harriet Tubman was. Their responses to my question the next day, "What do you know about Harriet Tubman?", took on a different dimension. Their responses included statements such as she was so brave, so strong, she had to fight her own fears, and she had to trick the police by being smart. The list went on and on as they shared more personal dimensions of her bravery.

It was clear that the students now had at least some appreciation of the significance of Harriet's acts of setting her people free. The teachers and I did not take the activity further by having the students create their own drawings, poetry, or written responses, but it would have been interesting to do so. Adding music of old spirituals, especially the song "Go Down Moses," would have also added a strong dimension. What we did do was engage students using some of their multiple intelligences—visual/spatial, linguistic, interpersonal, and kinesthetic. If the teachers continue with this activity next year, they may add more dimensions. Teachers can't create an elaborate range of activities for every reading activity they want students to complete (stories, topics in science, or integrated themes), but they can do much to stimulate students' minds more fully if they think about the range of options available to them for both receptive and expressive engagement. Listed below is a variety of such options that teachers can use. Many of these are included because I have watched good teachers engage their students in reading actively by using these powerful tools and activities.

1. Creating Visual Images

Asking students to draw their ideas can effectively stimulate their thinking and activate their visual intelligences in reading. Einstein once said, "If I can't picture it, I can't understand it." Helping students to use their visualizing abilities has been shown in a variety of studies to enhance their understanding.

Prereading Activation

Teachers can activate students' visual thinking even before they engage with a written text. Rather than asking for words during prereading brainstorming, teachers can ask students to draw what they think they know about the theme or topic. For example, before beginning a unit on arachnids or lepidoptera, teachers can ask students to draw what they think these animals look like and to illustrate their habitat.

"If I can't picture it, I can't understand it."

Visualizing Images While Reading

As students are reading they can also be encouraged to periodically create drawings of what they learn. This is effective with both fiction and informational materials. They can do this as an ongoing activity after each paragraph or section or for larger chunks of meaning. Key images can be used regularly to indicate specific ideas; for example, conflict could be represented by two heads banging into each other.

A social studies teacher encouraged students to draw images while reading about the Constitutional Convention. Some drew line pictures of James Madison and Ben Franklin in the stifling Philadelphia heat. Some created a floor plan of the room and marked key players in the debates. A few created a mock draft of their own Constitution and put deckle edging on their copy.

Consolidating Ideas

After reading, students again consolidate what they have learned or create an image for the whole text by drawing.

Short, Harstee, and Burke (1996)developed one form of this activity, called *Sketch to Stretch.* Students work in teams of four or five. After reading the selected text, each member of the team draws an illustration of the key idea or theme. The students then share their drawings with the group one at a time. As each picture is shown, each group member has an opportunity to say something about the drawing, and when they are done, the artist who created it has an opportunity to talk about his or her own work. This sharing continues until all members have shared their own sketch.

Students may find it easier to create a collage of pictures and artifacts to represent ideas rather than drawing them. This artistic activity can be used before reading, but seems to work best as an adjunct to the reading of a longer text. For example, during the reading of the play *Romeo and Juliet,* ninth graders collected pictures and small artifacts that reminded them of the characters and setting of the play. While studying the '50s in American history, a class of eighth graders created a large bulletin board of images—and included a few old 45 record jackets. Individually created character collages of main characters can help students think more deeply about stories they are reading.

2. Writing and Representing Ideas While Reading

Students who become accustomed to actively creating images and responses to what they read are going to be more engaged readers.

Students who become accustomed to actively creating images and responses to what they read are going to be more engaged readers. Many texts do not lend themselves to the creation of pictures but can be more actively read when students make notes or create graphic representations of the relationships between ideas. Several forms of engagement have been developed. Most of us, as adults, read books we take seriously by using a pencil to underline sentences, writing comments in the margins, or marking the pages in some way. Students also need opportunities to learn some forms of physically engaged reading.

Marginal Notation

Two basic forms of marginal notation will serve students well. While reading a text that does not belong to them, students can make light notes with a pencil in the margins. The *Insert* method of notemaking is simple and effective. Students learn to use symbols for their responses to parts of the text as they read. There is no one set of symbols that is essential, but an easy way to start is to suggest the following symbols:

! = a new insight or interesting point
+ = something important to be remembered

? = something unclear that I want to go back to or discuss
- = something I disagree with

After reading a text selection, students often find it interesting to work with a partner and compare how they have marked the text. They can make a list of the ideas they marked with each symbol or discuss their responses more generally. Later, the whole class can share their responses, and questions can be addressed to the teacher and others in the classroom to clarify any remaining confusion.

Mind Mapping and Graphic Organizers

Mind mapping and graphic organizers are terms used separately, but the basic idea of both is that students think about the text as a whole and try to create a graphic representation of the relationship between the main ideas. While reading a section that contrasts two regions, two countries, or two approaches to a mathematical problem, students can graphically represent the two ideas. They might use a Venn diagram, create a matrix to look at the aspects of the subject, or use other forms of lines, boxes, or drawings to capture what the relation of the ideas seems to be. After each student creates his or her own representation, he or she can share with a partner or with small groups of students. In this way, students review the ideas found in the text and get an opportunity for clarification. Students begin to see how others construct the relationship between ideas and what others consider important.

Sticky Notes and Bookmarks

Some students can't write lightly in a text and some teachers don't have the confidence to ask students to "mark up" school textbooks this way. Sticky notes can also be used to help students respond to ideas as they read. Teachers simply put a small number of sticky notes on each desk. After modeling the process, teachers encourage students to read and engage with the material whenever they come to something they want to remember about their own thinking—either a connection they make, a question they have, or an image or idea that comes to mind. After the reading, students can share their notes either with partners or in larger groups. This can also lead to metacognitive analysis of how the students "think" as they read.

Bookmarks that are disposable pieces of paper can also encourage student engagement. On a small piece of paper teachers can ask

Bookmark of __________

I predict . . .

I feel . . . and connect . . .

I wonder . . .

I don't understand . . .

Figure 1

students to write some key words to stimulate their thinking as they read and then to put these pieces in their book. Teachers may also prepare these ahead of time and have them copied for ease of use. A sample bookmark is shown in Figure 1.

3. Physical Engagement with Text

Large muscle involvement in learning is effective for many students. Yet, teachers rarely use it, which is probably due to concerns for management. However, when large muscle involvement is introduced correctly it can be a powerful component of literacy instruction. Pantomime and bodily representations of topics being studied are effective and easy to use.

Students can learn to create the representation of a vocabulary term or the meaning of a story or text they are reading. Teachers can begin by asking pairs of students to physically represent the same idea. When all have created the idea with their bodies, teachers can let the groups look at each other and comment on the poses. Seeing a variety of ways of representing the same idea can deepen student thinking about the idea. If it's a story or text that is being pantomimed, this is a good time for students to make predictions about upcoming events. A key to using pantomime is selecting a stopping point where there is some conflict or ambiguity that students can think about and discuss. The students read a few pages, then create a pantomime of what they think is happening.

Some middle school teachers have had great success using pantomime as a tool to help students learn vocabulary. A project in Chicago, called Whirlwind Arts Partnership (1997) uses pantomime as a tool to help students represent their understanding of stories. In a formal study, students in classes that learned to pantomime while reading showed significant gains in general reading comprehension.

Some texts, especially poems, lend themselves to pantomime *after* they have been read. This can help students become more aware generally of how texts work in space, but it won't deepen the particular reading of the text unless the teacher gives students time to go back and revisit it.

4. Oral Reading of Texts

For many students, hearing a text and reading it orally is important to their learning. For second-language learners, the need to hear English spoken adds a specific reason for more oral reading in classes. Four forms of oral reading follow. The first, dynamic duo reading, involves partners reading a text together. The second, radio reading, capitalizes on the traditional practice of oral, round-robin reading that goes on in many classes, but changes it to a rehearsed form of oral reading. The third, choral reading, is a larger group activity and involves multiple reading of the same text or play. Finally, readers' theater provides yet another option for students to participate in an oral reading.

Dynamic Duo Reading

Many forms of partner reading of text have been developed. Generally, they involve specific roles for each partner. One reads the first paragraph orally and the other serves as listener. When the reader is finished, he or she asks the listener one or two questions about the text. For the next paragraph, the partners switch roles and the former listener now becomes the reader and questioner. As teachers develop partner reading they need to spend some time focusing students on asking good questions (e.g., fat vs. thin questions, think and search or author and me; interpretive vs. literal, and so forth.). When students are reading and answering questions, opportunities for thinking deeply about the material are more likely to arise. The text reading proceeds in this shared way until the passage is completed.

Dynamic duo reading adds another dimension to this form of shared reading. It asks students to take roles as they read. These roles should come from the text itself. For example, if students are reading a social studies text, roles might include a newspaper commentator and/or a TV anchorperson. Students reading a novel might take roles from characters in the story, shifting their voices to match what they think the characters would sound like. In this way, students engage in more than just informational processing of text by adding an emotional, personalized voice to what they read.

Radio Reading

Students learn to read and listen to oral reading as if they were listening to the radio. First, the teacher divides the text into small segments and assigns a part to each student. Then, students are given time to prepare their reading of this segment. If they need help pronouncing some words, there is time for them to use the glossary or ask another person for help. Students think about how to read the text so it sounds professional, like a radio commentator or dramatic reader. When students are ready, the reading proceeds. During this period, only the reader has the book open. All other students listen, as if they were listening to the radio. One by one, students take their turns, reading for an audience. Their production accuracy is important and they know they are the source of the text for others, so motivation and care are high.

Choral Reading

Students read together as if they were a chorus, only instead of singing they say the text. Poetry is a great tool for choral reading, and different stanzas can be assigned to different students in small groups or to individuals. Students can create their own poetry or rap and use this for choral reading, too. The groups should practice their section of the poem before the whole text is put together and try out different inflections and emphases. The whole group can read some sections together, so the variety makes the reading interesting. Some teachers use an audiotape to record their students while they are reading so students can return to the "sounds of the language" later and reflect on their version of the text. Educators have found that this form of purposeful oral reading with rehearsal is a great help to second-language students and less-confident readers.

Readers' Theater

Students love to be a part of plays, yet it is time-consuming and difficult for teachers to create a "stage" and control large groups of students during drama in most classrooms. A nice alternative is for teachers to create a more controlled and less demanding way for students to perform a play script. In readers' theater, the actors sit on chairs or stools and read their parts. They may put on hats or some small piece of clothing to represent their character, but basically they are reading without full body movement. They rehearse and determine how to present their parts and then present them to the rest of the class or another audience (often other classes in the school).

Many good stories have been turned into the readers' theater format, and students can learn to create their own readers' theater by transferring stories they read into play form. Student magazines often contain plays that can be read orally as readers' theater.

5. Musical Association

Sounds and music are often associated with what individuals learn and remember. While it takes a little extra time, teachers who help students engage with material through music often find their efforts well-rewarded. To introduce this connection to reading, teachers can bring in music to set a mood for a new theme or topic. For example, when introducing the novel, *The Ramsey Scallop* (1995), Frances Temple's wonderful story of the medieval pilgrimages to Santiago de Compostela, teachers can play Gregorian chants as students enter the room to create a context for the story that other prereading activities cannot achieve.

The key to learning is the affective engagement of the brain.

As students become accustomed to thinking of musical associations they can bring in their own ideas on tape or compact disc for the class to hear. One science teacher began a unit on the rain forest with a tape of the sounds of the rain forest. Another used radio clips from WWI to introduce a unit on this subject. Hearing can build great lasting associations with what is read.

6. Engaging Affectively

The key to learning is the affective engagement of the brain. Teachers who begin learning activities by honoring what students already know and listening for their interests and connections help students feel affectively involved. Asking questions of identification and feelings also brings in this necessary component. Reducing the "guessing game" quality of some teacher-led discussions by encouraging students' own questions is also essential.

KWL

This framework for informational reading puts students at the center of their own learning. Using a three-column format (teachers can have students fold their paper in thirds lengthwise, draw lines on paper, or create a prepared form for students to use), students activate what they *K*now during a group discussion while the teacher writes these pieces of information on the board under the *K* column.

During this discussion, disagreements on some points should emerge and the teacher guides students to turn these into questions, what we *W*ant to learn, which go in the *W* column. Finally, as students read they make notes of information they *L*earn, which goes in the *L* column. Teachers can add to the *L* column by asking the students how they will learn the material and what sources they will need. This helps students assess their texts and think of appropriate resource materials and people.

7. Poetry

One of the easiest ways teachers can stimulate this important affective component is to involve students in writing (and responding to) poetry. Personal connections, feelings, and images can be shared freely through poetry. Teachers can encourage students to work together as partners, as this may make the activity easier for some. Some of the forms of poetry teachers can use are listed below.

Cinquain

A cinquain is a five-line poem that encourages synthesis of ideas and impressions.

The first line is a one-word description of the topic (usually a noun).

The second line is a two-word description of the topic (two adjectives).

The third line contains three words expressing action of the topic (usually "ing" words).

The fourth line is a four-word phrase showing feelings about the topic.

The last line is a one-word synonym capturing the essence of the topic.

Phrase Poems

An easy and freeing form of poetry writing is creating phrase poems. Each student thinks of phrases about the theme or topic. (They can contribute one or several phrases.) These are then collected and put on the board. From this list of phrases, individuals, partners, or the whole class can then create a collective poem.

This form of poetry lifts the fear some non-native language students have that their grammar and sentence structure is not accurate.

They can express ideas without full sentences and thus participate more fully in the sharing and creation of the poem. Many versions of poems can be created using the same basic phrases.

Examples

Tom Bean (1999) shares part of a rap his daughter and five other students collaborated to write, perform, and make an audiotape of in response to an assignment that gave them choices about how to come to an understanding of a period of history. This is part of their 20-verse rap about the exploration of the Western hemisphere.

> Pizarro another conquistador bold
> Came to Peru searching for gold
> Indians of Peru already there
> Called the Incas but Pizarro didn't care
> He ripped them off every chance he got
> Stole gold and silver from the New World's pot[ex]

This cinquain can be found in Steele, Meredith, and Temple (1999).

> Teaching
> Complex, tough
> Challenging, invigorating, rewarding
> Tying new to known
> Educating

The following phrase poem is from C. Kuner's world history class at Farragut High School in Chicago, IL, as they began studying WWI. The teacher asked students to come up with phrases to describe war. From those that were shared, the class created a group phrase poem.

> WAR
> Off today to foreign lands,
> Try to help our common man.
> Never think of the good-byes,
> Never think of people and their cries.
> People lose hope—
> "I wish it would stop!"
> I am just sitting asking, why?

CONCLUSION

The act of reading is complex and demanding on the brain. Teachers can make reading more accessible to students and more enjoyable if they make efforts to engage students' intelligences more fully as they read—whether in subject areas like science, social studies, and literature, or as students read for their own purposes and pleasure on their own time. Teachers can do much to honor and then develop the range of intellectual strengths and talents of their students. In response, students often reward their teachers with increased interest and success in their learning efforts.

REFERENCES

Anderson, R.C. and P.D Pearson. 1984. "A schema-theoretic view of basic processes in reading comprehension," in P.D. Pearson, R. Barr, M.L. Kamil & P. Mosenthal (Eds.) *Handbook of Reading Research,* vol. I: pp. 255–291. White Plains, NY: Longman.

Bean, T. 1999. Intergenerational conversations and two adolescents' multiple literacies: Implications for redefining content area literacy. *Journal of Adolescent and Adult Literacy* 42(6): pp. 438-44.

Bruner, J. 1986. *Actual minds: Possible worlds.* Cambridge, MA: Harvard University Press.

Gardner, H. 1993. *Multiple intelligences: The theory in practice.* New York: Basic Books.

Goleman, D. 1995. *Emotional intelligence.* New York: Bantam Books.

Lawrence, J. 1993. *Harriet and the promised land.* New York: Simon & Schuster.

Ogle, D. 1989. The Know, Want to Know, Learn Strategy in Muth, D. (Ed.) *Children's comprehension of text: Research to practice.* Newark: DE International Reading Association.

Paivio, A. 1986. *Mental representation: A dual coding approach.* New York: Oxford University Press.

Piaget, J. 1959. *The language and thought of the child.* (3rd edition). London: Routledge and Kegan Paul.

Short, K.G., J. C. Harstee, and C. Burke. 1996. *Creating classrooms for authors and inquirers.* 2nd ed. Portsmouth, NH: Heinemann.

Steele, J., C. Meredith, and C. Temple. 1999. *Methods for promoting critical thinking, Guidebook II.* Newark, DE: Reading and Writing for Critical Thinking Project of the University of Northern Iowa and International Reading Association.

Temple, F. 1995. *The ramsey scallop.* New York. Harper Trophy.

Whirlwind Arts Parntenrship. October 23, 1997. Press release Whirlwind improves leading scores in Chicago public schools. http://www.whirlwind-results.org

Section 4

Questioning and Problem Posing: Innate Human Curiosity and the Capacity for Healthy Skepticism

One of the distinguishing characteristics between humans and other forms of life is humans' inclination and ability to find problems to solve. Effective problem solvers know how to ask questions to fill in the gaps between what they know and what they don't know. Effective questioners are inclined to ask a range of questions, which fall into several categories.

Effective questioners make requests for data to support others' conclusions and assumptions.

- "What evidence do you have . . .?"
- "How do you know that's true?"
- "How reliable is this data source?"

They pose questions about alternative points of view.

- "From whose viewpoint are we seeing, reading, or hearing?"
- "From what angle, what perspective are we viewing this situation?"

Their questions search for connections and relationships.

- "How are these people/events/situations related to each other?"
- "What produced this connection?"

And, they pose hypothetical problems characterized by "iffy"-type questions.

- "What do you think would happen *if*. . .?"
- "*If* that is true, then what might happen if . . .?"

Inquirers recognize discrepancies and phenomena in their environment and probe into their causes.

In section four, all the authors pose perturbing questions intended to provoke greater thought and debate. They do not take things on face value; rather they critically probe, inviting readers to examine the issues, reveal their assumptions, and provide data to substantiate their assertions.

Jane Healy questions society's rush toward technology in schools by suggesting that society may be losing its focus on what is valued in youth education.

Ron Brandt asks some serious questions about the value of brain research in education by suggesting that society may be making some unfounded assumptions based on this research, and that the data from research in neuroscience may be too "soft" to build sound, educational practices.

Finally, Joe Renzulli questions traditional assumptions about working with students who are deemed gifted. Should an educator's job be to develop gifted behaviors in all students rather than merely finding and certifying them?

These three authors all question traditional modes of thinking about intelligence and learning and probe educators to do the same.

The Mad Dash to Compute
Enriching or Eroding Intelligence?

by Jane M. Healy

"Technology! I feel as if we're being swept down this enormous river—we don't know where we're going, or why, but we're caught in the current. I think we should stop and take a look before it's too late." This comment, voiced plaintively by an assistant superintendent from Long Island, New York, was typical of many I recently collected in a three-year process of investigating the reality of our heavily hyped "technological revolution." Having started this saga as a wide-eyed advocate for educational computing, I must now admit that the gentleman is right: New technologies hold enormous potential for education, but before any more money is wasted, we must pause and ask some pointed questions that have been bypassed in today's climate of "competitive technophilia." (My district's hard drives are bigger than yours!)

Educators, who are seen as one of the ripest growth markets in hardware, software, and Internet sales, have been carefully targeted by an industry that understandably wants to convince us that its products will solve all our problems. (When did you ever before see multiple double-page ads in *Education Week* for any educational product? When have you been offered "free" equipment—which eventually demands as much upkeep and fiscal lifeblood as the man-eating plant in *Little Shop of Horrors.*) "As much technology as early as possible or kids will be left hopelessly behind" is the thrust of the advertising, which extends also to parents. Not appreciating the nonsense inherent in this assumption, they, in turn, put pressure on schools to "get with the program."

Surely, as educators, we should have the wit to evaluate these pressures, resist public opinion, and shun manipulative marketing. It

---

also becomes our obligation to interpret to the public what we know is really good for kids. Yet, three major issues are being largely overlooked as we rush to capture the trend. I will call them (1) the trade-offs, (2) the developmental questions, and (3) who wins in the long run?

THE TRADE-OFFS: COULD THIS BE YOUR DISTRICT?

I am visiting the flagship middle school of a district that prides itself on the scope of its technology budget. Yet I am having difficulty finding students using computers, since many expensive machines sit idle (and, increasingly, obsolete) in classrooms where teachers have not learned to incorporate them into daily lessons. ("When they break, I just don't get them repaired," one first-grade teacher confided.)

Finally, in the computer lab, I find thirty-two fifth graders lined up at two rows of machines. The technology coordinator—who is technologically adept but has virtually no background in either teaching or curriculum development—explains that this group comes four times a week to practice reading and math skills. Many are below grade level in basic skills.

I randomly select a position behind Raoul, who is using a math software program. The director—now occupied in fixing a computer that eager young fingers have crashed—hastily reminds the students to enter the program at the correct level for their ability, but I begin to suspect something is amiss when Raoul effortlessly solves a few simple addition problems and then happily accepts his reward—a series of smash-and-blast games in which he manages to demolished a sizable number of aliens before he is electronically corralled into another series of computations. Groaning slightly, he quickly solves the problems and segues expertly into the next space battle. By the time I move on, Raoul has spent many more minutes zapping aliens than he has in doing math. My teacher's soul cringes at the thought of important learning time squandered. I also wonder if what we are really teaching Raoul is that he should choose easy problems so he can play longer, or that the only reason to use his brain even slightly is to be granted—by an automaton over which he has no personal control—some mindless fun as a reward. I wonder who selected this software or if any overall plan dictates the implementation of this expensive gadgetry. Moreover, this "lab"—like so many others—has been morphed from a music room. In this system, cuts in arts, physical education, and even textbooks are used to beef up technology budgets.

The trade-offs inherent in this all-too-typical situation should be troubling to all of us:

- Haste and *pressure for electronic glitz replacing a carefully designed plan* based on sound educational practice. Grafting technology onto schools without good curriculum or excellent teaching guarantees failure. First things first.
- *Money on hardware, software, and networks instead of essential teacher education.* Informed estimates suggest it takes five years of ongoing inservice before teachers can fully integrate computer uses into lesson plans. They also must have *solid technical support* so that instructional time is not spent repairing machines.
- *Technology coordinators without adequate preparation in education instead of teachers adept in linking computer use to significant aspects of curriculum.* "The third graders made T-shirts in computer lab today," one techie boasted. "Why?" I asked. "Well, we can—and besides, the kids just loved it." If this sort of justification prevails in your schools, don't be surprised if your test scores start to drop!
- Cuts in vital areas used to finance technology purchases. *Computers, which have as yet demonstrated questionable effects on student learning, must not be bought at the expense of proven staples of mental development*—art, music, drama, debate, physical education, text literacy, manipulatives, and hands-on learning aids. One teacher in a western state told me her district "could be IBM for all the technology we have." She was refused money to purchase a set of paperback literature books for her classroom. Why? "The money had all been spent on the machines," she sighed.
- *Pie-in-the sky assumptions that computers—instead of proven interventions—will remediate basic skills.* Many of today's youngsters need solid, hands-on remediation in reading and math delivered by teachers trained in established programs such as Reading Recovery. Don't forget that those "studies proving" that electronic learning systems work and are cost-effective were conducted by people with a big product to sell.
- *Installing computers instead of reducing class size.* To my surprise, I found that good technology use is actually *more teacher-intensive* than traditional instruction and works best with smaller classes! Research is also beginning to show the skill/drill software that "manages" learning for large groups may actually limit students' achievement once the novelty wears off. We need good, objective

long-range data before committing money and growing minds to such programs.

- Funding *electronic glitz instead of quality early childhood programs.* Again, we must weigh a large expense of unproven value against proven "upstream" prevention of academic and social problems. Ironically, estimated costs for connecting all classrooms to the Internet could also provide every child with an adequate preschool program.
- *Time wasted vs. productive learning.* Without good planning and supervision, youngsters tend to use even the best educational programs for mindless fun rather than meaningful learning. Moreover, if you do not have a district policy on selecting software, implement one today! Poorly selected "edutainment" and "drill and practice" can actually depress academic gains, whereas well-implemented simulations and conceptually driven programs may improve learning—if a good teacher is in charge. Consider the following:

> The image is a little unclear, but the twelve year olds surrounding the computer don't complain. They are too busy following the action on the screen where a disheveled-looking young man in bicycling clothes stands amidst a jungle talking earnestly with someone in a bush jacket who appears to be a scientist.
>
> One of the students giggles, pokes another, and attempts a whispered comment, but he is rapidly silenced.
>
> "Shush, Damon. Don't be such a jerk. We can't hear!" hisses his neighbor.
>
> What has inspired such serious academic purpose among these kids? They and their teacher are involved in directing (along with others around the globe) a three-month bicycle expedition, manned by a team of cyclists and scientists, through the jungles of Central America in search of lost Mayan civilizations. At the moment, they are debating the possibility of sending the team through a difficult, untravelled jungle track to a special site. How fast can they ride? How far? What obstacles will they encounter? What are the odds of success? What plans must be made?
>
> Like others in a new breed of simulations, this activity utilizes online and satellite phone communications to establish real-time links between students around the world and the adventurers. Because students' votes actually determine the course of the journey, they must problem solve right along with the scientists. To acquire the necessary knowledge, the class has also plunged into a variety of real-life, hands-on learning: history, archeology, visual arts, math (e.g., Mayans calculated in base 20), science of flora and fauna, Mayan poetry, building a

miniature rain forest, reading the daily journals of the adventurers, researching, developing theories, and debating about why the civilization collapsed.

This example is only one of many powerful supplements to a well-planned curriculum. New technologies can be used wisely—or they can be a costly impediment to educational quality. As you debate the trade-offs of your technology choices, you might keep these questions in mind:

1. What can this particular technology do that cannot be accomplished by other less expensive or more proven methods?
2. What will we gain—and what will we lose?
3. How can we "sell" wise educational decisions to a public foolishly buying the message that computers are a magic bullet for education?

THE DEVELOPMENTAL QUESTION: ARE WE HARMING KIDS?

A question too rarely considered is what effect extended computer use will have on children's developing bodies and brains. Moreover, it is imperative to ask at what age this technology should really be introduced. My observations have convinced me that normally developing children under age seven are better off without today's computers and software; technology funds should be first allocated to middle and high schools where computer-assisted learning is much more effective and age-appropriate.

Physical Effects: Too little is known about physical effects on digitized youngsters, but troubling evidence of problems resulting from computer use include vision (e.g., nearsightedness), postural and orthopedic complaints (e.g., neck and back problems; carpal tunnel syndrome), the controversial effects of electromagnetic radiation emitted from the backs and sides of machines, and even the rare possibility of seizures triggered by some types of visual displays. Administrators should be on top of this issue, as there is a chance schools might someday be found liable for physical complaints resulting from unregulated classroom computer use. In fact, I found a woeful disregard—and even ignorance—in schools of even the basic safety rules mandated for the adult workplace. Clear guidelines exist, and before you consign all your third graders to laptops you would be wise to check them out.

Brain Effects: In terms of what happens to kids' brains—cognitive, social, and emotional development—as a function of computer use, even less is known. The brain is significantly influenced by whatever media we choose for education, and poor choices now may well result in poor thinkers in the next generation.

For children of any age, improper software choices can disrupt language development, attention, social skills, and motivation to use the mind in effortful ways.

In my book *Failure to Connect* (1998)[1], I trace the course of brain development with technology use in mind, and one thing is clear: Computers can either help or hurt the process. For younger children, too much electronic stimulation replaces important experiences during critical periods of development: physical exploration, imaginative play, language, socialization, and quiet time for developing attention and inner motivation. For children of any age, improper software choices can disrupt language development, attention, social skills, and motivation to use the mind in effortful ways. (The next time you see a classroom of students "motivated" by computer use, be sure to question whether they are motivated to think and learn—or simply to play with the machines!)

By mid-elementary school, students can start to capitalize on the multi-media and abstract-symbolic capabilities of computers—if a good teacher is present to guide the learning. For middle and high schoolers, new technologies can make difficult concepts (e.g., ratio, velocity) more accessible and provide new windows onto visual reasoning, creativity, and the challenges of research. Yet, the first step must still be the filtering process: What is worthwhile in support of the curriculum, and what is merely flashy? Districts that take this job seriously and gear computer use to students' developmental needs are beginning to show real benefits from technology use.

PREPARING FOR THE FUTURE: WHO WINS IN THE LONG RUN?

"Kids need computers to prepare them for the future." Like so many advertising slogans, this one bears a closer examination. First of all, learning to use a computer today is a poor guarantee of a student's future, since workplace equipment will have changed dramatically for all but our oldest students. Moreover, because so much current use is harming rather than helping students' brain power and learning habits, the computer "have-nots" today may actually end up as the "haves" when future success is parceled out.

But even more important is the question of what skills will really prepare today's students for the future. Surely the next decades will be ones of rapid change where old answers don't always work, where employers demand communication and "people" skills as well as the ability to think incisively and imagine creative solutions to unforeseen problems. Many of today's computer applications offer poor preparation for such abilities.

One skill of critical importance in a technological future is "symbolic analysis," with reading and writing the common entry point. Yet while cyberspace may be filled with words, "a growing portion of the American population will not be able to use, understand, or benefit from those words," state Burstein and Kline (1966) in their book, *Road Warriors*[2]. "Some of these people may be digitally literate, in that they feel at home with joysticks and remote controls and are perfectly capable of absorbing the sights and sounds of multimedia entertainment. But if you are not functionally literate, your chances of getting a significant piece of the cyberspace pie are slim, even if you have access to it."

Our future workers will also need other abstract-symbolic skills. As the creation of wealth moves farther and farther away from raw materials and hands-on labor, successful workers will need to synthesize information, juggle abstract numbers, acquire multiple symbol systems in foreign languages, math, or the arts—as well as be familiar with new digital languages and images. As software design improves, computers will doubtlessly help with such preparation, but the key will continue to lie in the quality of the teachers who plan, mediate, and interpret a thoughtful curriculum.

The future also will favor those who have learned how to learn, who can respond flexibly and creatively to challenges, and who can master new skills. At the moment, the computer is a shallow and pedantic companion for such a journey. We should think long and carefully about whether our purpose is to be trendy or to prepare students to be intelligent, reasoning human beings whose skills extend far beyond droid-like button clicking. If we ourselves cannot think critically about the hard sell vs. the real business of schooling, we can hardly expect our students to do so.

NOTES:

1 *Failure to Connect: How Computers Affect Our Children's Minds—And What We Can Do About It.* (Simon & Schuster/Touchstone, 1998).

2 From *The Warriers* by Daniel Burstein and David Klein. New York: Penguin Books, 1966, p. 176.

Educators Need to Know About the Human Brain

by Ron Brandt

In this response to John Bruer's article in the May 1999 *Kappan,* Mr. Brandt argues that, used in conjunction with knowledge from other sources, findings from neuroscience are yielding additional insights into the learning process—and that educators would be foolish to ignore this growing body of knowledge. Mr. Bruer was offered an opportunity to provide a rejoinder, but he chose instead to refer readers back to his May article.

In the May 1999 *Kappan,* John Bruer condemns irresponsible claims regarding the use of brain research in education.[1] A well-informed scientist, Bruer is right to critique what he considers misinterpretations, but I think he is mistaken when he discourages educators from trying to understand and apply what is known. Used in conjunction with knowledge from other sources, including cognitive science, educational research, and professional experience, findings from neuroscience are yielding additional insights into the learning process.

In earlier articles Bruer stated flatly, "Right now, brain science has little to offer educational practice or policy" and urged attention instead to cognitive science.[2] But there is no need to erect a Berlin Wall between cognitive science and neuroscience; they are two sides of the same coin. In his *Kappan* article, Bruer recognizes this, noting that, in the past 15 years or so, "theoretical barriers have fallen."

Neuroscientists complain that, historically, cognivists have shown little interest in the neurological substrate of the cognition they study. If true, such an attitude would be understandable, because until the last decade, few means were available for scientists to investigate the brain directly. Under the circumstances, according to

From *Phi Delta Kappan,* November 1999, vol. 81, no. 3, pp. 235–238.

Francis Crick, co-discoverer of the structure of DNA, cognitive psychologists adopted a "functionalist" perspective:

> Just as it is not necessary to know about the actual writing of a computer when writing programs for it, so a functionalist investigates the information processed by the brain, and the computational processes the brain performs on this information, without considering the neurological implementation of theses processes. He usually regards such considerations as totally irrelevant, or at best, premature.[3]

This may be unfair. As evidenced by the lucid explanations of brain research in his new book, *The Myth of the First Three Years* [4] Bruer is very knowledgeable about neuroscience. But as Crick and some other neuroscientists say, the field of cognitive science must now be broadened to incorporate the flood of new knowledge emerging from brain research. Neuroscientist Joseph LeDoux—contending that cognitive science has ignored emotions, the subject of his research—argues the need for a new, more inclusive field he calls "mind science."[5]

SCHOLARLY QUARRELS SERVE A PURPOSE

Educators are used to scholarly quarrels: positions advanced by some researchers are almost invariably contradicted by others. One result is that practitioners seldom look to research for guidance. With so many inconsistencies, how are they to know whose claims are right? But such disagreements are part of how science works. Leslie Brothers, a psychiatrist who writes about the relationships between neuroscience and other fields, notes that among brain researchers, "Unexpected findings strain existing paradigms. Back and forth struggles regarding the proper context and significance of the findings ensue. Ultimately—sometimes after many years of discussion—old frameworks for understanding are replaced by new ones."[6] In the meantime, those unwilling to wait must decide for themselves—after weighing contrasting views—what seems to make the most sense.

In my reading of the books scientists have been writing about the brain. I have come across several debates that are important to educators. I will briefly highlight two such disagreements and explain possible reasons for them. Then I will cite a few examples of why I think findings from neuroscience—when combined with other knowledge—can be enlightening.

ENRICHMENT IN EARLY CHILDHOOD

One of the brain-related issues especially interesting to educators is the place of "enrichment" in early education. Science writer Janet Hopson and anatomist Marian Diamond have written about research conducted since the 1960s establishing that rats allowed to play with toys and other rats have thicker, heavier brains than rats kept in isolation. The extra weight and thickness is mostly because their brains have formed more connections among neurons. Researchers have also found that the growth of rats' brains in response to experience (and apparent shrinkage from lack of it) occurs not just in the weeks following birth, but at all ages. Even more interesting, the same is true for humans. Bruer, who downplays the concept of "enrichment," nevertheless calls "the ability of the mature brain to change and reorganize . . . a new, exciting finding of brain science."[7]

So what is in dispute? Whether the findings justify calls for improving the care and education of children. Diamond and Hopson recommend a set of experiences at each age level from birth to adolescence that they believe constitute "enrichment" for humans.[8] Bruer cautions that enriched conditions for rats, which he prefers to call "complex," are really just approximations of rats' natural environment in the wild. Most human children are not kept in cages, so we have no way of knowing what would be the equivalent of an enriched environment for humans. Bruer wants educators to understand the possibility of cultural bias in a loaded word like "enrichment." Experiences like those suggested by Diamond and Hopson may be valuable, he implies, but they do not necessarily affect children's brains in the same way complex environments affect the brains of rats.

Michael Gazzaniga, a prolific author who worked with Roger Sperry on the well-publicized research on split-brain patients, also objects to the idea that certain experiences automatically improve children's brains. "[Following a] White House conference on babies and brains," Gazzaniga writes, "the *New York Times* published an editorial saying neuroscience had informed us that the brain needs crafting during development, and reading is the way to do it. . . . This kind of casual reasoning drives serious scientists to distraction."[9] Offering what he considers a more accurate position, Gazzaniga declares that "the brain is not primarily an experience-storing device that constantly changes its structure to accommodate new experience. From the evolutionary perspective it is a dynamic computing device that is largely rule driven; it stores information by manipulating the value of simple arithmetic variables."[10]

Educators concerned about the quality of child care in our society must decide which interpretation of the enrichment research seems most reasonable. The issue, they should remember, is not whether children's lives will be better if they have access to books, music, and interesting games—they will, of course—but whether these things are necessary for brain development.

CONSTRUCTIVISM WRONG?

Closely related to the enrichment issue (because it also involves the brain's plasticity) and having many implications for education is a controversy between researchers whose work builds on discoveries that many capabilities are "built in" and other scientists who are equally impressed with the brain's ability to change with experience. Diamond and Hopson say, "When you look at the way a child's brain develops, one thing becomes absolutely obvious . . . *input from the environment helps shape the human brain.*"[11] Gazzaniga, however, rejects the idea of "so-called plasticity." He claims that when "clever neuroscientists . . . intervene and stimulate neurons in abnormal and bizarre ways, . . . the brain simply responds differently, and hence the resulting networks are different. This response hardly suggests that the brain is plastic in the sense that it has rewired itself."[12]

Gazzaniga and other neuroscientists who emphasize the evolutionary perspective are so convinced that "brains accrue specialized systems (adaptations) through natural selection" that they ridicule the idea, much cherished by educators, of constructivism.[13] Gazzaniga attacks neuroscientist Terry Sejnowski, who he says

> marries the questionable neurobiology he reviews to the work of Jean Piaget, then suggests children learn domains of knowledge by interacting with the environment. . . . The constructivist view of the brain is that it has a common mechanism that solves the structure of all problems. . . . This sort of assertion leaves us breathless because if we know anything, it is that any old part of the brain can't learn any old thing.[14]

Another evolutionary scientist, Steven Pinker, blames educators for trying to teach mathematics and reading with a constructivist philosophy, which he describes as "a mixture of Piaget's psychology with counterculture and postmodern ideology." American students, he charges, perform poorly because they are taught in accord with this "wrong" idea. "The problem," Pinker writes, "is that the educational establishment is ignorant of evolution."[15]

Educators who understand what cognitive scientists mean when they describe learning as construction[16] have cause to resent Pinker's charges and to wonder who is ignorant of what. Beyond being offended, however, we need to understand the reason he takes such a position.

. . . [N]o . . . area holds sway over all the others, nor do all areas of the brain 'report' to an overall supervisory center.

THE EVOLVED MODULAR BRAIN

Richard Restak, a Washington neurologist who has written numerous books about the brain, provides a piece of the puzzle by describing the brain as "modular." Researchers now understand, he writes, that brains are "arranged according to a distributed system composed of large numbers of modular elements linked together. . . . [N]o . . . area holds sway over all the others, nor do all areas of the brain 'report' to an overall supervisory center."[17] This decentralized organization, which is presumably the result of millions of years of evolution, incorporates numerous systems for performing particular tasks, such as recognizing faces, throwing objects, and counting. Each ability probably developed in response to a particular environmental challenge.

It may be helpful for educators to understand that human brains are apparently "pre-wired" for capabilities such as oral language and rudimentary mathematics (in the sense that particular neurons seem dedicated to these purposes from birth). In other words, these capabilities are not created entirely through experience; children's brains are not blank slates.

Knowing that this is really their message, perhaps we can be tolerant of scientists who, as they seek to establish the concept of the evolved modular brain, think it necessary to wage verbal warfare on the equally valid idea that brains also learn from experience. Francis Crick summaries the interrelationship succinctly. "The brain at birth, we now know, is not a tabula rasa but an elaborate structure with many of its parts already in place. Experience then tunes this rough-and-ready apparatus until it can do a precision job."[18]

YOU CAN'T DERIVE PEDAGOGY FROM BIOLOGY, BUT . . .

With the conflicts over enrichment, plasticity, and evolved capabilities as background, I now return to the original question about the usefulness of brain research to education. My position is simply this: if we had no other knowledge about human behavior and learning, we could certainly not derive much pedagogy from findings about the physical brain. But that is not the case. We do have a great deal of knowledge about learning, which we have acquired in several different ways. As Bruer argues, psychology, especially cognitive psychology, is a key source of that knowledge. We can also draw on other social sciences, such as anthropology, along with educational research and professional experience. When brain research is combined with knowledge from these other sources, it can further illuminate our understanding.

A practical example is Fast ForWord, a research-based program for students with a particular kind of learning disability. Neuroscientists Paula Tallal and Michael Merzenich developed the program based on research documenting brain plasticity in monkeys and on findings that some children have difficulty hearing phonemes, especially consonants because their brains do not process spoken language quickly enough.[19] If they do not hear the difference between "*b*" and "*p*," for example, they cannot develop phonemic awareness, which reading experts now agree is an essential prerequisite for learning to read.

Fast ForWord consists of computer games that first teach students to distinguish between similar sounds, using artificially slowed speech, and then challenge them gradually to increase their recognition speed. Using the program several hours a day, many children are said to make as much progress in four to six weeks as they would in two years of intensive work with a therapist.

Fast ForWord is a good illlustration because it builds on what was already known about reading instruction and the problems of learning-disabled students. For example, in a comprehensive review of the voluminous research on reading, Marilyn Adams had already identified the critical necessity of phonemic awareness.[20] Without that kind of information, and without other knowledge, including that accrued in recent decades about the design of computer games, Fast ForWord might not have been as effective.

UNDERSTANDING OURSELVES AND OUR STUDENTS

Most of us, though, are not in a position to devise new programs or approaches. An important benefit for us of knowledge about the brain may be increased understanding of what we commonly observe about human behavior. I have begun keeping a list of questions that I think neuroscience is helping to answer. Here are three: Why do people often not use in one situation what they have learned someplace else? Why do people sometimes do things—such as buying a particular kind of car or picking a fight in school—for reasons they are not completely aware of? Why do students often not remember what they have been taught?

Information from brain research cannot provide definitive answers to questions such as these, but combined with what we already know, it can add to our understanding. For example, the problem of "transfer of training" has plagued educators for at least a century. School curricula were changed when researchers could find no evidence that Latin and other classical studies improved students' general academic abilities. Advocates of character education and thinking skills have found, to their chagrin, that students who have been taught a strategy often fail to use it when circumstances are different. Researchers even have labels to describe knowledge that is not transferred: it is called "inert" or "situational."

Evolutionary theory has generated the notion that we are a collection of adaptations—brain devices that allow us to do specific things.

The transfer problem becomes clearer when we know about the brain's modular structure explained above. As mentioned, many scientists now believe this structure is the result of evolution. "Evolutionary theory has generated the notion that we are a collection of adaptations—brain devices that allow us to do specific things. . . . Many systems throughout the brain contribute to a single cognitive function."[21] While these systems are certainly in communication with one another, they are also somewhat independent. Knowing this, educators must take steps to strengthen connections among cognitive functions that might otherwise remain relatively separate. Stanislaus Dehaene, a French mathematician turned neuroscientist, says a priority for mathematics teachers must be integration of the brain's various mathematics systems:

> If my hypothesis is correct, innumeracy is with us for a long time, because it reflects one of the fundamental properties of our brain: its modularity, the compartmentalization of mathematical knowledge within multiple partially autonomous circuits. In order to become proficient in mathematics, one must go beyond these compartmentalized modules and establish a series of flexible links among them. . . . A good teacher is an alchemist who gives a fundamentally modular human brain the semblance of an interactive network.[22]

Another commonly observed characteristic of people, including children in schools, is our tendency to do things without always knowing why. A contributing factor is probably our emotions, which, though still poorly understood, are now being studied by neuroscientists. They have identified connections among the amygdala, the hippocampus, and the frontal lobes, revealing that fear—and probably the emotions—are processed in the same approximate location (the frontal lobes) where personal and social decisions are made.[23] When we understand that emotions, which probably are the effects of various chemical neurotransmitters,[24] help determine what we remember but that they are usually unconscious (when they become conscious we call them feelings), we can begin to see how emotions may influence our decisions without our knowing it.

A third question that brain research helps answer is why we remember some things but forget others. Every teacher has been exasperated by students who insist they were never taught something when they obviously were. Knowing how memory works not only helps us understand this familiar problem but gives us some clues for what to do about it. The most fundamental thing scientists have learned about memory is that we do not store memories whole and therefore do not retrieve them that way either. When we remember something, we actually reconstruct it by combining elements of the original experience. Neuroscientist Antonio Damasio explains that a memory "is recalled in the form of images at many brain sites rather than at a single site. Although we have the illusion that everything comes together in a single anatomical theater, recent evidence suggests that it does not. Probably the relative simultaneity of activity at different sites binds the separate parts of the mind together."[25]

Our ability to re-create the memory—to recombine all or most of the elements (which are stored in millions of neurons)—depends on the strength of the original experience, including the emotional load. Daniel Schacter, an expert on memory and the brain, says it concisely: "For better or worse, our recollections are largely at the mercy of our elaborations; only those aspects of experience that are targets of elaborative encoding processes have a high likelihood of being remembered subsequently."[26] Why, then, do students forget what they have been taught? Because the information served no useful purpose in their lives, was thus devoid of emotional impact, and was not "elaborately encoded."

THINKING, LEARNING, AND FEELING ALL HAVE A 'NEURAL SUBSTRATE'

My purpose here is not to insist on the correctness of these interpretations or to argue that brain research alone tells us how to run schools. I wish only to show that knowledge about brain functioning is relevant, especially when used to supplement what we know from other sources. Today's educators are fortunate to be living at a time when we are finally beginning to really understand the learning process, including its neural substrate. We are coming to recognize, Francis Crick says in *The Astonishing Hypothesis,* that all our thoughts, behaviors, and feelings are the result of chemical and electrical activity in the brain and related neural structures. Never again should we talk about psychological phenomena without recognizing that all of them are "brain-based."

Much remains unclear, and we surely will misinterpret some findings as we try to make sense of the partial information currently available. If so, we must be open to clarification, some of which will come with newer findings. But with today's challenges, educators would be foolish to ignore the growing body of knowledge about our brains.

NOTES

1. John T. Bruer, "In Search of . . . Brains-Based Education," *Phi Delta Kappan,* May 1999, pp. 649–57.

2. John T. Bruer, "Brain Science, Brain Fiction," *Educational Leadership,* November 1998, p. 14. See also John T. Bruer, "Education and the Brain: A Bridge Too Far," *Educational Researcher,* November 1997, pp. 4–16.

3. Francis Crick, *The Astonishing Hypothesis: The Scientific Search for the Soul* (New York: Scribner, 1994), p. 18.

4. John T. Bruer, *The Myth of the First Three Years* (New York: Free Press, 1999).

5. Joseph Ledoux, *The Emotional Brain* (New York: Simon & Schuster, 1996), p. 68.

6. Leslie Brothers, *Friday's Footprint: How Society Shapes the Human Mind* (New York: Oxford University press, 1997), p. 48.

7. Bruer, "Brain Science, Brain Fiction," p. 18.

8. Marian Diamond and Janet Hopson, *Magic Trees of the Mind: How to Nurture Your Child's Intelligence, Creativity, and Healthy Emotions from Birth through Adolescence* (New York: Dutton, 1998).

9. Michael S. Gazzaniga, *The Mind's Past* (Berkeley: University of California Press, 1998), p. 29.

10. Ibid., p. 35

11. Diamond and Hopson, p. 63 (emphasis in the original).

12. Gazzaniga, p. 48.

13. Ibid., p. 9.

14. Ibid., pp. 13–15.

15. Steven Pinker, *How the Mind Works* (New York: Norton, 1997), pp. 341–42. When I complained to Pinker about these comments, he replied in a personal message sent in May 1999 that "ultimately we do not disagree on much" and that in his future writings he would take my observations into account.

16. *Learner-Centered Psychological Principles: A Framework for School Reform and Redesign* (Washington, D.C.: American Psychological Association, 1997).

17. Richard Restak, *The Modular Brain* (New York: Scribner, 1994), pp. 35, xvi–xvii.

18. Crick, p. 10.

19. Beverly A. Wright et al., "Deficits in Auditory temporal and Spectral Resolution in Language-Impaired Children," *Nature,* 8 May 1997, pp. 176–78.

20. Marilyn J. Adams, *Beginning to Read: Thinking and Learning About Print* (Urbana: Center for the Study of Reading, University of Illinois, 1990).

21. Gazzaniga, p. 10.

22. Stanislaus Dehaene, *The Number Sense: How the Mind Creates Mathematics* (New York: Oxford University Press, 1997), p. 139.

23. LeDoux, op. cit.

24. Candace Pert, *Molecules of Emotion* (New York: Scribner, 1997).

25. Antonio R. Damasio, *Descartes' Error* (New York: Grosset/Putnam, 1994), p. 84.

26. Daniel L. Schacter, *Searching for Memory* (New York: Basic Books, 1996), p. 56.

Raising the Ceiling for All Students

School Improvement from a High-End Learning Perspective[1]

by Joseph S. Renzulli

> Powerful learning strategies can most simply be thought of as what we presently do for gifted and talented children. What works for these students works just as well in at-risk situations.—Henry M. Levin (Founder of the Accelerated Schools Project, as cited in Hopfenberg 1993)

EDUCATION'S DIRTY LITTLE SECRET

If there is any single, unifying characteristic of today's schools, that characteristic is surely a resistance, if not an immunity, to change. The ponderous rhetoric about school improvement and the endless lists of mission statements, noble goals, and standards need to be tempered with a little common sense about the real purpose of schooling and the essentials needed to make learning enjoyable and satisfying as well as efficient. We also need to have practice precede policy so that we eventually adopt what works rather than what politicians and others far removed from classrooms try to ram down the throats of the persons who deliver the services. Finally, we need to adopt gentle and evolutionary approaches to change that school personnel can live with and grow with, rather than be threatened by.

Albert Einstein once said that problems cannot be solved at the same level of consciousness that created them. We must consider these words of wisdom very carefully if there is any hope whatsoever of turning around a public education system that is slowly but surely deteriorating into a massive warehouse of underachievement, unfulfilled expectations, and broken dreams. The factory model of school-

---

ing that gave rise to the clear and present danger now facing our schools cannot be used to overcome the very problems that it has created. And yet, as we examine reform initiatives, it is difficult to find creative and innovative plans that are qualitatively different from the old top-down patterns of policy making that were based almost exclusively on rigidly prescribed curriculum, endless lists of state regulations, and statewide testing programs. We delude ourselves into thinking that the "new standards movement" is different from the behavioral objectives movement of the 1960s or the mastery learning and minimum competency movements of the 1970s and 1980s. And most of today's so called *performance tests* differ very little from what we have previously called achievement tests, criterion-referenced tests, and competency-based tests. Nor have we made significant progress beyond the traditional models of learning that have dominated our schools. We must also face up to a reality that almost everyone understands, but no one is willing to talk about because it has become education's "dirty little secret." Ram, remember, and regurgitate has become the learning "model" that desperate policy makers think will allow them to tell the public that our schools are improving. The appearance of school improvement that may result from hosing students down with the facts and figures that prepare them for what we now call "high-stakes testing" may show small and temporary gains in scores, but such improvements are a far cry from the kinds of higher-level thinking skills and problem-solving capacities that will prepare our young people for productive lives in an ever-demanding world of higher education and job performance.

Ram, remember, and regurgitate has become the learning "model" that desperate policy makers think will allow them to tell the public that our schools are improving.

Those that are not smart enough to learn from history are doomed to repeat their mistakes over and over and over. Since the onset of the compensatory education movement in the early 1960s, billions of federal, state, and local dollars have been spent on deficit-based, compensatory learning models. Not only have these models failed to produce significant improvements in schooling, they actually have been counterproductive! In an effort to capitalize on the deficit-driven models of school reform, textbook publishers have engaged in a marketplace practice so extensive and pervasive that it has earned its own name—the dumbing down of curriculum. In a study dealing with reading achievement, Taylor and Frye (1988) found that 78 percent to 88 percent of fifth- and sixth-grade average readers could pass pretests on basal comprehension skills before they were covered in the basal reader. The average readers were performing at approximately 92 percent accuracy while the better readers were performing at 93 percent accuracy on the comprehension skills pretests.

One reason that so many average and above-average students demonstrate mastery of the curriculum is because contemporary textbooks have been dumbed down, a phrase coined by Terrel Bell, former secretary of education. Chall and Conard concur with Bell's assessment, documenting a trend of decreasing difficulty in the most widely used textbooks over a thirty-year period. "On the whole, the later the copyright dates of the textbooks for the same grade, the easier they were, as measured by indices of readability level, maturity level, difficulty of questions and extent of illustration" (1991, 2). Kirst (1982) also believes that textbooks have dropped by two grade levels in difficulty over the last 10 to 15 years. Most recently, Philip G. Altbach, noted scholar and author on textbooks in America, suggests that textbooks, as evaluated across a spectrum of assessment measures, have declined in rigor.

> Textbooks are a central part of any educational system. They help define the curriculum and can either significantly help or hinder the teacher. The "excellence movement" has directed its attention to textbooks in the past few years. American textbooks, according to the critics, are boring and designed for the lowest common denominator. They have been "dumbed down" so that content is diluted and "readability" is stressed. Textbooks have evolved over the past several decades into "products" often assembled by committees in response to external pressures rather than a coherent approach to education. Most important to many of the critics, textbooks do not provide the knowledge base for American schools in a period of reform, renewal and improvement (Altbach et al. 1991, 2).

Researchers have discussed the particular problems encountered by students when textbooks are "dumbed down" because of readability formulas or the politics of textbook adoption. Bernstein summarizes the particular problem that current textbooks pose for learners whose performance levels vary: "Even if there were good rules of thumb about the touchy subject of textbook adoption, the issue becomes moot when a school district buys only one textbook, usually at 'grade level,' for all students in a subject or grade. Such a purchasing policy pressures adoption committees to buy books that the least-able students can read. As a result, the needs of more advanced students are sacrificed" (1985, 465). Chall and Conard (1991) also cite particular difficulties for the above-average student with regard to less difficult textbooks.

Another group not adequately served was those who read about two grades or more above the norm. Their reading textbooks, especially, provided little or no challenge since they were matched to students' grade placement, not their reading levels. Many students were aware of this and said, in their interviews, that they preferred harder books because they learned harder words and ideas from them. Since harder reading textbooks are readily available, one may ask why they were not used with the more able readers, as were the easier reading textbooks for the less able readers. This practice of using grade-level reading textbooks for those who read two or more grades above the norms has changed little through the years, although it has been repeatedly questioned (see Chall 1967; Chall and Conard 1991). It would appear that, for various administrative reasons, teachers do not use a reading textbook above the student's grade placement. The reason most often mentioned is really a question: If the third-grade teacher uses fourth-grade books, what is the fourth-grade teacher going to do?

Further, Chall and Conard stress the importance of the match between a learner's abilities and the difficulty of the instructional task, stating that the optimal match should be slightly above the learner's current level of functioning. When the match is optimal, learning is enhanced. However, "if the match is not optimal [i.e., the match is below or above the child's level of understanding/knowledge], learning is less efficient and development may be halted" (1991, 19). It is clear that the current trend of selecting textbooks that the majority of students can read is a problem for higher-achieving students, but also has a negative impact on all students because of the boredom that typically results from a lack of challenge.

Recent findings by Usiskin (1987) and Flanders (1987) indicate that not only have textbooks decreased in difficulty, but also that they incorporate a large percentage of repetition to facilitate learning. Usiskin argues that even average eighth-grade students should study algebra since only 25 percent of the pages in typical seventh- and eighth-grade mathematics texts contain new content. Flanders corroborated this finding by investigating the mathematics textbook series of three popular publishers. Students in grades 2 through 5 who used these math textbooks encountered approximately 40 percent to 65 percent new content over the course of the school year which equates to new material two to three days a week. By eighth grade, the amount of new content had dropped to 30 percent, which translates to encountering new material once every one and one half days a week. Flanders suggests that these estimates are conservative because days for review and testing were not included in his analysis, and concludes, "There should be little wonder why good students get bored: they do the same thing year after year" (1987, 22).

There should be little wonder why good students get bored: they do the same thing year after year.

In light of the findings by recent researchers, a mismatch seems to exist between the difficulty of textbooks, the repetition of curricular material in these texts, and the need to engage and challenge learners at various achievement levels. Far too many students spend too much of their time in school practicing skills and learning content they already know. All of these factors are causing students at all levels to learn less and proceed haltingly in their development, thereby creating or encouraging their underachievement. The problem is most pervasive in schools that serve at-risk populations. Pressure in these schools to "get-the-scores-up" forces needless repetition and practice and an overreliance on remedial instructional models. These deficit-oriented practices are far less tolerated in schools that serve more affluent communities, and thus, what seems to be a logical approach to dealing with disadvantaged populations only serves to widen the gap between poor and middle class schools.

TRANSCENDING PREVIOUS LEVELS OF CONSCIOUSNESS

Transcending previous levels of consciousness will not be an easy task because moving away from a deficit-oriented model is counterintuitive (i.e., it goes against common sense). If students are not learning basic material, doesn't it make sense to give them more drill and practice? And if more drill doesn't work, let's just give them ever-increasing doses! It seems so logical and reasonable, but it simply has not worked. And unfortunately, the major effect of such approaches has been to turn schools into dreary and punitive places rather than places where personal and creative growth and the joy of learning become not only valued, but the necessary precursors to academic attainment. Deficit-oriented models also lead to increased top-down punitive practices that, once again, have proven to produce results that are opposite from what was intended. Witness the current trend toward grade-level retention for underachieving students and denying graduation to high school students who fail to pass state tests. Both practices have no basis in research and only serve to increase the number of unengaged and disaffected students, many of whom become the potential dropouts and push-outs of a system that is now failing them for a second time. Retention and the denial of graduation may provide good public relations material for the "get tough" rhetoric of policy makers, but such practices do not address the problem of students who are not learning. Rather than examining ways to make schools more inviting, friendly, and enjoyable places, we seem predisposed to looking for ways of blaming and punishing the victim!

Rather than examining ways to make schools more inviting, friendly, and enjoyable places, we seem predisposed to looking for ways of blaming and punishing the victim!

If we are to transcend the deficit/punitive level of consciousness that has characterized so much of our efforts to improve schools, we need to look at models of learning that pay more attention to the full development of the learner rather than merely how much we can stuff in their memory banks for the next round of standardized testing. More books, articles, and papers have been written about the process of learning than perhaps any other topic in education and psychology. And when we add the vast amount of material that has been written about models of teaching and theories of instruction, the sheer volume of literature is nothing short of mind boggling! It is not my intention to review this multitudinous literature as background for the discussion on high-end learning that follows, nor will I argue about the number of unique theories that actually exist, or the advantages and disadvantages of various paradigms for guiding the learning process. I will argue, however, that in spite of all that has been written, every theory of teaching and learning can be classified into one of two general models. There are, obviously, occasions when a particular approach transcends both models; however, for purposes of clarifying the main features of high-end learning, we will treat the two main models as polar opposites. Both models of learning and teaching are valuable in the overall process of schooling, and a well-balanced school program must make use of both of these general approaches to learning and teaching.

Although many names have been used to describe the two models that will be discussed, we will simply refer to them as the deductive model and the inductive model. The deductive model is the one most educators are familiar with and the one that has guided the overwhelming majority of what takes place in classrooms and other places where formal learning is pursued. The inductive model, on the other hand, represents the kinds of learning that take place outside of formal school situations. A good way to understand the difference between these two types of learning is to compare how learning takes place in a typical classroom with how someone might learn new material or skills in real-world situations. Classrooms are characterized by relatively fixed time schedules, segmented subjects or topics, predetermined sets of information and activity, tests and grades to determine progress, and a pattern of organization that is largely driven by the need to acquire and assimilate information and skills imposed from above and from outside the classroom. The major assumption in the deductive model is that current learning will have transfer value for some future problem, course, occupational pursuit, or life activity.

Contrast this type of learning with the more natural chain of events that take place in inductive situations such as a research laboratory, business office, or film studio. The goal in these situations is to produce a product or service. All resources, information, schedules, and sequences of events are directed toward this goal, and evaluation (rather than grading) is a function of the quality of the product or service as viewed through the eyes of a client or consumer. Everything that results in learning in a research laboratory, for example, is for present use, and, therefore, looking up new information, conducting an experiment, analyzing results, or preparing a report is focused primarily on the present rather than the future. Even the amount of time devoted to a particular project cannot be determined in advance because the nature of the problem and the unknown obstacles that might be encountered prevent us from prescribing rigid schedules.

The deductive model has dominated the ways in which most formal education is pursued, and the "track record" of the model has been less than impressive. One need only reflect for a moment on his or her own school experience to realize that with the exception of basic language and arithmetic, much of the compartmentalized material learned for some remote and ambiguous future situation is seldom used in the conduct of daily activities. The names of famous generals, the geometric formulas, the periodic table, and the parts of a plant are quickly forgotten; and even if remembered, they do not have direct applicability to the problems that most people encounter in their daily lives. This is not to say that previously learned information is unimportant, but its relevancy, meaningfulness, and endurance for future use is minimized when it is almost always learned apart from situations where the application of knowledge is as important as the knowledge itself.

Nowhere is change more evident than in the emphasis that is being placed currently on thinking skills and interdisciplinary approaches to curriculum.

Deductive learning is based mainly on the factory model or human engineering conception of schooling. The underlying psychological theory is behaviorism, and the central concept of this ideology is that schools should prepare young people for smooth adjustment into the culture and workforce of the society at large. A curriculum based on deductive learning must be examined in terms of both what is taught and how it is taught. The issue of what is (or should be) taught has always been the subject of controversy, ranging from a conservative position that emphasizes a classical or basic education curriculum to a more liberal perspective that includes contemporary knowledge and life adjustment experiences (e.g., driver education, sex education, computer literacy). By and large, American schools have been very effective in adapting what is taught to changes taking place in our society. Recent concerns about the kinds of skills that will be required in a rapidly changing job market have accelerated curricular changes that will prepare students for careers in technological fields and what has been described as a post-industrial society. Nowhere is this change more evident than in the emphasis that is being placed currently on thinking skills and interdisciplinary approaches to curriculum. These changes are viewed as favorable developments so far as schoolwide enrichment is concerned; however, the deductive model still places limitations on learning because of restrictions on how material is taught.

Although most schools have introduced teaching techniques that go beyond traditional drill and recitation, the predominant instructional model continues to be a prescribed and presented approach to learning. The teacher, textbook, or curriculum guide prescribes what is to be taught, and the material is presented to students in a predetermined manner. Educators have become more clever and imaginative in the teaching models employed, and it is not uncommon to see teachers using approaches such as discovery learning, simulations, cooperative learning, inquiry training, problem-centered learning, concept learning, and a host of variations on these basic models. More recent approaches include simulated problem solving through the use of interactive videodiscs and computer programs. Some of these approaches certainly make learning more active and enjoyable than traditional, content-based deductive learning, but the "bottom line" is that there are certain predetermined bodies of information and thinking processes that students are expected to acquire. The instructional effects of the deductive model are those directly achieved by leading the learner in prescribed directions. As indicated above, there is nothing inherently "wrong" with the deductive model; however, it is based on a limited conception of the role of the learner, it fails to consider variations in interests and learning styles, and it always places students in roles of lesson learners and exercise doers rather that authentic, firsthand inquirers.

Inductive learning, on the other hand, focuses on the present use of content and processes as a way of integrating material and thinking skills into the more enduring structure of the learner's repertoire. And it is these more enduring structures that have the greatest amount of transfer value for future use. When content and processes are learned in authentic, contextual situations, they result in more meaningful uses of information and problem-solving strategies than the learning that takes place in artificial, preparation-for-the-future situations. If persons involved in inductive learning experiences are given some choice in the domains and activities in which they are engaged, and if present experience is directed toward realistic and personalized goals, this type of learning creates its own relevancy and meaningfulness.

If we agree that people do, in fact, learn when they are outside of schools and classrooms, in the "real-world" as it is sometimes called, then we need to examine the dimensions of this type of learning and the ways that real-world learning can be brought into the school. But we must also be extremely cautious whenever we think about "bringing" anything into the school. Our track record in this regard has been one of structuring and institutionalizing even the most innovative approaches to learning. We recall how the much heralded concept of discovery learning ended up being what a colleague called "sneaky telling"; and how a focus on thinking skills and creative thinking fell prey to the same types of formulas and prescribed activities that characterized the content-based curriculum that has been criticized so strongly by thinking skills advocates. Even our present fascination with computers and videodiscs is, in some cases, turning out to be little more than "electronic worksheets."

High-end learning is essentially an inductive approach to learning; however, it draws upon selected practices of deductive learning. My argument is not an indictment of deductive learning, but, rather, a need to achieve balance between the two major approaches. Introducing inductive learning into the school is important for several reasons. First, schools should be enjoyable places that students want to attend rather than places they endure as part of their journey toward assimilation into the job market and the adult world. Second, schools should be places where students participate in and prepare for intelligent, creative, and effective living. This type of living includes learning how to analyze, criticize, and select from among alternative sources of information and courses of action; how to think effectively about unpredictable personal and interpersonal problems; how to live harmoniously with one another while remaining true to one's own emerging system of attitudes, beliefs, and values; and how to confront, clarify, and act upon problems and situations in constructive and creative ways. Finally, inductive learning is important because our society and democratic way of life are dependent upon an unlimited reservoir of creative and effective people. A small number of rare individuals have always emerged as the thinkers and problem solvers of our society. But we cannot afford to leave the emergence of leaders to chance, nor can we waste the undeveloped talents of so many of our young citizens who are the victims of poverty and the negative consequences that accompany being poor in America. All students must have the opportunity to develop their potentials and to lead constructive lives without trampling on or minimizing the value of others in the process.

Perhaps the best way to summarize the difference between deductive and inductive learning is to examine each model in terms of the three components that portray the act of learning. If we place each of these components on a continuum ranging from highly structured learning on the left side to unstructured learning on the right side, what emerges is a contrast such as the type portrayed in Figure 1. There is, obviously, a middle ground for each continuum, and each point on the continua has implications for the ways in which we organize learning situations. I do not believe that all learning should favor the right side of each continuum presented in Figure 1. Some learning situations are undoubtedly more efficient when carried out in structured settings, and even drill and worksheets have value in accomplishing certain goals of learning. But because I believe that schools are first and foremost places for talent development, there are times within the overall process of schooling when we can and should make a conscious commitment to apply high-end learning methods to selected aspects of schooling.

There is, obviously, a middle ground for each continuum, and each point on the continua has implications for the ways in which we organize learning situations.

HIGH-END LEARNING DEFINED

High-end learning, or what I have also called enrichment learning and teaching, is based on the ideas of a small number of philosophers, theorists, and researchers. Although it is beyond the scope of this chapter to review the work of these eminent thinkers, the following four principles summarize their beliefs:

1. Each learner is unique, and, therefore, all learning experiences must be examined in ways that take into account the abilities, interests, and learning styles of the individual.

2. Learning is more effective when students enjoy what they are doing, and, therefore, learning experiences should be constructed and assessed with as much concern for enjoyment as for other goals.

3. Learning is more meaningful and enjoyable when content (i.e., knowledge) and process (i.e., thinking skills, methods of inquiry) are learned within the context of a real and present problem, and, therefore, attention should be given to opportunities to personalize student choice in problem selection, the relevance of the problem for individual students at the time the problem is being addressed, and strategies for assisting students in personalizing problems they might choose to study.

Figure 1. The Structured to Unstructured Continuum of Instructional Practices

The Deductive Model ("Direct Frontal Teaching")	**The Inductive Model** ("Enrichment Learning and Teaching")
The Teacher's Role	
Teachers initiate, determine, control, and micromanage learning	Students play a leading role in topic/problem selection and pacing
Teachers provide feedback in the form of grades based on normative criteria	Teachers and students are partners informative evaluation based on progress toward goals
Teachers as instructors (disseminators of knowledge)	Teachers as coaches, patrons, resource procurers, probers, editors, ombudsmen, and colleagues
Teachers view content as objective, impersonal, and value free	Teachers personalize, criticize, and emphasize the value-laden character of content (artistic modification)
The Curriculum	
Predetermined by textbooks or courses of study	Derived as a result of individual or small-group student interests
Content driven	Process and product driven
Problems are prescribed, presented, and usually previously solved	Self-selected, open-ended, real-world problems
Information is presented for (possible) future use	Information is sought only when needed to help solve a present problem
Knowledge is presented as factual material	Knowledge serves as a vehicle for confrontation with events, issues, ideas, and beliefs
Classroom Organization and Management	
Predetermined daily time blocks and the weekly allocation of time are determined on the size of units of instruction	Time is determined by the evolving nature of the task, project, or end product
Whole group activities	Individual and small-group activities
Age/grade grouping	Interest, problem, and common task grouping
Predetermined and usually fixed classroom arrangements	Classrooms are arranged to facilitate the accomplishment of the task or the completion of products
Classrooms are the places where learning takes place	Learning takes place wherever relevant information is gathered or experiences are pursued
The Student's Role	
Students as lesson learners and consumers of knowledge	Students as first-hand inquirers and producers of knowledge
Students accumulate and store knowledge for possible future use	Student confronts and constructs knowledge for present use
Students pursue common tasks and activities	Students' tasks and activities are based on divisions of labor
Students use knowledge to study about problems	Students use knowledge to *find* and *focus* problems and to *act on* problems
Students passively accept knowledge as objective, factual, and correct	Students personalize, interpret, criticize, and dissect knowledge

4. Some formal instruction may be used in high-end learning, but a major goal of this approach to learning is to enhance knowledge and thinking skill acquisition gained through teacher instruction with applications of knowledge and skills that result from students' construction of meaningfulness.

The ultimate goal of learning that is guided by these principles is to replace dependence and passive learning with independence and engaged learning. Although all but the most conservative educators will agree with these principles, much controversy exists about how these (or similar) principles may be applied in everyday school situations. A danger also exists that these principles might be viewed as yet another idealized list of glittering generalities that cannot easily be manifested in schools that are overwhelmed by the deductive model of learning. Developing a school program based on these principles is not an easy task. Over the years, however, we have achieved a fair amount of success by gaining faculty, administrative, and parental consensus on a small number of easy-to-understand concepts and related services, and by providing resources and training related to each concept and service delivery procedure. In the ensuing years, numerous research studies (Renzulli and Reis 1994) and field tests in schools with widely varying demographics have been carried out. These studies and field tests provided opportunities for the development of large amounts of practical know-how that are readily available for schools that would like to implement this approach to school improvement.

THE SCHOOLWIDE ENRICHMENT MODEL

I describe here the rationale for a plan that has demonstrated its effectiveness in bringing about significant changes in schooling. That plan, the Schoolwide Enrichment Model (SEM), is a systematic set of specific strategies for increasing student effort, enjoyment, and performance and for integrating a broad range of advanced learning experiences and higher-order thinking skills into any curricular area, course of study, or pattern of school organization. The details and know-how for implementing a school improvement program based on this plan are beyond the scope of this article; however, key resource books can be found in the references. The general approach of the SEM is one of infusing more effective practices into existing school structures. This research-supported plan is designed for general education, but it is based on instructional methods and curricular practices that originated in special programs for high-ability students. These programs have been an especially fertile place for experimentation because prescribed curriculum guides or traditional methods of instruction usually do not encumber them. It was within the context of these programs that the thinking-skills movement first took hold in American education and the pioneering work of such notable theorists as Benjamin Bloom, Howard Gardner, and Robert Sternberg first gained the attention of the education community.

Research opportunities in a variety of special programs have allowed me along with my colleagues to develop instructional procedures and programming alternatives that emphasize the need (1) to provide a broad range of advanced-level enrichment experiences for all students and (2) to use varied student responses to these experiences as steppingstones for relevant follow-up. This approach is not viewed as a new way to identify who is or is not "gifted"; rather, the process simply identifies how subsequent opportunities, resources, and encouragement can be provided to support the continuous escalation of student involvement in both required and self-selected activities. This approach seeks to develop high levels of multiple potentials in a broad range of students.

Practices that have been a mainstay of many special programs for "the gifted" are being absorbed into general education by reform models designed to upgrade the performance of all students. This integration of know-how from programs for the gifted is a favorable development for two reasons. First, the adoption of many of these practices is indicative of the viability and usefulness of both the know-how of special programs and the role that enrichment specialists can and should play in total school improvement. Second, all students should have opportunities to develop higher-order thinking skills, to pursue more rigorous content than is typically found in today's "dumbed-down" textbooks, and to undertake firsthand investigations. The ways in which students respond to enriched learning experiences should be used as a rationale for providing all students with advanced level follow-up opportunities. The SEM approach reflects a democratic ideal that accommodates the full range of individual differences in the entire student population, and it opens the door to programming models that develop the talent potentials of many at-risk students—those often excluded from anything but the most basic of curricular experiences.

The transfer of know-how from special programs into general education is supported by a wide variety of research on human abilities (Bloom 1985; Gardner 1983; Renzulli 1978; Sternberg 1984). This research clearly and unequivocally endorses much broader conceptions of talent development. And these broader conceptions argue against the restrictive student selection practices that guided identification procedures in the past. Laypersons and professionals at all levels have begun to question the efficacy of programs that rely on IQ scores and other measures of cognitive ability as the primary methods for identifying which students can benefit from differentiated services. Traditional identification procedures have restricted services to small numbers of high-scoring students and have excluded large numbers of at-risk students.

Special services should be viewed as opportunities to develop gifted behaviors rather than merely to find and certify them.

Special services should be viewed as opportunities to develop gifted behaviors rather than merely to find and certify them. In this regard, we should judiciously avoid saying that a young person is either "gifted" or "not gifted." It is difficult to gain support for talent development when we say such things as "Elaine is a gifted third grader." Such statements offend many people and lead to the accusations of elitism that have plagued special programs. But note the difference in orientation when we focus on the behavioral characteristics that brought this child to our attention in the first place: "Elaine is a third-grader who reads at the adult level and who has a fascination with biographies about women scientists." And note the logical and justifiable services that we might provide for Elaine under the guidance of her classroom teacher: Elaine is allowed to substitute for the third-grade reader more challenging books in her interest area; she leaves the school two afternoons a month to meet with her mentor, a local journalist specializing in gender issues; and during time made available through curriculum compacting in her strength areas (i.e., reading, language arts, and spelling), the schoolwide enrichment teaching specialist helps Elaine prepare a questionnaire and an interview schedule to be used with local women scientists.

Could even the staunchest opponent of programs for the gifted argue against the logic or the appropriateness of these services? When programs focus on developing the behavioral potentials of individuals or of small groups whose members share common interests, we can avoid the controversies surrounding the "G word" by labeling the services rather than the students. Through the use of the Schoolwide Enrichment Model, we can serve both traditional high-achieving students, and students who show their talents in a variety of other ways. A detailed description of the model is beyond the scope of this article, but as mentioned earlier, the plan is based on a thorough assessment of students' strengths through the Total Talent Portfolio, and it offers a broad continuum of services purposefully designed to capitalize on various strengths.[2]

Most efforts to make major changes in schooling have failed.

SCHOOLWIDE ENRICHMENT AND EDUCATION REFORM

Most efforts to make major changes in schooling have failed. Although there is endless speculation about why schools are so resistant to change, most theorists and policy makers have concluded that tinkering with single components of a complex system will give only the appearance of improvement rather than the real and lasting change so desperately sought by educational leaders. Examples of tinkering are familiar to most educators. For instance, more rigorous curriculum standards, without improved curricular materials and teachers able to use them, will not yield significantly improved academic performance. Similarly, tinkering designed to force change in classrooms (e.g., high-stakes testing) may create the illusion of improved achievement, but the reality is increased pressure on schools to expand the use of compensatory learning models that, so far, have contributed only to the "dumbing down" of curriculum and the lowering of academic standards. Teacher empowerment, school-based management, an extended school day and year, and revised teacher certification requirements are merely illusions of change when state or district regulations prescribe the curriculum through the use of tests that determine whether schools get high marks for better performance.

How, then, do we establish an effective change process—one that overcomes the long record of failed attempts? The leverage we need to make meaningful change cannot be had without doing away with two mindsets: (1) that one person or one group knows the right answer, and (2) that change is linear. The only reasonable solution is to develop a process in which the adoption of policy and the adoption of practice proceed simultaneously! Policy makers and practitioners need to collaborate during all phases of the change process by examining local capacity and motivation in conjunction with the desired changes. Thus, neither policy makers nor practitioners can reform schools by themselves; instead, both must come together to shape a vision and develop the procedures that will be needed to realize and sustain that vision.

Peter Senge compares "visioneering" to a hologram, a three-dimensional image created by interacting light sources:

> When a group of people comes to share a vision . . . each sees his or her own picture. Each vision represents the whole image from a different point of view. When you add up the pieces of the hologram, the image does not change fundamentally, but rather becomes more intense, more lifelike, more real in the sense that people can truly imagine achieving it. The vision no longer rests on the shoulders of one person [or one group], but is shared and embodies the passion and commitment of all participants (1990, 312).

The Schoolwide Enrichment Model has been developed around a vision that my colleagues in the Center for Talent Development at the University of Connecticut and I have shared for a number of years. This vision is also embraced by thousands of teachers and administrators with whom we have worked in academic programs and summer institutes dating back to the 1970s. Simply stated, this vision is that schools are places for talent development.

Academic achievement is an important part of the vision and of the model for school improvement. However, we also believe a focus on talent development places the need for improved academic achievement into a larger perspective about the goals of education. The things that have made our nation great and our society productive are manifestations of talent development at all levels of human activity. From the creators and inventors of new ideas, products, and art forms to the vast array of people who manufacture, advertise, and market the creations that enrich our lives, there are levels of excellence and quality that contribute to our standard of living and way of life. Our vision of schools for talent development grows out of the belief that everyone has an important role to play in the improvement of society and that everyone's role can be enhanced if we provide all students with the opportunities, resources, and encouragement to develop their talents as fully as possible.

The SEM is a practical plan for making our vision of schools for talent development a reality. We are not naive about the politics, personalities, and financial issues that often supersede the pedagogical goals that are the focus of the model. At the same time, we have seen this vision manifested in schools located in places ranging from struggling urban areas and isolated and often poor rural areas to affluent suburbs. We believe that the strategies are flexible enough for making any school a place for talent development.

Everyone has a stake in having public schools that provide all our young people with high-quality education.

There are no quick fixes or easy formulas for transforming schools into places where talent development is valued and vigorously pursued. However, our experience has shown that, once the concept of talent development catches on, students, parents, teachers, and administrators begin to view their school in a different way. Students become more excited and engaged in what they are learning; parents find more opportunities to become involved in all aspects of their children's learning; teachers begin to discover and use a variety of resources that, in the past, seldom found their way into classrooms; and administrators start to make decisions that affect learning, rather than merely enforce "tight ship" efficiency.

Everyone has a stake in having public schools that provide all our young people with high-quality education. Parents benefit when their children are happy and successful in school. Employers and colleges benefit when they have a steady supply of young people who are competent, creative, and effective in the work they do and in the higher learning they undertake. Political leaders benefit when good citizens and a productive population contribute to a healthy economy, a satisfying quality of life, and respect for the values and institutions of our democracy. And professional educators at all levels benefit when the quality of schools for which they are responsible is high enough to create respect for their work and generous financial support for the educational enterprise.

Everyone has a stake in good schools because schools create and re-create a successful modem society. Renewed and sustained economic growth and the well-being of all citizens require investment in high-quality learning in the same way that previous generations invested in machines and raw materials. Our schools are already dumping millions of functionally illiterate young people into the workforce, and more and more colleges are teaching remedial courses that deal with material once taught in high school.

Although everyone has a stake in good schools, America has been faced with a "school problem" that has resulted in declining confidence in schools and in the people who work in them. This decline has manifested itself in drastic limitations in the amount of financial support for education and in general public apathy toward or dissatisfaction with the quality of education our young people are receiving. The parents of poor children have largely given up hope that education will enable their sons and daughters to break the bonds of poverty. And middle-class parents, perhaps for the first time in our nation's history, are exploring government-supported alternatives such as vouchers and tax credits for private schools, home schooling, charter schools, and summer and after-school programs that enhance their children's chances for admission to competitive colleges.

A great deal has been written about America's "school problem."

A great deal has been written about America's "school problem." Studies, commissions, and reports have been issued, and even a governors' summit conference has been held—all in pursuit of solutions to the problems facing our schools. But the hundreds if not thousands of conferences, commissions, and meetings and the tons of reports, proclamations, and lists of goals have yielded only minimal results, mainly because they have generally focused on tinkering with traditional methods of schooling.

THREE KEY INGREDIENTS OF SCHOOL IMPROVEMENT

If the traditional methods of schooling have failed to bring about substantial changes, we must look to different models that show promise of achieving the types of school improvement that we so desperately need. New models must focus their attention on three major dimensions of schooling: the act of learning, the use of time, and the change process itself.

The act of learning. School improvement must begin by placing the act of learning at the center of the change process. Such organizational and administrative structures as vouchers, site-based management, school choice, multiaged classes, parent involvement, and extended school days may be important considerations, but they do not address directly the crucial question of how we can improve what happens in classrooms, where teachers, students, and curriculum interact with one another.

One of the things we have done in developing the SEM is to base all recommendations for school improvement on the learning process. It is beyond the scope of this article to explain this process in detail, but we must take into account the important components that students bring to the act of learning. Thus, when examining the learner, we must take into consideration (1) present achievement levels in each area of study, (2) the learner's interest in particular topics and the ways in which we can enhance present interests or develop new interests, and (3) the preferred styles of learning that will improve the learner's motivation. Likewise, the teacher and learner dimensions have subcomponents that must be considered when we place the act of learning at the center of the school improvement process (Renzulli 1992).

Use of time. Although it would be interesting to speculate about why schools have changed so little over the decades, at least part of the reason has been our unwillingness to examine critically the issue of school time. If the ways we currently use school time were producing remarkably positive (or even adequate) results, there might be an argument for maintaining the traditional schedule and calendar. But such is not the case.

The universal pattern of school organization that has emerged over the years has contributed to our inability to make even the smallest changes in the overall process of learning. This pattern is well-known to educators and laypeople alike. The "major" subject areas (reading, mathematics, science, language arts, and social studies) are taught on a regular basis, generally five days a week. Other subjects, sometimes called "the specials" (such as music, art, and physical education) are taught once or twice a week. So accustomed have we become to the rigidity of this schedule that even the slightest hint of variation is met with a storm of protest from administrators and teachers. "We don't have time to cover the regular curriculum now." "How will we fit in the specials?" "They keep adding new things like drug, education and sex education for us to cover."

Our unthinking acceptance of the elementary and secondary school schedules causes us to lose sight of the fact that at the college level, where material is ordinarily more advanced and demanding, we routinely drop from five class meetings per week, to three or even two. And our adherence to the "more time is better" argument fails to take into account research that shows just the opposite. For example, international comparison studies report that schools in eight of the eleven nations that surpassed the United States in an assessment of mathematics achievement spend less time on math instruction than do American schools (Jaeger 1992). In the SEM, a number of alternative scheduling patterns are based on selectively "borrowing" one or two class meetings per month from the major subject areas. This approach guarantees that a designated time will be available each week for advanced-level enrichment clusters.

Schools are constantly being bombarded with flavor-of-the-month proposals for change.

The change process itself. The approach to school improvement being recommended here is a realistic one because it focuses on those aspects of learning and development over which schools have the most influence. Therefore, the probability of achieving success is greatly increased.

Schools are constantly being bombarded with flavor-of-the-month proposals for change. These proposals range from total "systemic reform" to tinkering with bits and pieces of specific subjects and teaching methods. Often the proposals are little more than lists of intended goals or outcomes, and only limited direction is provided about how these outcomes are to be achieved. Even less information is provided about the effectiveness of recommended practices in a broad range of field-test sites. Worse yet are the mixed messages that policy makers and regulators are beaming to schools at an unprecedented rate, messages that often are incompatible with one another. For example, one state mandated a core set of standards for students but then evaluated teachers on the basis of generic teaching skills that had nothing to do with the standards. In some places, schools are encouraged to raise standards and advocates of site-based management urge teachers to become more active in curriculum development. But, these same schools are rated on the basis of test scores tied to lists of state-specified, outcome-based competencies. A recent study showed that the most widely used tests measure low-level skills and knowledge and that teachers are under pressure to emphasize such material because it shows up on the tests (Madaus 1992). The study also reported that teachers and administrators believed that the tests forced them to compromise their ideals about good teaching.

I believe that school improvement can be initiated and built upon through gentle and evolutionary strategies for change. These strategies must concentrate first on the act of learning as represented by the interactions of learners, teachers, and the curriculum. In the early stages of the change process, these strategies should make minimal, but specific, changes in existing schedules, textbook usage, and curricular conventions. And these strategies should be based on practices that have already demonstrated favorable results in places where they have been used for reasonable periods of time and with groups from varying ethnic and economic backgrounds.

I also believe that the individual school is the appropriate level at which to address school improvement and that effective and lasting change can occur only when it is initiated, nurtured, and monitored from within the school itself. Regulations and remedies brought in from outside the school seldom have changed the daily behavior of students and teachers or dealt effectively with solutions to inside-of-school problems (Barth 1990). A simple but sincere waiver of top-down regulations—a plan that involves consensus and shared decision making on the arts of administrators, parents, and teachers—and incentives for specific contributions to the change process must be the starting points and are the only "big decisions" policy makers need to make in order to initiate a gentle and evolutionary school improvement process.

Our goal in the Schoolwide Enrichment Model is not to replace existing school structures, but rather to apply the strategies and services that define the model to improve the structures to which schools already have made a commitment. Thus, for example, if a school has adopted national standards, whole-language learning models, or site-based management, the purpose of the SEM is to help these structures become maximally effective. I view this process as an infusion approach to school improvement rather than as an add-on or replacement approach. The main targets of the process are those factors that have a direct bearing, on the act of learning. Evaluations of SEM programs have indicated that the model is systematic, inexpensive to implement, and practical in a commonsense sort of way that makes it appealing to both professionals and laypeople (Olenchak and Renzulli 1989).

HOW TO START A SCHOOL IMPROVEMENT PROCESS

As is always the case with any change initiative, a person or a small group of people becomes interested in something that seems likely to be good for the school. I hope that those who read this article and the longer materials cited in the references list will play this role. If that happens, I recommend the following series of actions for examining and implementing the model.

I hope that those who read this article and the longer materials cited in the references list will play this role.

The principal and representatives of groups in the school's nuclear family should form a steering committee. There are only three guidelines for the steering committee as it embarks on a process for exploring the plan presented in this model. (I emphasize exploring because consensus must be reached at each step of the committee's process in order for the plan to work.) First, all steering committee members should be provided with information about the Schoolwide Enrichment Model so that they are well-informed and can engage in an intelligent discussion about whether or not they are interested in the plan. All steering committee members should have equal rights and opportunities to express their opinions. If a majority decision is reached to recommend the plan to the school community at large, information should be made available to all faculty members and parents. Older students (middle grades and above) should also be asked to participate in the discussions.

Second, the steering committee should arrange a series of discussion group meetings that include members of all subgroups in the school's nuclear family. In setting up the discussion groups, it is important to avoid having separate parent groups, teacher groups, and administrator groups. Grouping by role is a classic error that has plagued communication in the school community, and it is the main contributor to the "us-versus-them" mentality that pits one group against another. Printed information, research findings, key diagrams and charts, and the results of steering committee deliberations should be brought to the attention of the discussion groups.

The discussion groups should elect a chair and a recorder. They should remain intact for the duration of the examination process, and they should set a mutually acceptable schedule of dates and times for meetings. The meetings should continue until everyone has had a chance to express his or her opinions, after which a vote should be taken as to whether or not to proceed with the plan. The voting outcomes from each discussion group should be reported to the steering committee, and a report of all the votes should be issued to the school's nuclear family. The report should also contain each group's suggestions and concerns.

Any plan for school change is a lightning rod for naysayers, self-proclaimed experts, and people who are reluctant to endorse almost anything involving thinking or doing something differently.

If at least two-thirds of those voting express an interest in going ahead with the plan, the steering committee should make arrangements to meet with the superintendent or appropriate central office personnel. Once again, descriptive material about the model should be provided, and the model should be characterized as a pilot or experimental venture. Assurances should be given that there is no intention to replace any of the programs or initiatives that the district has already adopted. The fastest way to get a polite but firm rejection from the central office is to threaten existing programs or policies to which decision makers already have made a commitment. It is worth repeating that the goal is to infuse exemplary learning and teaching opportunities into the existing school frameworks.

A third guideline concerns strategies for overcoming roadblocks that might present themselves during the examination process. Any plan for school change is a lightning rod for naysayers, self-proclaimed experts, and people who are reluctant to endorse almost anything involving thinking or doing something differently. The problem is an especially sticky one if these people occupy positions of formal or informal authority in the school community or if they are particularly adept at creating negative energy that is not easily overcome. Like everyone else, such people must have an opportunity to express their opinions in a democratic process. But in order for a majority opinion to be the deciding factor in determining whether or not the model is adopted, it may be necessary to pursue strategies that ensure majority rule.

WHAT'S IN IT FOR ME?

Although everyone has a stake in good schools, it would be naive to assume that already overburdened professionals or parents who historically have had a limited impact on school change will find it easy to make a commitment to a new initiative that requires time, energy, and participation in activities that are a departure from the status quo. Each person examining the SEM should ask himself or herself a few questions: What's in it for me? What will I have to do? What will I have to give or give up? What will I get out of it?

Policy makers and administrators should examine these questions with an eye toward building the kinds of public support necessary for an adequate financial commitment to public education. The tide of criticism that constantly is being directed toward our schools has taken its toll in the extent to which the public is willing to pay for public education, and it also has resulted in low morale at all levels of the profession. Because of this criticism, education is rapidly becoming a profession without an ego. Schools in other nations are constantly being held up to us as mirrors for pointing out our own inadequacies; hardly a month passes without someone writing yet another article or news story about the crisis in educational leadership. It would be nice to think that some magical force will "save us," but the reality is that leadership for better schools can come only from people who are responsible for schools at the local level.

Almost every teacher has—or at one time had—a notion of what good teaching is all about.

More than any other group, teachers will have to ask themselves some hard questions. Almost every teacher has—or at one time had—a notion of what good teaching is all about. And yet it is not an exaggeration to say that most teachers are dissatisfied with their work and with the regulations and regimentation imposed on their classrooms. A recent report on teachers' response patterns to classroom practices indicated that teachers who adapt to traditional practices "become cynical, frustrated, and burned out. So do their students, many of whom fail to meet expectations established for the classroom" (McLaughlin and Talbert 1993, 6). However, we must still raise the questions: Are there benefits for teachers who are willing to take on the challenge of variations in traditional practice? Can we avoid the cynicism, frustration, and burnout that seem to be so pervasive in the profession? The SEM is designed to provide opportunities for a better brand of teaching through the application of more engaging teaching practices.

Finally, parents must examine the above questions with an eye toward the kind of education they want for their sons and daughters. The SEM is not intended to replace the focus of the schools on traditional academic achievement, but it does emphasize the development of a broader spectrum of the multiple potentials of young people. Schools do not need to be places to which so many of our young people dread going, but if we are to make schools more enjoyable places, parents must have an understanding of and a commitment to an education that goes beyond the regimentation and drill that are designed only to get the scores up.

Schools are places for developing the broadest and richest experiences imaginable for young people. The atmosphere is favorable for a broader application of the strategies and techniques that originated in special programs, and they can serve as a basis for making all schools into laboratories for talent development.

NOTES:

1 The work reported herein was supported under the Education Research and Development Centers Program, PT/Award Number R206R50001, as administered by the Office of Educational Research and Improvement, U.S. Department of Education. The findings and opinions expressed do not reflect the positions or policies of the National Institute on the Education of At-Risk Students, the Office of Educational Research and Improvement, or the U.S. Department of Education.

2 For descriptive information about the School Enrichment Model and about related research, see Joseph S. Renzulli and Sally M. Reis, "Research Related to the Schoolwide Enrichment Model," *Gifted Child Quarterly*, vol. 38, 1994, pp. 2–14 and *The Schoolwide Enrichment Model: A How-To Guide for Educational Excellence*, 2d ed. (Mansfield Center, CT: Creative Learning Press, 1997).

REFERENCES

Altbach, P. G., G. P. Kelly, H. G. Petrie, and L. Weis. 1991. *Textbooks in American society.* Albany, NY: State University of New York Press.

Bernstein, H. T. 1985. The new politics of textbook adoption. *Phi Delta Kappan* 66(7): 463–466.

Bloom, B. S., Ed. 1985. *Developing talent in young people.* New York: Ballantine.

Chall, J. 1967. *Learning to read: The great debate.* New York: McGraw-Hill.

Chall, J. S., and S. S. Conard. 1991. *Should textbooks challenge students? The case for easier or harder textbooks.* New York: Teachers College Press.

Flanders, J. R. 1987. How much of the content in mathematics textbooks is new? *Arithmetic Teacher* 35: 18–23.

Gardner, H. 1983. *Frames of mind.* New York: Basic Books.

Hopfenberg, W. S., and H. M. Levin. 1993. *The accelerated schools resource guide.* San Francisco: Jossey-Bass.

Jaeger, R. M. 1992, October. World class standards, choice and privatization: Weak measurement serving presumptive policy. Paper presented at American Educational Research Association.

Joyce, R. B., and B. Showers. 1983. *Power in staff development through research in training.* Alexandria, VA: Association for Supervision and Curriculum Development.

Kirst, M. W. 1982. How to improve schools without spending more money. *Phi Delta Kappan* 64(1): 6–8.

Olenchack, F. R, and J. S. Renzulli. 1989. The effectiveness of the schoolwide enrichment model on selected aspects of elementary school change. *Gifted Child Quarterly* 32: 44–57.

McLaughlin, M. W., and J. E. Talbert. 1993. *Contexts that matter for teaching and learning.* Stanford, CA: Center for Research on the Context of Secondary School Teaching.

Renzulli, J. S. 1978, November. What makes giftedness? Reexamining a definition. *Phi Delta Kappan,* 180–184.

Renzulli, J. S. 1992. A general theory for the development of creative productivity through the pursuit of ideal acts of learning. *Gifted Child Quarterly* 36: 170–82.

Renzulli, J. S., and S. M. Reis. 1994. Research related to the schoolwide enrichment triad model. *Gifted Child Quarterly* 31(1): 7–20.

Senge, P. M. 1990. *The fifth discipline.* New York: Doubleday.

Sternberg, R. J. 1984. Toward a triachic theory of human intelligence. *Behavioral and Brain Science* 7: 269–316.

Taylor, B. M., and B. J. Frye. 1988. Pretesting: Minimize time spent on skill work for intermediate readers. *The Reading Teacher* 42(2): 100–103.

Usiskin, Z. 1987. Why elementary algebra can, should, and must be an eighth-grade course for average students. *Mathematics Teacher* 80: 428–438.

Section 5

Striving for Accuracy, Precision, and Elegance: The Human Yearning for Craftsmanship

Embodied in the stamina, grace, and elegance of a ballerina or a shoemaker is the desire for craftsmanship, mastery, flawlessness, and economy of energy, which produces exceptional results. People who value accuracy, precision, and craftsmanship take time to check over their products. They review the rules by which they are to abide; they review the models and visions they are to follow; and they review the criteria they are to employ and confirm that their finished product matches the criteria exactly. To be craftsman-like means to know that one can continually perfect one's craft by working to attain the highest possible standards, and one can pursue ongoing learning to bring a laser-like focus of energies to tasks. These people take pride in their work and demonstrate their desire for accuracy as they take time to check over their work. Craftsmanship includes exactness, faithfulness, and fidelity.

In this fifth section, the authors invite educators to consider raising their standards, to become more exacting, and to become more craftsman-like in their educational practices.

Kay Burke opens with an overview of how standards of learning can contribute to higher achievement. She invites educators to become explicit about their curriculum expectancies, to align their practices and assessments with desired outcomes, and to use clarity and precision when communicating about their accomplishments.

Jeni Pollack Day and Richard Allington, drawing on research in effective instruction, invite educators to become more thorough in their expectations about teaching abilities.

Clifford Hill suggests that educators become more definitive about performance and that test scores communicate with greater accuracy, precision, and reliability what is meant by success using standards-based testing.

Finally, Carolyn Chapman and Rita King propose that if educators are truly are to find merit in their testing efforts, they should become more exacting about what contributes to students' test success. They offer a range of sound instructional standards that will prove valuable to any school or teacher intent on raising students' test scores and making achievement more meaningful.

These authors all agree that standards can be applied to different learning situations to help educators to become craftsmen of teaching, and they discuss ways that educators can hone their skills and attain their highest capabilities.

Learning Standards

by Kay Burke

WHAT ARE LEARNING STANDARDS?

any districts and states across the nation are developing standards for student learning that describe what students should know and be able to do as a result of their schooling. These standards are intended to provide educators with guidelines for curriculum and teaching that will ensure that students have access to the knowledge believed to be necessary for their later success" (Darling-Hammond and Falk 1997, p. 190). Standards help educators focus on clear expectations for all students to achieve.

Most educators attribute the publication of *A Nation at Risk* (National Commission on Excellence in Education) in 1983 as the impetus for setting standards at a national level. The concern over education was also the focus of the first education summit, held in Charlottesville, Virginia, in September 1989, where the nation's fifty governors and President George Bush adopted National Educational Goals for the year 2000. One of the goals was to establish challenging national achievement standards for five school subjects—English, mathematics, science, history, and geography. As a result of the summit, a number of national organizations representing various subject areas published numerous documents (Marzano and Kendall 1996).

Diane Ravitch, former Assistant Secretary of Education, is recognized as one of the chief proponents of the standards movement. Ravitch wrote the book *National Standards in American Education: A Citizen's Guide* (1995), in which she explains the rationale for standards:

"Americans . . . expect strict standards to govern construction of buildings, bridges, highways, and tunnels; shabby work would put lives at risk. They expect stringent standards to protect their drinking water, the food they eat, and the air they breathe . . . standards are created because they improve the quality of life" (Ravitch 1995, cited in Marzano and Kendall 1996, p. 1).

Darling-Hammond (1997), in her book *The Right to Learn,* agrees that standards of practice are used to license professionals and guide the work of architects in constructing sound buildings, accountants in managing finances, engineers in assembling space shuttles, and doctors in treating patients. She adds, however, "These standards are not prescriptions; instead they reflect shared norms and knowledge about underlying principles of practice, the effects of various techniques, and decision-making processes" (p. 213). Standards, therefore, clarify expectations and consensus about what constitutes quality products and practice.

Standards, therefore, clarify expectations and consensus about what constitutes quality products and practice.

The challenge involves the lack of experience educators in the United States have in transmitting standards. Since professional organizations, standards boards, and accrediting agencies have been weak or non-existent, unexamined standards exist by default. Darling-Hammond (1997) suggests that teachers are rarely involved in the professional activities of standard setting, curriculum development, or assessment. Instead, the standards are "the aggregations of decisions made by textbook makers, test publishers, individual state agencies, legislatures, and school boards, often uninformed by professional knowledge, shared ideals, or consensual goals for education" (p. 213). Educators need to take more active roles in determining the key learnings and the developmentally appropriate levels of student attainment of standards.

National Standards

Standard-setting efforts have been undertaken by a number of national organizations representing various subject areas as well as the U.S. Department of Education. The documents published by such organizations as the National Council of Teachers of English (NCTE) and the National Council of Teachers of Mathematics (NCTM) offer their versions of standards in their subject areas.

Many of these standards documents vary because of the differing definitions of standards. Some standards are very general, such as "Understanding the arts in relation to history and cultures" proposed by the National Standards for Arts Education, 1994. Other standards, however, are more specific, such as "Students should understand the causes of the Civil War" as proposed in the National Standards for United States History: Exploring the American Experience (Marzano and Kendall 1996, p.22). In addition to the wide variance in the specificity of standards, Marzano and Kendall (1996) describe the problem of "varying levels of subordination," in which some standards have a complex structure in terms of subordination (topic, understandings, elements, components, example of student achievement) and others, as shown below, map out a general area and then provide benchmarks that describe appropriate expectations at specific grade levels.

- Mathematics Content Standard. The student demonstrates number sense and an understanding of number theory.
- Middle School Benchmark. The student understands the relationship of decimals to whole numbers.
- High School Benchmark. The student understands the characteristics of the real number system and its subsystems. (Marzano and Kendall 1996, pp. 24–25)

Format of Standards

The lack of uniformity in national standards makes it difficult for school districts to adopt the subject-specific national documents for all subject areas and organize their schools around them. Some standards deal with content, while others address curriculum, performance, or lifelong learning skills. This format inconsistency among the various national organizations who have set standards has caused many states, districts, and schools to use the national standards as models to create their own standards, which they construct with the same type of format to allow for more consistent application and assessment. Despite the inconsistency in the format of standards, the basic concepts and key learning components are very similar from state to state. Almost all language arts standards address expectations related to communication skills—reading, writing, speaking, technology. Differences occur when the standards are written as content skills, procedural skills, or performance skillls.

Management Issues

Theorist Elliot Eisner (1995) noted the similarity of the standards movement to the efficiency movement that began in 1913 when Frederick Taylor, the inventor of the time-and-motion study, was hired by industrialists to make plants more efficient and profitable. According to Eisner, school administrators soon found that the basic concept underlying the efficiency movement—routine mechanization of teaching and learning—did not work. Eisner concludes that educators will no doubt come to the same conclusions about standards (cited in Marzano and Kendall 1996). Many teachers can still remember the 1960s and 1970s, when they had to prepare lesson plans that targeted hundreds of behavioral objectives for each of their students. The paperwork involved in documenting the objectives occupied much of teachers' time, often at the expense of effective teaching and meaningful learning.

Darling-Hammond (1997) is afraid the sheer number of the performance indicators in the new standards documents would create expectations for drill and skill "content coverage" at the expense of in-depth understanding and application of key ideas. The 1993 draft standards for social studies outlined more than one thousand performance indicators for students at each benchmark level. She describes many of the performance indicators as "laundry lists" of facts to be identified, described, or defined. Darling-Hammond notes "In geography, for example, fourth graders are expected to be able to describe the physical characteristics of Earth; biosphere, atmosphere, lithosphere, hydrosphere, and Earth-Sun relationships; explain volcanic eruptions; draw a map of the world from memory; predict population patterns; and do more than three hundred other things" (p. 228).

Standards have the potential to increase student achievement, but the process of development and implementation must be examined carefully so that learning standards are used to enhance learning, not to create a paperwork management nightmare.

TYPES OF STANDARDS

Standards pervade education, but the most commonly identified standards address the following: *content, curriculum, performance, lifelong, and opportunity to learn.* Almost all standards also contain *benchmarks or specific performance indicators,* which represent the specific learning that will be demonstrated by the students at varying levels of their cognitive development.

Content Standards

Content standards refer to knowledge and skills belonging to a particular discipline. The content standards depict the key elements in the program through a focused and clear approach to the subject (Foriska 1998).

Examples:

Science Standard
- Explain the relationships among science, technology, and society

Physical Education Standard
- Demonstrate individual development in swimming and water safety

(Foriska 1998, p. 49)

The knowledge itself is usually divided into two types: content and process. *Content knowledge* is classified into a hierarchy ranging from facts about specific persons, places, things, and events to concepts and generalizations. The *processes* are identified as skills or strategies that can be applied to many types of situations (Marzano, Pickering, and McTighe 1993, cited in Foriska, 1998, p. 53).

Following the development of content standards, *benchmarks* are developed. "Benchmarks detail the progression of reasonable expectations for acquiring the skills and knowledge needed to reach the content standards" (Foriska 1998, p. 31). The desired student performance related to the benchmark is a key connection for linking assessment and instruction. Benchmarks are often targeted at specific grade levels or stages.

Curriculum Standards

Curriculum standards are more specific and more detailed than content standards. They represent the specific activity that occurs in the classroom when the teacher instructs. Foriska (1998) describes the four steps that define the curriculum structure as follows:

1. Standards Identification
2. Benchmark Development
3. Comprehensive Assessment
4. Planned Course Development

(p. 33)

Benchmarks

The design begins with the identification of standards, then benchmarks are developed along a K–12 continuum. Appropriate assessments are created to evaluate students' success in meeting the standards and benchmarks. The process then evolves into the development of planned courses of study for each grade level.

Marzano and Kendall (1996) maintain that standards are generally broad and contain somewhat arbitrary categories of knowledge. *Benchmarks,* however, represent the real substance of standards construction. Marzano and Kendall state that *benchmarks* can be written in three general formats: (1) as statements of information and skills (declarative and procedural); (2) as *performance activities*; and (3) as *performance tasks* (p. 53).

Foriska (1998) describes benchmarks as the guideposts that "identify a progression of reasonable expectations detailing what students are capable of learning at different ages with regard to the content standards. This makes the structure of the curriculum appropriate for the cognitive development of the students" (pp. 31–32). Benchmarks provide the framework for teaching and assessing key concepts because they are more specific and concrete than most standards.

For example, a current state foreign language standard in Illinois is that students "demonstrate knowledge of manners and customs." The Stage One Learning Benchmark is "Use common forms of courtesy, greetings, and leave-taking appropriate to the time of day and relationship (adult, peer, parent) in their immediate environment."

Illinois English Language Arts Standard

Learning Standard 4b
Speak effectively using language appropriate to the situation and audience.

Middle/Junior High School Benchmark
Deliver planned oral presentations using language and vocabulary appropriate to the purpose, message, and audience; provide details and supporting information that clarify main ideas; and use visual aids and contemporary technology as support.

(**Source:** Illinois Learning Standards, 1st edition, adopted July 25, 1997, Illinois State Board of Education, page 11)

As shown on page 188, another example from the Illinois Standards addresses an English language arts standard and the more specific Middle School Benchmark that describes specific criteria. These criteria can be developed into a checklist or rubric later—to use for assessment purposes.

Checklists

At this point in the assessment process for language arts, a checklist could be developed that lists the criteria described in the Benchmark shown above. Later, students and teacher could develop the indicators of quality that list specific characteristics of each rating.

Checklist Rubric to Assess Speech				
Criteria	0	1	2	3
Language • Grammar • Sentence structure				
Vocabulary • Technical terms • Appropriateness				
Main Ideas • Thesis • Topic sentences				
Support • Examples • Explanations • Definitions				
Visual Aids • Graphics • Color • Appropriateness				
Technology • PowerPoint • Slides • Videotape				

Performance Standards

Performance standards focus on "students applying and demonstrating what they know and can do while defining the levels of learning that are considered satisfactory. Performance standards seek to answer the question: How good is good enough?" (Foriska 1998, p. 3). Marzano and Kendall (1996) describe how the term *standards* was formalized in the 1993 report to the National Education Goals Panel, commonly referred to as the Malcom Report because Shirley W. Malcom was chair of the planning group. The report makes a clear distinction between *content standards* and *performance standards.*

Rubrics are guidelines that measure degrees of quality.

Content standards specify "what students should know and *be able to do.*" They indicate knowledge and skills—the ways of thinking, working, communicating, reasoning, and investigating, and the most important and enduring ideas, concepts, issues, dilemmas, and knowledge essential to the discipline—that should be taught and learned in school.

Performance standards specify "how good is good enough." They relate to issues of assessment that gauge the degree to which content standards have been attained. . . . They [performance assessments] are indices of quality that specify how adept or competent a student demonstration must be (Marzano and Kendall 1996, p. 64).

A common convention to refer to a set of performance levels is a rubric. Rubrics are guidelines that measure degrees of quality. Solomon (1998) writes that an evaluation of a student's achievement of a standard can be in terms of levels of progress toward the level of the bar or the result of overall quality of the achievement when compared to the quality of others. "Rubrics can be defined as a set of guidelines for distinguishing between *performances or products* of *different quality.* . . . Rubrics should be based on the results of stated performance standards, and be composed of *scaled descriptive levels of progress* towards the result" (p. 120). Criteria for creating rubrics and sample rubrics are discussed in detail in Chapter 5.

Lifelong Learning Standards

Lifelong learning standards help students become lifelong learners and are commonly associated with the world of work. Marzano and Kendall (1996) describe how attention was focused on these workplace-related skills in 1991 when the Secretary's Commission on Achieving Necessary Skills (SCANS) published the report "What Work Requires of Schools: A SCANS Report for America 2000." The commission members spent twelve months talking to business owners and public employees to determine the types of skills that would make students productive members of the workforce.

The SCANS report identified a three-part foundation of skills and personal qualities, as follows:

- The first part of the foundation involved traditional academic content such as reading, writing, arithmetic, mathematics, speaking, and listening;
- The second part of the foundation involved the thinking skills of thinking creatively, making decisions, solving problems, seeing things in the mind's eye, knowing how to learn, and reasoning.
- The third part of the foundation involved lifelong learning skills, such as individual responsibility, self-esteem, sociability, self-management, and integrity.

(Marzano and Kendall 1996, p. 40).

Marzano and Kendall (1996) compiled a comprehensive record of many of the lifelong learning skills identified in national and state documents.

Lifelong learning skills

Working With Others

1. contributes to the overall effort of a group
2. uses conflict-resolution techniques
3. works well with diverse individuals and in diverse situations
4. displays effective interpersonal communication skills
5. demonstrates leadership skills

Self-Regulation

1. sets and manages goals
2. performs self-appraisal
3. considers risks
4. demonstrates perseverance
5. maintains a healthy self concept
6. restrains impulsivity

(Marzano and Kendall 1996, p. 41. Reprinted with permission.)

Parents, business leaders, and administrators feel competencies such as punctuality, dependability, self-discipline, and interpersonal skills are critical attributes for students' success in school and life.

Opportunity-to-Learn Standards

Opportunity-to-learn standards focus on the conditions and resources necessary to give student an equal chance to achieve standards. When all students are to be held to the same set of learning standards, there must be ways to ensure they have access to all the conditions needed for them to meet the standards. Often legislatures, community members, and state organizations plan punitive measures to punish school districts, principals, teachers, and, sadly, children if they do not meet the standards. Schools can be put on probation or even taken over by the state; principals can be removed, teachers can be penalized financially, and students can be retained if they don't meet the standards.

Darling-Hammond and Falk (1997) advocate that "along with standards for student learning, school systems should develop 'opportunity-to-learn' standards—standards for delivery systems and standards of practice—to identify how well schools are doing in providing students with the conditions they need to achieve and to trigger corrective actions from the state and district" (p. 196). Oakes (1989) has argued that information about school resources and practices is essential if policymakers plan to use standards in the quest for accountability (p. 182). The "standards for delivery systems" should identify key resources that enable student learning. These include:

- school funding levels adequate to support the program of study outlined by content and performance standards;
- access to well-prepared, fully qualified teachers;
- reasonable class sizes; and
- access to materials and equipment necessary for learning, including texts, libraries, computers, and laboratories, among others (Oakes 1989, in Darling-Hammond and Falk 1997, p. 196)

Students should not be penalized because the system has not provided them with the resources to meet standards. Provisions must be made to assist the student in meeting the standards rather than retaining the student. Students can be given extra help, taught in different ways, or given more time, but they should not have to suffer if the system has failed them. As Shepard and Smith (1986) conclude in their review of research on grade retention, "Contrary to popular beliefs, repeating a grade does *not* help students gain ground academically and has a negative impact on social adjustment and self-esteem" (cited in Darling-Hammond and Falk 1991, p.191).

Wolk (1998) warns that standards-based school reform is on "a collision course with reality" because half the states hold schools accountable and apply sanctions to those whose students fail to meet standards, despite the fact "a great many high school and middle school students, especially in urban districts, cannot read well enough to pass these tough courses and tests" (p. 48).

WHY DO WE NEED STANDARDS?

"A coherent view of curriculum, assessment, and teaching is at the core of any vision of more effective education. Education standards have become a major policy vehicle in part because they can reflect changes in goals including, for example, the major shift in the kind of learning our society desires of young people, which in turn requires a major shift in teaching and schooling" (Darling-Hammond 1997, p. 211).

Marzano and Kendall (1996), in their book *A Comprehensive Guide to Designing Standards-Based Districts, Schools, and Classrooms*, cite at least four reasons that standards represent one of the most powerful options for school reform:

1. Erosion of the Carnegie Unit and the Common Curriculum
2. Variation in Current Grading Practices
3. Lack of Attention to Educational Outputs
4. Competing Countries Do it.

(Marzano and Kendall 1996, pp. 11–18. Reprinted with permission.)

Erosion of the Carnegie Unit and the Common Curriculum

Veteran educators remember the shift away from the standard concept of credit hours (based on the Carnegie unit—a measure of class time) and proliferation of elective courses in the 1960s and 1970s. It was not unusual for students to elect to take "Science Fiction Short Stories" or "Gothic Mystery Writers" in lieu of American literature or composition. Furthermore, studies have shown a disparity among teachers concerning the amount of time spent teaching a particular subject area or skill. How many teachers have spent six weeks covering the Civil War in a history class, and then not have sufficient time for World War I or II? Because teachers sometimes make arbitrary decisions regarding what they teach, there is often a lack of uniformity in a given district's or state's curricula and little consistency in the knowledge and skills covered within subject areas.

Variation in Current Grading Practices

Grading has always been an ambiguous process. What does a "B" really mean? How many teachers average effort, behavior, cooperation, and attendance into the academic grade, thus conveying an inaccurate portrayal of a student's achievement? O'Connor (1999) contends it is difficult to know how a teacher arrives at a grade because grades are often imprecise and sometimes are not indicative of what students know and can do in a subject area.

Lack of Attention to Educational Outputs

The outcomes-based education movement attempted to focus attention not so much on the input of instructional delivery but on the outcome of the results. Unfortunately, some of the outcomes were difficult to measure objectively, and some parents felt educators should not be measuring outcomes that included values. Glickman (1993, in Schmoker 1996) feels too much emphasis has been placed on new instructional strategies, the innovation or the "hot topic" rather than on the results for the learner. Having the entire school wired for technology is wonderful. Integrating the theory of multiple intelligences into each lesson is motivating. However, the bottom line should always be "How does it affect student achievement?" Today, schools are paying more attention to results, not intentions. The "A" word of the twenty-first century is accountability.

Competing Countries Do It

The fourth reason for implementing standards for school reform addresses the issue of competition with other countries. Proponents of standards often point to countries such as China, Japan, France, and England to show how setting standards and developing a national curriculum, national exams, and cut-off scores can help students attain academic excellence. Many business and community leaders have vigorously supported the establishment of student performance standards to create a world-class workforce. Behind this expectation is the assumption that higher educational standards and student performance are keys to higher workplace productivity (Marzano and Kendall 1996).

Levin (1998), however, reviewed evidence and found only a weak relationship between test scores and economic productivity and virtually no evidence on the predictive validity of the newer performance standards. He suggests that "the educational standards movement has relied on the economic rationale largely because of its persuasiveness in stimulating educational reform rather than any compelling evidence on the links between specific educational standards and economic performance" (p. 4). Noted labor economist Clark Kerr (1991) examined a range of evidence on the contention that education is the key to the nation's competitiveness and concluded, "Seldom in the course of policy making in the United States have so many firm convictions held by so many been based on so little proof" (cited in Levin 1998, p. 5).

Noddings maintains the real task is not to find out *what* kids are supposed to do, but instead *how* do we get them to do it!

The standards movement has gathered momentum on the basis of these four reasons as well as the public's dissatisfaction with the quality of students the public schools are producing. Headlines about scores on international tests showing the placement of the United States have fueled the ground-swelling of support for high standards for academic excellence. Moreover, the members of the business community have expressed concern over the skills their employees lack and the inordinate amount of time and money they are spending to teach their employees what they feel they should have learned in public schools.

These reasons, as well as many more, serve to form the "compelling why" behind the standards movement.

HOW CAN WE USE STANDARDS?

Adopting a standards-based curriculum will not be the "magic bullet" to solve all the educational problems. Noddings (1997) remembers the 1970s, when school districts spent an enormous amount of time and money rewriting curricula to include behavioral objectives: "We were supposed to say exactly what students would do (content standards?), to what level of proficiency (performance standards?), and under what conditions (opportunity to learn standards?)" (p. 188). The behavioral objective movement produced little demonstrable improvement. Noddings maintains the real task is not to find out *what* kids are supposed to do, but instead *how* do we get them to do it!

Rather than creating another whole system, Management by Standards (MSS), to replace the Management by Objectives (MBO), educators should follow Darling-Hammond's (1997) advice. She says standards can be most useful when used as "guideposts not straitjackets for building curriculum assessments and professional development opportunities, and when they are used to focus and mobilize system resources rather than to punish students and schools" (p. 213).

Standards are not the end; they are a means to achieve the end—improved student achievement.

Standards as Guideposts

Even if a school or district does not develop a systemic standards-based curriculum and assessment program, it could still utilize standards as effective guideposts to improve student achievement. Standards can target nine important goals, as follows:

Synthesize Educational Goals

Educators need to focus on attaining important goals that will benefit all students. Establishing a few clear and specific goals can focus a faculty on developing action plans and unify efforts to achieve the goals. Schmoker (1996) says "Goals themselves lead not only to success, but also to the effectiveness and cohesion of a team" (p. 19). Educators need to set goals in their strategic plans in order to later measure their success in meeting the goals.

Target Student Achievement

The primary purpose for standards is to focus attention on student work and improved student achievement. Cohen (1995) states, "It is student work that we want to improve, not standards or scholars' ideas about standards" (p. 755). The emphasis is changing from the "input" of what teachers teach to the "output" of what students learn. Standards are not the end; they are a means to achieve the end—improved student achievement.

Align Curriculum Systemically

The "erosion of the common curriculum" has caused teachers to pick and choose what they want to teach without always being aware of essential learnings in the subject area. The standards and benchmarks provide guideposts and key concepts that help focus teachers on a relatively small set of core ideas. The curriculum has become so

Standards as Guideposts

Standards can benefit students by helping educators to:

S ynthesize educational goals

T arget student achievement

A lign curriculum systemically

N otify the public of results

D etermine criteria for quality work

A nalyze data

R efocus instructional methodology

D edicate resources to professional development

S erve the needs of a diverse population

overwhelming, teachers are forced to either cover a great deal of information superficially, or as Costa says, "selectively abandon" their curriculum. Many districts are also working on curriculum mapping to develop a blueprint of not only *what* essential skills are taught, but also *when* they are taught. A curriculum aligned to meaningful standards and aligned with authentic assessments is a powerful predictor of increased student achievement.

Notify the Public of Results

One of the reasons the public is demanding standards is because they are concerned about the quality of the schools. Newspaper headlines about how students in the United States compare with students in other countries and the decline of Scholastic Assessment Test (SAT) scores cause alarm among parents and business leaders. Schmoker (1996) advocates emphasizing results so all the stakeholders know there is accountability for educators. "Results should be understood as a thoughtfully established desired end product, as evidence that something worked (or did not work). In this sense, all results—good or bad—are ultimately good because they provide feedback that can guide us, telling us what to do next and how to do it better" (p. 3).

Determine Criteria for Quality Work

One of the most important by-products of the standards movement is the emphasis on establishing specific criteria for all student work. Teachers are involving their students in determining the criteria for assignments and the indicators of quality to determine, "How good is it?" Conversations among teachers, parents, and students about what constitutes "A" work and the creation of checklists and scoring rubrics to guide the students have "demystified" the grading process. Students know not only the expectations, but also the steps they need to take to meet the expectations. The emphasis on performance assessments helps students internalize the criteria and become critical self-evaluators of their own work.

Analyze Data

School personnel have found that if they use standards to drive student achievement, they need to measure a school's progress with hard data—something schools have not done well. Schmoker (1996) believes educators fear data because of its capacity to reveal strengths and weaknesses, failures and success. Harrington-Lueker (1998) maintains that districts engaged in standards-based reform must "routinely analyze data on student achievement—the number of students completing algebra and geometry, the number enrolled in Advanced Placement classes, the number receiving D's and F's and so on" (p. 21). By collecting and analyzing data, educators can become better informed about what works and what doesn't work, and then take proactive steps to revise their curriculum, instruction, assessment, or data collection procedures accordingly.

Refocus Instructional Methodology

The most comprehensive standards in the world will not, by their very existence, improve education. The key to improving student achievement is instruction. In order to meet the needs of a diverse student population, teachers need to integrate a repertoire of instructional strategies to help all students learn. The "drill and skill" lecture method may appeal to some of the parents and students, but more and more of the students do not respond to that method. Instructors are utilizing Gardner's multiple intelligences theory to prepare lessons and assessments to address students' learning styles and interests. Other teachers are using cooperative learning techniques, problem-based learning approaches, integrated curricula lessons, and portfolios to promote teamwork, thinking skills, and connections among subject areas. Research on brain-compatible learning is providing strategies teachers can implement to enrich the learning environment, foster reflection and self-evaluations, and stimulate student interest in new areas of study. Darling-Hammond (1997) believes real improvement will come about because "the standards come alive when teachers study student work, collaborate with other teachers to improve their understanding of subjects and students' thinking, and develop new approaches to teaching that are relevant and useful for them and their students" (p. 236).

The most comprehensive standards in the world will not, by their very existence, improve education.

Dedicate Resources for Professional Development

The standards movement goes way beyond standards for students. It takes a dedicated and competent teacher to implement the instructional strategies to help students learn. The statistics about the number of uncertified teachers, especially in the fields of science and mathematics and in urban districts, are staggering. One report shows one-third of mathematics teachers have neither a college major or minor in mathematics; half of all high school physical science teachers don't have any background in any of the physical sciences; and one in five high school English teachers did not have a minor in English (Messacappa 1998).

The standards-based reform movement may drive education in the twenty-first century—or it could be abandoned by 2020.

It is evident that the professional development of teachers is critical if students are going to meet the standards. Professional development could include certification in content areas, workshops and courses in instructional strategies and classroom management, study groups, action research teams, cognitive coaching, and professional portfolios. The proposed reforms require educators to reinvent teaching and schooling. Solomon (1998) warns "Dealing with multiple intelligences and student goals and building classroom dialogues that encourage metacognitive strategies require us to learn and practice all the new knowledge available" (p.132).

Serve the Needs of a Diverse Population

One of the biggest paradoxes of the standards movement is requiring *all* students to meet the same standards, regardless of their reading ability, socio-economic status, or quality of their education. Not every student enters school with the same abilities, and Darling-Hammond (1997) says we must allow for "differing starting points and pathways to learning so that students are not left out or left behind" (p. 231). Establishing the standard will *not* help a student meet the standard. Teachers will have to work with a diverse group of students and experiment with a wide variety of instructional and assessment strategies to see which ones work best. Rubrics that state expectations and criteria for success provide students of all abilities clear guidelines for meeting goals. All students may not reach the standard, but they know where they are and what they still need to do. Portfolios also document the growth and development of a student over time. A student may not achieve the standard, but the portfolio provides evidence that he is progressing toward the standard as well as provides the student's insight and reflections about the learning process. Until all students have the same opportunity to learn standards, it would be ludicrous to punish them for having an inadequate education.

Final Thoughts

Arthur Costa once addressed an audience at an educational conference and asked, "How many of you in the audience are old enough to have been through three back-to-basic movements?". The audience members laughed and nodded their heads. The members of that audience, like so many veteran teachers, recognize how many educational movements have come and gone, sometimes sapping the strength and enthusiasm of those involved and making teachers somewhat cynical of "innovations" and "systemic reform." "The new math," "transformational grammar," "time on task," "outcomes-based education," and "whole language" are just a few of the many educational reforms that have been implemented and, in some cases, abandoned. The standards-based reform movement may drive education in the twenty-first century—or it could be abandoned by 2020. The real question for educators today is whether to adopt part or all of the standards movement to help teachers teach and to help students learn. Standards will probably not be the panacea for improving education overnight, but they can become valuable guides to focus attention on teacher quality and student achievement.

REFERENCES

Burke, Kay. 1999. *The mindful school: How to assess authentic learning.* Arlington Heights, IL: SkyLight Training and Publishing Inc.

Cohen, D. K. 1995. What standards for national standards? *Phi Delta Kappan 76:* 751–757.

Darling-Hamond, L. 1997. *The right to learn: A blueprint for creating schools that work.* San Francisco, CA: Jossey-Bass Publishers.

Darling-Hammond, L. and B. Falk. 1997, November. Using standards and assessments to support student learning. *Phi Delta Kappan* 79(3): 190.

Eisner, E. W. 1995. Standards for American schools: Help or hindrance? *Phi Delta Kappan* 76(10): 758–764.

Foriska, T. J. 1998. *Restructuring around standards: A practitioner's guide to design and implementation.* Thousand Oaks, CA: Corwin Press, Inc. A Sage Publications Company.

Harrington-Lueker, D. 1998, June. Now local school districts are accountable for results. *The American School Board Journal,* 17–21.

Illinois Learning Standards. Adopted July 25, 1997. Springfield, IL: Illinois State Board of Education.

Levin, H. M. 1998, May. Educational performance standards and the economy. *Educational Researcher* 27(4), *American Educational Research Association,* 4–10.

Marzano, R. J., and J. S. Kendall. 1996. *A comprehensive guide to designing standards-based districts, schools, and classrooms.* Association for Supervision and Curriculum Development and Mid-Continent Regional Educational Laboratory.

Marzano, R. J., D. Pickering, and J. McTighe. 1993. *Assessing student outcomes: Performance assessment using the dimensions of learning model.* Alexandria, VA: Association for Supervision and Curriculum Development.

Messacappa, D. 1998, July 12. A lesson in mediocrity: How teachers are trained and chosen. *Philadelphia Inquirer* [Online]. Available: http://www.phillynews.com/inquirer/98/Jul/12/frontpage/TEAC12.htm [1998, July 13].

Noddings, N. 1997, November. Thinking about standards. *Phi Delta Kappan* 79(3): 184.

Oakes, J. 1989. "What educational indicators?: The case of assessing the school context. *Educational Evaluation and Policy Analysis* 11: 182.

O'Connor, K. 1999. *The mindful school: How to grade for learning.* Arlington Heights, IL: SkyLight Training and Publishing Inc.

Ravitch, D. 1995. *National standards in American education: A citizen's guide.* Washington, DC: Bookings Institution.

Schmoker, M. 1996. *Results: The key to continuous school improvement.* Alexandria, VA: Association for Supervision and Curriculum Development.

Shepard, L., and M. L. Smith. 1986, November. Synthesis of research on school readiness and kindergarten retention. *Educational Leadership,* 86.

Solomon, P. G. 1998. *The curriculum bridge: From standards to actual classroom practice.* Thousand Oaks, CA: Corwin Press, A Sage Publications Company.

Wolk, R. A. December 9, 1998. Commentary: Education's high-stake gamble. *Education Week* XVIII(15): 48.

What Sorts of Standards for Teachers?

Focusing on Exemplary Elementary Teaching

by Jeni Pollack Day and Richard L. Allington

> The best school year I ever had was in Mrs. Worthing's fourth grade class. I remember collecting water from the creek to look for amoebae under a microscope, watching in wonder as she modeled the movement of the earth by spinning around a lamp in the center of the room, and busily working on some question or problem she posed to us. Mostly what I remember about fourth grade was feeling really smart, rare for me in elementary school. I wasn't afraid to ask questions that year because I wasn't worried about being laughed at. When we made mistakes, Mrs. Worthing assured us it was OK, that that's what learning is all about. She was patient when we didn't understand, and took the time to work with everyone. When Jimmy didn't know to capitalize the word "I", Mrs. Worthing sat at his desk, next to mine, for an entire spelling period teaching him why and how. After that I never looked at Jimmy, or my teacher, in the same way again.—Jeni Pollack Day

While the higher standards and new assessments for students have gained much attention, new standards and assessments for teachers are also being implemented in many states. Similar to the standards for students, these teacher standards also seem targeted at raising the intellectual bar, but the teacher standards seem a lot like the old minimum competency standards for students—the ones that have been replaced with more challenging outcomes. No one would likely argue against requiring that teachers demonstrate their capacity to read, write, and know basic educational terminology—we wouldn't. But at the same time, what about the other characteristics of exemplary teachers—the characteristics that made Mrs.

Worthing's fourth grade class so memorable? Will the new minimum standards for teachers increase the number of teachers who will be remembered as fondly as Mrs. Worthing was?

We wondered what the research said about memorable, influential, exemplary elementary teachers like Mrs. Worthing. So, we searched the literature and located ten studies of such teachers. These studies ranged from small, historical efforts to large-scale national surveys; from a handful of teachers to hundreds; from paper-pencil survey studies to careful classroom observational studies. The teachers studied were selected in a variety of ways, from student nomination to supervisor and peer recommendation. We read each of these studies closely and carefully and listed each and every characteristic reported by each of the researchers. Once this listing was completed, we read and reread the list of traits and dispositions and worked to merge common features into a single comprehensive listing. Our efforts are displayed in Figure 1, which depicts the characteristics we located by frequency of their appearance in the studies we reviewed.

	Haberman (1995)	Ladson Billings (1996)	Moll (1988)	Pedersen, et al. (1978)	Pressley, Rankin, Yokok (1996)	Pressley, et al. (1997)	Pressley, et al. (1998)	Ruddell (1995)	Thomas & Barksdale-Ladd (1995)
1. High expectations	x	x	x	x		x		x	x
2. Student ownership of learning internal motivation	x		x		x	x	x	x	x
3. Martial made relevant, engaging to learner	x	x	x		x			x	x
4. Curriculum determined by observing and knowing student		x	x		x		x	x	x
5. Teacher knowledge of theory and practice	x		x			x		x	x
6. Passionate about teaching and learning	x	x		x	x			x	
7. Skills taught through modeling, scaffolding		x			x	x	x		x
8. Discipline approach: collaboration over authority	x	x					x	x	
9. Subjects integrated across curriculum			x			x	x		x
10. Contextualized skills taught within authentic tasks						x	x	x	x
11. Sensitive and concerned for students as people		x		x				x	
12. Higher-order understanding emphasized		x	x					x	
13. Risk-free environment	x				x				x
14. High paced		x				x	x		
15. Excellent classroom management	x					x	x		
16. Able to work within bureaucracy	x		x						
17. Count on support from colleagues	x		x						
18. Cooperation emphasized over competition		x							x
19. Students engaged in much reading and writing					x				x
20. Print-rich environment					x				x

Of these characteristics, the first four were cited by more than half of the researchers and merit further description. They were high expectations, student ownership, material made relevant, and curriculum determined by knowing students.

CHARACTERISTICS OF EFFECTIVE TEACHERS

Effective teachers have high expectations—they believe that every student can and will learn, and they convey this belief to their students through both their words and actions. Teachers with high expectations often mention to their students the potential each student possesses. They also give more and more complex assignments that challenge students' abilities, implying that students are capable of doing the work. They require that students do their best in all assignments. Pedersen, Faucher, and Eaton (1978) and Moll (1988) further mention that effective teachers gave extra time to students who were having trouble, even putting in time after hours to make sure students understood new topics. Effective teachers also expect that students will be successful and engaged. Ladson-Billings (1994) notes these teachers took the time to try diverse approaches to search out hidden abilities in otherwise low-achieving students.

Effective teachers have high expectations—they believe that every student can and will learn, and they convey this belief to their students through both their words and actions.

Exceptional teachers create classrooms where students own their learning, and where students are given choices and input into activities in exchange for greater responsibility. This creates internal motivation and students who care more about learning and less about merely completing an assignment. Haberman (1995) notes that effective teachers gave their students options whenever possible and used questions and ideas proposed by students as leads to further activities and topics of study. This does not mean the classroom was an educational free-for-all, but rather that effective elementary teachers gave students flexibility in noncritical aspects of a task. Block and Pressley (1998) describe teachers who allowed students to choose their topic and genre in a writing assignment, but were very specific about the skill, content, or strategy they wanted students to master.

Students of effective teachers are encouraged to regulate themselves and monitor the quality of their work. These teachers expect and teach students to create their own goals and keep track of their own progress toward those goals, such as maintaining records of progress in math, reading, and writing, or determining if daily goals have been met. This greater responsibly encourages students to evaluate their own progress and recognize qualifications for success.

Exceptional teachers make material relevant, engaging, and meaningful to students by relating new content to student interests and prior knowledge, and by placing knowledge within a purposeful context. These teachers start by determining what students know and relate what they are teaching to that level of knowledge. Through prompting and questioning, they make students aware of knowledge they did not know they had. Ladson-Billings (1994) provides the example of a teacher of African-American students who used the students' knowledge of the governing structure of their Southern Baptist church to help them understand the legislative bodies in the federal and state governments. Effective teachers also provide a context for what they are teaching, relating ideas such as math concepts to more global issues such as the historical context in which they were discovered. These teachers make subjects such as history or current events relevant to their students by helping them to see connections between world affairs and their own lives and neighborhoods. Haberman notes that teachers used what he describes as "hot topics" to relate student learning to current issues that have more relevance to students. He gives the example that the topics of "spread of disease" and "property rights" are not typically relevant to students, while "chemical waste in my neighborhood and how it might cause disease and other problems" (1995, 31) makes the learning more personal. These students do not learn about a static world outside of their control, but rather of a world that they belong to and are responsible for.

Exemplary teachers determine their curriculum in no small part by observing their students and determining their needs and interests.

Exemplary teachers determine their curriculum in no small part by observing their students and determining their needs and interests. This includes having thorough knowledge of children's developmental levels, as well as the observation skills to know where individual students are functioning and the ability to adapt activities to different student needs. Thomas and Barksdale-Ladd (1995) note that effective teachers use "student-centered planning" in which they base their plans on student needs identified through reading and writing portfolios, and by determining what students are learning, missing, and misunderstanding in the curriculum. Pressley, Rankin, and Yokoi (1996) note that effective teachers do a great deal of assessment as they teach so that they can adjust and reteach as necessary, and they monitor constantly for that purpose.

Effective teachers integrate curriculum, creating natural connections across subject areas and relating what students are learning in different disciplines.

Other characteristics on the list were not mentioned as frequently but were integral parts of effective teaching and are interrelated with the characteristics mentioned. Effective teachers are aware of educational theory and can relate what they are doing on a daily basis to their overarching goals for students. They are passionate about what they do and convey the seriousness and importance of learning and education to their students. They teach by modeling skills for students, including where and when to use a skill, and scaffold student learning by providing supports, hints, and prompts as students work to acquire new abilities. Effective teachers don't use power to gain control, but earn authority by building equitable relationships with students based on cooperation, respect, and kindness. They are concerned for students as individuals and work to build a relationship with each of them.

Effective teachers integrate curriculum, creating natural connections across subject areas and relating what students are learning in different disciplines. They teach skills explicitly, but do so within authentic contexts, and they teach students to think and question what they know and what is considered knowledge. They give students opportunities for much reading and writing throughout the day and surround them with motivating print materials at an appropriate level of complexity. The classroom environment of an effective teacher is high paced, in which much is expected, yet it is also risk free, where students are allowed to make mistakes and effort is valued over innate ability. Cooperation among students is emphasized over competition, and students are taught to work together and to be responsible for one another. Effective teachers are well prepared each day so that their class runs like clockwork. They are able to work within difficult circumstances, including mind-numbing bureaucracies and critical colleagues, often because they draw strength from professional support groups that they maintain membership in.

ENGAGING INSTRUCTION

If we had to reduce this long list of characteristics, our focus would be on the **engagingness** of these classrooms. More research is needed to clarify just what features of the instruction offered make these classrooms places where students routinely and voluntarily engage in reading, writing, discussion, and learning. But if we were to bet our hunches at this point, we would bet that the combination of personalized teaching developed from a close understanding of each child as a person as well as an understanding of each child as a reader, writer, and learner would be the key. These teachers teach children, not subjects. They seem to have not only a rich, technical expertise about teaching and learning, but also a very real respect for children and their curiosity. The technical knowledge is not unimportant—knowing which book best "fits" a child, the level of explicitness a given child will need to develop and maintain the use of an effective decoding or composing strategy, or how to develop a sense of classroom community are all essential aspects of exemplary teaching. But the technical expertise is not enough. There also is an ethic of caring, of personal and professional responsibility for all students. So how do educational administrators write this into a teacher standard? How will they test this mix of technical and personal characteristics?

SUMMARY

The characteristics generated in our review of the research on exemplary teachers seem to describe the Mrs. Worthings of America's elementary school classrooms (although, as Pressley et al. [1998] have noted, creating a mosaic seems a fitting metaphor for describing how any exemplary teacher incorporates this list of features into a classroom plan). So how will the new standards for teachers work to ensure that the supply of exemplary teachers increases? We are not sure that the efforts put into effect to date will enhance the likelihood that more exemplary teachers get classrooms of their own. And this seems truly unfortunate.

The new teacher standards are reminiscent of the old minimum competency standards for students that were widely implemented in the 1970s. Those standards had little positive impact on fostering the sort of higher-order understandings that the new student standards require. In fact, it could be argued that those minimum competency standards misdirected instructional efforts, with all the attention being given to lower-order skill development. Perhaps the same fate will befall the teacher standards—more minimally qualified teachers will be accepted while attention and fiscal resources are directed away from fostering teaching excellence. We hope not.

But, until it is more widely understood that exemplary teaching is "rocket science," and until the focus shifts away from setting minimal standards for teachers, we see little support for efforts focusing on the hard work of fostering exemplariness in all teachers. In the end, nothing matters more than the quality of the teachers students encounter. Refocusing attention—on teacher exemplariness rather than minimal competence—is essential if students are to have a chance at meeting the new, higher academic standards.

Authors' Note: This study was supported in part by a grant to the National Research Center on English Learning and Achievement, which is a research development center funded by the Office of Educational Research and Improvement (OERI), U.S. Department of Education. The center is headquartered at University at Albany, State University of New York, and The University of Wisconsin, Madison. (Grant #R305A60005). The contents of this report do not necessarily reflect the position or policies of OERI, the Department of Education, or any agency of the U.S. Government.

REFERENCES

Block, C., and M. Pressley. 1998. Differences between the philosophies and instructional actions of exemplary and typical first grade teachers. Unpublished manuscript.

Haberman, M. 1995. *Star teachers of children of poverty.* West Lafayette, IN: Kappa Delta Pi.

Ladson-Billings, G. 1994. *The dreamkeepers: Successful teachers of African American children.* San Francisco, CA: Jossey-Bass.

Moll, L. 1988. Some key issues in teaching Latino students. *Language Arts* 65: 465–472.

Pedersen, E., T. A. Faucher, and W. W. Eaton. 1978. A new perspective on the effects of first-grade teachers on children's subsequent adult status. *Harvard Educational Review* 48: 1–31.

Pressley, M., R. Wharton-McDonald, R. Allington, C. Block, L. Morrow, D. Tracey, K. Baker, G. Brooks, J. Cronin, E. Nelson, and D. Woo. 1988. *The nature of effective first grade literacy instruction.* Albany, NY: University at Albany, National Research Center on English Learning and Achievement.

Pressley, M., J. Rankin, and L. Yokoi. 1996. A survey of instructional practice of primary teachers nominated as effective in promoting literacy. *The Elementary School Journal* 96: 363–384.

Pressley, M., R. Wharton-McDonald, and J. Mistretta-Hampton. 1997. The development of literacy, part 3: Expert primary-level teaching of literacy is balanced teaching. In *Reading instruction that works: The case for balanced teaching,* edited by M. Pressley. New York: The Guilford Press.

Ruddell, R. 1995. *Teaching children to read and write: Becoming an influential teacher.* Boston, MA: Allyn & Bacon.

Ruddell, R. 1997. Researching the influential literacy teacher: Characteristics, beliefs, strategies, and new research directions. In *Inquiries into literacy theory and practice: Forty-sixth yearbook of the National Reading Conference,* edited by C. K. Kinzer, K. A. Hinchman, and D. J. Leu. Chicago, IL: National Reading Conference.

Thomas, K. F., and M. A. Barksdale-Ladd. 1995. Effective literacy classrooms: Teachers and students exploring literacy together. In *Perspectives on literacy research and practice: Forty-fourth yearbook of the National Reading Conference,* edited by K. A. Hinchman, D. J. Leu, and C. K. Kinzer. Chicago, IL: National Reading Conference.

Constructivist Assessment in Early Childhood Education

by Clifford Hill

INTRODUCTION

At the 1998 Teaching for Intelligence Conference, I made a presentation in which I challenged the use of the national reading test at the fourth grade level (Hill 1999). This challenge was based on a large-scale study of how such tests are structured and how children from varying ethnocultural backgrounds respond to them (Hill and Larsen 1999). I introduced representative material from this study to show that such tests have traditionally required children to respond from an acommunicative perspective: that is to say, children need to suppress their constructive responses to text and engage in such activities as recycling passage information or defining a vocabulary item.

Such acommunicative tasks can be difficult for children for various reasons. To begin with, the reading passage may be taken from material such as children's literature that calls for a more communicative style of reading. Moreover, if the passage is excerpted—as it often is—from a larger text, its incomplete nature may stimulate children to expand it. As researchers such as van Dijk and Kintsch (1983) have shown, comprehension necessarily depends upon our assimilating what we read to various schemata built around our experience not only of the real-world but also of text itself. In effect, we draw on both *real-world schemata* and *textual schemata* in order to make sense out of what we read.

A communicative response can be stimulated not only by the way in which the passage is structured but also by the way in which it

---

From presentation at the Teaching for Intelligence Conference in San Francisco, April 1999.

interfaces with the tasks. As already indicated, these tasks tend to call for an acommunicative target response but they also often include what Hill and Larsen describe as *communicative distractors* (1999, 34). Such distractors tend to be based on inferences, which though textually stimulated, introduce information, which, strictly speaking, is not contained in the passage. Hill (1992) points out that children from certain ethnocultural backgrounds are more prone to select such distractors, partly because they have been less socialized to the restrictive model of literacy that the test makers work with.

Although I focused on problems of standardized testing in last year's presentation, I did briefly introduce an alternative assessment model known as the *Progress Profile,* which is built around a constructivist model of literacy. Given the strong interest in this model, this year's presentation has been designed to show in more detail how it can be used to assess children's knowledge and skills with respect to emergent literacy and numeracy. What I would like to do in this presentation is to

1. describe the development of this model
2. provide an overview of its major components
3. illustrate activities within these components at the kindergarten level

I will then conclude the presentation with a brief discussion of major benefits and problems in using this model.

THE PROGRESS PROFILE

How the Model Was Developed

The Progress Profile was initially developed for use in the school district of Newburgh, New York where the student body is culturally diverse: much as in New York City itself, about one-third of the students are European-American, one-third African-American, and one-third Latino-American. Teachers in early childhood education had become increasingly dissatisfied with using the Iowa Test of Basic Skills and were looking for an alternative approach. The district superintendent invited me to work with the teachers in order to develop such an approach. I agreed to undertake the project on the condition that what we produced would be used in place of the Iowa Test. I had observed in previous work that whenever a standardized test is in place, it is difficult for students, teachers, and parents to make a sufficient investment in alternative assessment. The superintendent agreed to this condition but imposed a condition of his own: that we come up with an approach that could yield quantitative results. Each school district is required by state law (Chapter 53 legislation) to have in place some kind of assessment for identifying both "gifted students" and "students with learning disabilities."

The teachers and I agreed to this condition and began our work together. Our goal was to build an assessment model that would emphasize:

1. a constructivist approach to learning (but one also attentive to mastery of basic skills)
2. problem-solving activities that are familiar to children since they are centrally placed within the curriculum
3. the best practices that individual teachers were using throughout the district
4. a dynamic model of assessment in which the test giver can provide systematic cues to a child who is unable to perform a certain task (Feuerstein, Feuerstein, and Schur 1997).

The teachers and I called the model that we developed the *Progress Profile* in order to focus on the child's past performance as the comparative basis for assessment rather than the performance of other children or certain criteria (i.e., our approach to assessment can be described as *self-referenced* rather than *norm-referenced* or *criterion-referenced).*

How the Model Is Structured

The Progress Profile has two major components: testlike activities and documentation activities. We describe the first component as *testlike,* since although it reflects basic features of a testing situation (e.g., students respond individually to a common set of tasks), it does introduce certain features that extend the traditional testing paradigm: if individual children are not, for example, able to respond appropriately to a particular task, the test giver—typically the teacher—can introduce certain cues to help them. In effect, the testlike component reflects Feuerstein's model of dynamic assessment in that it is designed to establish how well children, when unable to respond, can make use of appropriate cues. These cues have been preestablished and so can be factored into the evaluation of children's performance.

As for the documentation activities, they are divided into two major components: (1) portfolios of work samples that children maintain, with guidance from teachers and parents, and (2) records of children's activities that teachers and parents jointly maintain. Figure 1 summarizes the major components of the Progress Profile.

testlike component
documentation component
  portfolio (child maintained)
  records (school/home maintained)

Figure 1

How Assessment Activities Are Conducted at the Kindergarten Level

In illustrating the major components of the Progress Profile, I will provide examples of assessment activities at the kindergarten level, the initial point at which a profile is developed of an individual child. I will show examples, first, of testlike activities and, then, of documentation activities (throughout this section, activities for emergent literacy will be presented before those for emergent numeracy).

Testlike Activities

Figure 2 provides an overview of various testlike activities used to assess kindergarten children's emergent literacy knowledge and skills (all major domains of the curriculum are covered).

As can be seen, all the activities—whether they involve reading, writing, or drawing—revolve around the children's experience of a storybook, which provides a natural anchoring that increases the validity of the assessment. These activities are initiated by the test giver presenting the child a collection of storybooks and encouraging him or her to choose one. The child is then asked to read the book if (s)he is able to; if not, the test giver reads to the child. We do not have time to describe all the activities so I will concentrate on those dealing with comprehension. As soon as the reading has been completed, the child is asked to retell the story to provide a baseline for subsequent comprehension tasks. The test giver then notes on a retelling form salient features of what the child does.

To illustrate how this process works, let us turn to *Bread,* a small storybook by Joy Cowley about twins whose mother sends them to buy bread. After buying the bread, the twins, on their way home,

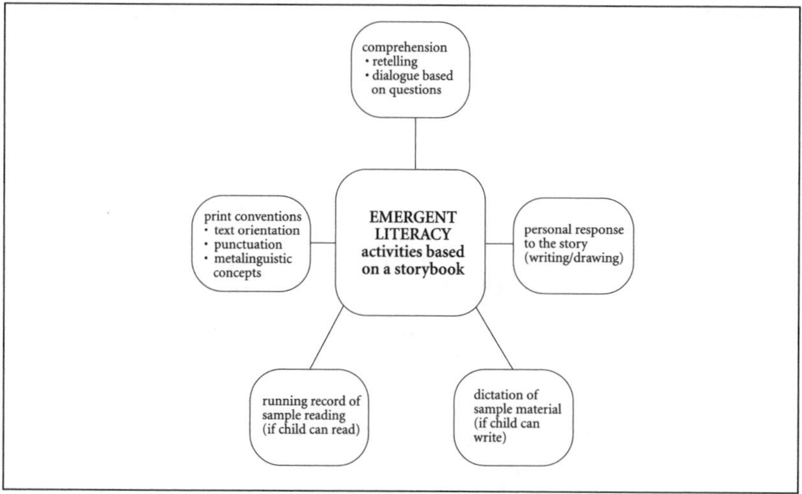

Figure 2

share it with various hungry animals. The twins reach home with only a bit of bread, but with a flock of animals following them. Their mother exclaims: "Where's the rest of the bread?" to which their father replies, pointing to the smiling animals outside the door, "Here it is." This story, like others we have selected, has a particular appeal to children. After all, the twins pursue a higher good in failing to fulfill their mother's request; it's as if children really know better than their parents anyway.

Figure 3 shows two retellings of the story *Bread,* which we have labeled as *summary style* and *performance style* respectively.

Summary style:
The mother sent the twins to buy bread. They gave it to the animals. They got home and their mother wanted the whole bread.

Performance style:
The mom said to the kids, "Go and get some bread." They went to get that bread. They saw a hungry dog. "Here, have some bread." They saw a hungry duck. "Here, have some bread." They saw a hungry goat. "Here, have some bread." The Mom said, "Where's the rest of the bread?" The Dad said, "It's in the animals' tummies."

Figure 3

The second retelling is by an African-American child who displayed considerable mimetic skill in representing the speech of the various characters. The teacher was especially pleased with his performance, for she thinks of him as a child who has trouble concentrating on what he hears.

We are especially interested in documenting the style that children use in the retelling, and so the test giver can note on the retelling form whether the style tends to be summary or performance (if the style is not clearly one or the other, the space can be left blank). The test giver then checks off whether the child included the major elements of the story; next to each element is a place to note any distinctive features of the child's performance. To give you an idea of how this form is used, Figure 4 shows the test giver's documentation of the second retelling shown in Figure 3.

	Yes/No	Comments
Story Style		
• Summary		
• Performance	x	dramatic style
Story elements		
• Mother sends twins to buy bread	x	
• Twins buy bread	x	
• Twins feed hungry animals	x	
• Dog	x	
• Duck	x	
• Goat	x	
• Mother asks where bread is	x	
• Father explains where it went	x	"animal tummies"

Figure 4

After the retelling has been completed, the test giver then engages the child in a series of comprehension tasks, which build on and extend the comprehension model developed by Bloom (1984). Figure 5 gives examples of the tasks used with the story *Bread.*

Children's responses to the factual and inferential tasks are numerically scored, but their responses to the holistic and experiential tasks are simply documented on forms that resemble the retelling form. This approach to evaluation exemplifies a basic principle fol-

Factual
- Where was the rest of the bread?

Inferential
- How did Dad know where the bread was?

Holistic
- What do you think happened next in the story? Tell me about it.

Experiential
- Have you ever got in trouble for doing something to help others? Tell me about it.

Figure 5

lowed in the Progress Profile: children's responses to all tasks are documented, but they are scored only when a task elicits responses sufficiently constrained to justify this kind of evaluation. I should note that we clearly separate factual and inferential tasks in order to avoid the confusion generated by multiple-choice tasks that often force children to choose between a factual and an inferential response.

Figure 6 provides an overview of various testlike activities used to assess kindergarten children's emergent numeracy knowledge and skills (all major domains of the kindergarten curriculum are covered).

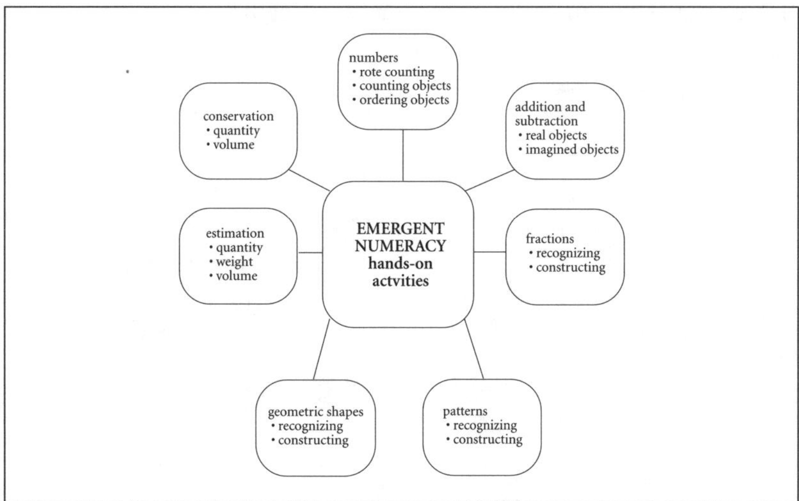

Figure 6

Just as the emergent literacy activities are anchored in familiar experience (e.g., children reading a story book), so the emergent numeracy activities are anchored in familiar experience as well. Children engaged in a wide range of acclivities across the seven domains, many of which involve their interacting with building blocks. In fact, children interact with blocks even in emergent literacy activities that deal with spatial terms. Here, for example, is an activity that focuses on orientational terms. A single red block is placed directly in front of the child and the test giver who gives the child a blue block and asks him or her to place it

1. in front of the red one
2. in back of the red one
3. to the left of the red one
4. to the right of the red one

Researchers in language development (e.g., Harris and Strommen 1972) have established that young children do not necessarily reflect adult patterns in their deictic use of orientational terms (a use in which these terms are anchored in their own spatial location). When using *front* and *back* to describe relations between objects that do not have intrinsically marked orientation, adult speakers of standard English generally construct a field oriented toward themselves, in which case the nearer object is viewed as *in front* of the further one, the further object as *in back* of the nearer one (see Figure 7).

'There's my pen *in front* of the ball.'

Figure 7

The construction of such a field is based on what can be called *mirror imagery* (i.e., the field reflects back toward the language user).

A significant number of young children, especially at the preschool stage, construct an opposing field in which the nearer object is viewed as in back of the further one, the further object as in front of the nearer one (see Figure 8).

'There's my pen *in back* of the ball.'

Figure 8

The construction of such a field is based on what can be called *in-tandem imagery* (i.e., the language user and the field are both oriented toward a further point). It is significant that children who use in-tandem imagery construct the same kind of field for both *front/back* and *left/right* constructions, as illustrated in Figure 9.[1]

As cross-linguistic research has demonstrated (Abubakar 1984; Hill 1974, 1975a and b, 1977; Ho 1999; Isma'il; Mahmoud 1996; Mshelia 1985; Wei 1996), adult speakers of many Asian and African languages who have not adapted to Western norms use in-tandem imagery for both 'front/back' and 'left/right' relations. Moreover, the use of such imagery has been documented for African-American and Asian-American students who are not acculturated to the norms of standard English (Hill 1982, 1991a and b, 1998; Ji 1998, Kim 1997; McKenna 1985; Mooney and Goldstein 1980). In administering the orientational task to African-American children in Newburgh, we discovered that nearly three-quarters of them used in-tandem imagery for both *front/back* and *left/right* (the research by McKenna docu-

'There's my pen *to the left* of the ball.'

Figure 9

mented a comparably dominate use of in-tandem even at the high school level for African-American students).

Given such ethnocultural variation, test givers obviously do not score the use of one kind of deictic imagery as right and the use of the other as wrong; rather they simply record which kind of imagery an individual child uses. Such information can be useful in indicating whether African-American children have acculturated to the commutative norms of standard English (and if they have, at what point). We have discussed this task at some length, for it illustrates well that the *Progress Profile* is designed not simply to provide quantitative results, but also to provide teachers deeper insight into the ethnocultural framing that children use.

In illustrating emergent numeracy activities, I will present (1) an activity in the *numbers* domain, in which children use ordinal terms such as *first* and *second,* and (2) an activity in the *estimation* domain, in which children first estimate the length of an object and then verify whether their original estimate was accurate.

In order to carry out the ordering task, the child is presented with six colored blocks arranged in a row. The test giver then asks the child four questions:

1. Which color is first?
2. Which color is second?
3. Which color is third?

4. Which color is last?

Once the child has answered these questions, the test giver then asks the child why (s)he started where (s)he did. On the ordering form, the test giver records

1. whether the child used the four ordinal terms consistently
2. the direction—left to right or right to left—which the child followed
3. the child's explanation of the direction followed.

This task provides information about not only children's knowledge of ordering terms but also the underlying frame that they use. During preschool years, children tend to favor their dominant hand as they engage in various play routines: right-handed children, for example, tend to push a car from right to left; left-handed children from left to right. As right-handed children engage in literacy-based activities, however, many show an increasing tendency to adopt a left-to-right frame. This particular task provides a subtle cue, at least for right-handed children, as to whether they are using such a frame.

The cross-linguistic research described earlier has also dealt with the interaction of literacy frames and the use of deictic imagery. In conducting research in Nigeria, I presented Hausa students with a task in which they were asked to draw a circle either *gaba* 'in front of/before' or *baya* 'behind/after' certain words (Hill 1991a and 1991b). This task was presented in Hausa written in

1. Roman script for students in Western schools
2. Arabic script for students in Islamic schools.

Nearly all the students responding to Roman script drew the circle to the right of the words, whereas nearly all the students responding to Arabic script drew the circle to the left of the words. In effect, the students projected in-tandem imagery on to the particular axis in the textual field—left/right for Roman script and right/left for Arabic script.

Let us now turn to the other emergent numeracy task in which children are asked to estimate length and then verify their estimate. Children are presented with paper clips, a ruler, a pencil, and a piece of paper on which the pencil and the ruler have been traced. The test giver first asks the children to match the pencil and the ruler to the tracings on the paper. (S)he then gives them the paper clips and asks them to estimate the number of clips that would equal the length of each object. After the children have recorded each estimate, the test giver then asks them to measure each tracing with the paper clips and to record each measurement. The test giver takes notes on the children's performance, with particular attention to the degree to which they preserve their original estimate. If children measure inaccuractely in an effort to preserve their original estimate, the test giver, drawing on Feuerstein's model of dynamic assessment, asks them to measure again with greater attention to the actual length of the object. If their second measurement is more accurate, they receive partial credit, since they have demonstrated a capacity to respond to coaching (the test giver also asks them why they think their first measurement was less accurate). This task provides valuable information about not only how well children can estimate length but also the degree to which they are willing to conduct objective measurement that they contradict their original estimate. This task, as one teacher put it, gives a sense of "whether children are more interested in preserving their own view of things or finding out how things really are. It gives us a great context for introducing the values of science."

These stories help to develop children's understanding that ultimately their human heritage is global rather than national or ethnic.

Documentation Activities

The portfolios that children maintain with the help of teachers and parents include a range of work samples. In assembling the portfolio, children are encouraged to maintain a balance between assigned activities and freely chosen activities. An assigned activity has the virtue of establishing a common context (for example, children drawing a human figure), which can be repeated at regular intervals throughout the first five years of schooling. We are now developing an assigned activity in which kindergarten children select a story from a collection of aetiological tales that come from various parts of the world (i.e., those that explain natural phenomena ranging from why humans die to why a dog wags (its tail). From a pedagogical perspective, these stories help to develop children's understanding that ultimately their human heritage is global rather than national or ethnic. As the world becomes increasingly interdependent, this lesson takes on an ever greater urgency.

Once the child has selected the story, (s)he and the teacher read it together and (s)he then retells it. Since this procedure is repeated at regular intervals, it allows us to discern development in children's sense of how a story works. In this way we obtain valuable information about individual children's growth, though, as experienced teachers have wisely counseled, our ordinary notions about progress can be misleading. As children try to do the same task in a more complex way, they may not appear to be moving forward in all respects.

It is important that the portfolio contain work that children choose to do on their own. Teachers have shown ingenuity in helping students display personal work; for example, they help children convert stories, replete with drawings, into small books. Figure 10 presents one of these books, titled *My Mother Is Great* (each of its seven pages contains a drawing by the child together with the words he dictated to his teacher, Jon Yettru). As can be seen, the initial words—*my mother is great*—are recycled at the end. In the final drawing, the child, however, appears in place of the mother, though he is now larger and seems to have taken over her eyes. Perhaps there's a lesson here—every great mother may have to recede as the child grows.

Once children's books have been completed, Jon helps put in a pocket for a library card. He then puts the books in a small classroom library so that the children can check them out and read each other's stories at home. As I have pointed out elsewhere, "As children participate in this activity, they acquire a good deal of knowledge about literacy: for example, how an individual book is organized (images and words working together to make meaning) and how books are organized in a library. Here they get early exposure to the alphabetical principle of organization basic to the western experience of literacy; the alphabet becomes something more for children than a string of letters to recite. But apart from this practical knowledge of literacy, children learn an even more important lesson—that they can bring their personal worlds to the classroom" (Hill 1992, 38–39).

As for the emergent numeracy portfolio, it, too, is balanced between assigned activities and activities that are freely chosen. In order to provide documentation on children's capacity to work in groups, one assigned activity repeated in regular intervals is for the teacher to give two children a tangerine and ask them to share it. The teacher uses a preestablished form designed to document not only the procedures that the children follow but also what the outcome ultimately is. Did the children manage to divide the tangerine evenly? If not,

Page	Child's Drawing	Child's Words
1	a tall mother with long brown hair, green eyes, and a large red mouth	My mother is great.
2	a short roundish child holding a baby (the baby appears to be slipping away)	She lets me hold my little brother and I don't drop him.
3	the child with a robust smile	She loves to read to me every day.
4	the mother with somewhat bluish eyes (her hair has become decidedly bouffant)	She has brown hair and eyes that change color.
5	the mother with hair rising to a sharp point above her head	My mother is beautiful.
6	the child appearing more roundish	She is a great cook—hamburgers and hot dogs are my favorite.
7	the child even more expanded and now possessing the mother's brightly colored eyes	My mother is great.

Figure 10

who gets the larger share? The form also contains a space in which various kinds of social interaction can be noted. Did one child try to coerce the other? If so, in what way?

Just as freely constructed stories are included in children's emergent literacy portfolios, so freely constructed objects are included in their emergent numeracy portfolios. Moreover, just as teachers preserve the stories by converting them into small books, so they preserve the objects by photographing them. The photographs can then be placed in the emergent numeracy portfolios in order to provide a more permanent record of children's work. As children move on to a higher level, their teachers can use such documentation to gain a clearer picture of their development.

It is especially important that these portfolios be presented in an intelligible fashion, and technology has an important role to play in facilitating such intelligibility (e.g., photographs of children's constructed objects can be scanned into computer files). It is, of course, difficult for young children to maintain such files, so at one school middle school students, as part of a technology project, work with kindergarten children to develop and maintain computer files.

As for the school/home-maintained records, teachers have worked with parents to develop a range of methods for keeping track of children's emergent literacy and numeracy activities at home. Teachers use, for example, a method developed by Judy Duquette for documenting children's reading at home. When children take home books to read, they take along a small notebook in which entries can be made: whoever reads with the child—a parent, a grandparent, an older sibling, a visiting friend or relative—can write comments about how the child responds to the book. Figure 11 shows a couple of excerpts from what one mother wrote:

> Darryl did real excellent with this book. He read it to me, his big sister, and two little brothers. He knew about all the words. And at the same time, he learned two new words, *else* and *hugs*. He's doing wonderful.
>
> Darryl read this book to his grandma. She says he read the words real good at the end. He liked that the cars be moving real slow because they were fat.

Figure 11

As teachers write personal responses to these comments, they are able to maintain a dialogue with those at home around the child's reading. Such a dialogue has a number of advantages, a couple of which I can mention here. It encourages those at home to be more active in reading with the child and, at the same time, provides teachers greater understanding of the child's home life (emergent numeracy activities are documented in a parallel notebook).

CONCLUSIONS

Benefits in Using the Model

It is the children themselves who benefit most greatly from the use of the Progress Profile. As for the testlike activities, since they are anchored in familiar routines, children do not run the risk of an impoverished performance simply because they do not understand what they are to do. Moreover, the test giver's use of a dynamic model of assessment ensures that children leave these activities with a sense of accomplishment. As for the documentation activities, they are designed to provide a sense of children's development over time. Since the children are involved in maintaining their own portfolios, they learn important lessons not only about organizing their work but also about evaluating it. Indeed, of children's capacity to evaluate their own work responsibly, may well be the most important outcome of any assessment activity.

Indeed, children's capacity to evaluate their own work responsibly, may well be the most important outcome of any assessment activity.

The teachers also benefit from using the Progress Profile. To begin with, it represents a pooling of their best practices and so encourages a sense of collaboration. As Stefanakis (1998) has pointed out in her aptly titled *Whose Judgment Counts?*, when teachers develop and administer an assessment program, they authenticate their own judgment: they are, after all, the persons who are best placed to evaluate the individual child's knowledge and skills. It is also important to note that since the teachers are themselves the test givers, they are in a position to develop a more refined capacity for careful clinical observation. Such greater refinement carries over into their everyday interaction with children.

Finally, parents benefit from the Progress Profile as well. The various methods used to facilitate home-school communication leads to a richer and more comprehensive documentation of the individual child's development of knowledge and skills. The systematic documentation of a child's literacy and numeracy experience at home leads to increased involvement of parents and other family members in the child's school experience. We have found that such increased involvement is a source of great motivation for young children. A particular benefit to parents derives from the collection of a child's work on a regular basis. From our vantage point, all the artifacts in the child's portfolio ultimately belong in the home, since technology can be used to maintain a record of these artifacts at school.

Problems in Using the Model

Despite the many benefits associated with the use of the Progress Profile, substantial problems remain. The most basic problem has been to sustain districtwide use of the model, especially now that new standard-based tests have been introduced in New York State. District superintendents no longer have the freedom to use locally developed alternative assessment in place of externally developed tests. Since these tests place heavy demands on children, teachers, and even parents, it has become difficult to maintain the level of commitment that the Progress Profile requires.

All the artifacts in the child's portfolio ultimately belong in the home . . .

Advocates of standard-based testing claim that it reflects a constructivist approach to assessment and thus can be used in place of locally constructed models such as the Progress Profile. Although such testing is designed according to constructivist principles, it still reflects three major limitations. To begin with, it is not generally complemented by any systematic use of documentation activities. Moreover, teachers are less involved in designing such tests and in evaluating students' performance, and so their own professional development does not take place in the same way. Finally, the standards-based tests, at least as they are currently designed and administered, often require children to carry out a series of complex tasks in a limited time frame and thus force children to respond at a superficial level. On the fourth grade test in New York, children are required, within a span of forty-five minutes, to listen to a test giver read a folktale twice (only after the second reading are they allowed to take notes) and then respond to three short-answer tasks, which are followed by two tasks that call for extended writing. The limited time frame necessarily leads to hurried writing with little or no planning, which is frustrating not only to children but also to teachers and parents.

As content standards are used to develop more complex tasks, we must be willing to allow children to carry out these tasks apart from the limited time frame traditionally associated with multiple-choice testing. As indicated in our description of the Progress Profile, test givers are not limited to a strict time frame when administering testlike activities. From our perspective, time pressure is counterproductive if the goal is to document reliably children's capacity to carry out complex activities such as writing; and, of course, the Progress Profile also includes documentation activities in which children can work on a single project over an extended period of time.

In closing, I would like to mention one other problem: the public has been conditioned to expect numbers in evaluating the educational performance of individual students. As long as this expectation is in place, alternative assessment is subject to the criticism that it does not achieve a high degree of psychometric reliability. To counter such criticism, it is important that the public be educated on two fronts. First, it must become more aware of what psychometric reliability means in standardized testing: this reliability is purchased at the cost of reducing complex activities, such as reading comprehension, to artificial exercises in which students learn to respond acommunicatively to the multiple-choice format. Second, the public needs to learn more about what to expect from alternative assessment. It is not realistic, given the range and complexity of its various activities, to achieve the kind of psychometric reliability that has been purchased at great cost by standardized testing. Rather the public must be educated to think about reliability in a new way, to associate it with the more comprehensive understanding of individual students that alternative assessment can provide. This new way of thinking is especially important in early childhood education, where the basic role of assessment is to provide comprehensive understanding of individual children that can be used in facilitating their exploration of knowledge and their development of skills.

Author's Note: I would like to acknowledge the support of the U.S. Department of Education, where I served as a visiting research fellow at the National Institute on Student Achievement, Curriculum, and Assessment. The views expressed in this article do not necessarily reflect the position of the U.S. Department of Education.

NOTES

1. By the way of contrast, adult speakers of standard English (and, for that matter, adult speakers of standard forms of other European languages) use mirror imagery for *front/back* and in-tandem imagery for *left/right* (see Hill, 1999, for discussion of such contrasting imagery).

REFERENCES

Abubakar, A. 1985. The acquisition of 'front' and 'back' among Hausa children: A study in deixis. Unpublished doctoral dissertation. Teachers College, Columbia University.

Aronowitz, R. 1977. A pilot study on the encoding of spatial relations in Israel. Unpublished manuscript.

Bloom, B. 1984. A taxonomy of educational objectives. New York: Longman.

Feuerstein, F., F. Feuerstein, and Y. Schur. 1997. Process as content in education of exceptional children. In *Supporting the spirit of learning when education is content,* edited by A. Costa and R. Liebmann. Thousand Oaks, CA: Corwin Press.

Harris, L. and E. Strommen 1972. The role of front-back features in children's placement of objects. *Merrill-Palmer Quarterly* 18: 259–271.

Hill, C. 1974. Spatial perception and linguistic encoding: A case study in Hausa and English. *Studies in African Linguistics* 4: 135–148.

Hill, C. 1975a. Variation in the use of 'front' and 'back' by bilingual speakers. *Proceedings of the Berkeley Linguistics Society* 1: 196–206.

Hill, C. 1975b. Sex-based differences in cognitive processing of spatial relations among bilingual students in Niger. *Working papers in linguistics: patterns in language, culture, and society.* Ohio State University 19: 185–198.

Hill, C. 1978. Linguistic representation of spatial and temporal orientation. *Proceedings of the Berkeley Linguistics Society* 4: 524–538.

Hill, C. 1982. Up/down, front/back, left/right: a contrastive study of Hausa and English. In *Here and there: Cross-linguistic studies on deixis and demonstration,* edited by J. Weissenborn and W. Klein. Amsterdam: John Benjamins Press.

Hill, C. 1991a. Recherches interlinguistiques en orientation spatiale. *Communications* 53: 171–207.

Hill, C. 1991b. *Spatial and temporal orientation: African and African-American continuities.* LC Report 1991-1, Literacy Center, Teachers College, Columbia University.

Hill, C. (1992). *Testing and assessment: an ecological approach.* Inaugural lecture for the Arthur I. Gates Chair in Language and Education. New York: Teachers College, Columbia University.

Hill, C. 1998. Semiotic perspectives on space and time. Unpublished manuscript.

Hill, C. 1999. A national reading test for fourth graders: A missing component in the policy debate. In *Teaching for intelligence I: A collection of articles,* edited by B. Presseisen. Arlington Heights, IL: Skylight Training and Publishing.

Hill, C., and E. Larsen. 2000. *Children and reading tests.* Stamford, CT: Ablex Press.

Ho, Y. 1999. Textual orientation and problem solving in mainland China and Taiwan. Unpublished manuscript.

Isma'il, T. 1979. *Cross-cultural variation in spatial and temporal constructs: Hausa speakers' use of spatial and temporal constructs in English.* Unpublished doctoral dissertation. Teachers College, Columbia University.

Ji, J. 1998. Spatiotemporal orientation among Chinese immigrants in Metropolitian New York. Unpublished doctoral dissertation, Teachers College, Columbia University.

Kim, S. 1997. *Variation in Koreans' use of spatial and temporal constructs.* Unpublished doctoral dissertation, Teachers College, Columbia University.

Mahmoud, H. 1998. *Variation in the use of spatial constructs among secondary school students in Chad.* Unpublished doctoral dissertation. Teachers College, Columbia University.

McKenna, S. 1985. *7th, 9th, and 11th grade mainstream and minority students' use of patterns for the deictic interpretation of orientational prepositions across the two modes of oral and written language.* Unpublished doctoral dissertation, Teachers College, Columbia University.

Mooney, W. and L. Goldstein. 1980. Pilot study in a Harlem high school: Language variation based on interlocutor shift. Unpublished manuscript.

Mshelia, A. 1985. *The influence of cognitive style and training on depth picture perception among non-western children.* Unpublished doctoral dissertation. Teachers College, Columbia University.

Reyes, M. 1994. Variation in the use of spatial constructs by Puerto Rican students. Unpublished doctoral dissertation. Teachers College, Columbia University.

Stefanakis, E. 1998. *Whose judgment counts?* Portsmouth, NH: Heinemann.

van Dijk, T., and W. Kintsch. 1983. *Strategies of discourse comprehension.* New York: Academic Press.

Wei, Y. 1996. Linguistic representation of spatial and temporal orientation: Structured variation among Chinese university students. Unpublished doctoral dissertation, Teachers College, Columbia University.

Test Success in the Brain-Compatible Classroom

by Carolyn Chapman and Rita King

THE CURRENT TESTING SCENE

Is there a learning experience that generates more negative feelings than standardized testing? When the word *test* is simply mentioned, the connotation creates deep-rooted negative reactions from teachers, administrators, and parents. These feelings of anxiety and stress are transferred directly and indirectly to students during testing experiences.

Across the country, negative comments and attitudes are accepted as common reactions to tests. The following scenarios (Clovis 1999) are examples of the pervasive negativity related to testing:

> Before the achievement tests a principal asked a class of fourth-grade students how they were feeling about the tests. One boy immediately responded with one word. He said, "Sick!" Later the boys and girls were asked how they felt during the test, and the same student's response was "Sick." (Rita King interview with Kenny Hoff 1999)

> In a similar situation a Philadelphia middle school student reported that he immediately started sweating, had stomach cramps and thought he would be sick when the teacher told the class to take out their No.2 pencils. (Clovis 1999, p. 28)

> A second-grade teacher said, "On the morning of the first test day my students acted as though they had stage fright. They did not seem to remember anything we had practiced during the last few days. It was an extremely frustrating day for me." (Rita King interview with Betsy Esa 1999)

> A college senior said, "When I take a test, I feel like my stomach is in my throat. I talk to myself to calm myself down and say, "I am not on

my way to the electric chair." (Rita King interview with Marcia Leech 2000)

Teachers don't need to ask *why* these attitudes exist; they know.

Effective teachers are using performance-based tests as authentic measures of achievement, but standardized tests are viewed as the most important assessment performances each year. Most states mandate annual standardized achievement tests for elementary, middle, and high schools. Reading, writing, math, science, and social studies are the subjects tested in the majority of schools. Some states also include spelling, health, and communication. Local school systems receive the legislated requirements and materials for the standardized test from the state. These requirements are then passed on to school administrators. The administrators forward the information and materials to classroom teachers who are responsible for directing the test. It is the teachers who are accountable for the scores.

Many legislators and administrators believe that teachers work harder to increase achievement scores when they are accountable for the results. Such accountability may include rewards for high scores or sanctions for low scores. The current national trend is to connect salary increases or merit pay to achievement gains.

Test scores are published in newspapers and various media for public scrutiny. Owners of businesses and industries analyze test results to choose new locations. Realtors use the test scores to promote home and property sales. In many instances the public uses the published test scores as the sole criteria to judge the quality of teaching, schools, and districts in a certain area.

Achievement tests will not become obsolete in the next few years. State and local districts will continue to demand annual tests, but school administrators, teachers, and parents have the autonomy to create relaxed learning environments, to provide meaningful experiences, and to help students develop positive attitudes toward test-taking experiences.

The Testing Scene through New Eyes

A major paradigm shift in attitudes and practices toward testing experiences is needed. This call for major changes in testing approaches is based on the authors' review of current cognitive research, which reveals that the brain operates best in a state of mental relaxation and relaxed alertness. Thus, for optimal learning to occur in test preparation and during tests, negative attitudes and practices must be abandoned. We don't have to look to research to reach this conclusion—it is common sense.

Brain-compatible environments are based on cognitive research related to "how one learns." Studies related to learning illustrate that positive classroom climates and positive home environments are necessary for successful test-taking experiences. Past beliefs, values, and views regarding tests must be replaced with positive approaches, language, and attitudes. In brain-compatible environments everyone involved in the student's education provides lessons and activities from a positive perspective.

According to cognitive scientists, the learning climate provided in brain-compatible classrooms is conducive to positive attitudes, fewer mental blocks, more neural brain connections, more student responsibility for learning, and more feelings of success. When this learning environment is provided, the ultimate payoff is a higher rate of test success. It is obvious that this change constitutes a major transformation in test preparation. What is there to lose?

THE RESEARCH PERSPECTIVE

The rationale for shifting to positive approaches to teaching test-taking skills is grounded in brain-based research. A brief description of significant research findings and their relationship to the test-taking scene are outlined below.

Costa's Thinking Skills Model

Art Costa's strategy for teaching a thinking skill can be easily adapted and applied to teaching a test-taking skill. Teachers can use the following outline of the Costa model as a guide to help students transfer knowledge from prior experiences to the testing format.

CAINE AND CAINE'S RESEARCH ON RELAXED ALERTNESS

Renate Nummela Caine and Geoffrey Caine (1994) provide extensive research related to understanding the value of nonthreatening, relaxed environments for learning. Formal test settings do not reflect relaxed atmospheres. However, teachers have the tools necessary to present test-taking skills in new and exciting ways to make test-taking experiences more relaxed, comfortable, inviting, and challenging.

Gill's Perspective on Learning to Learn

Effective teachers know that their goal is to help students *learn how to*

TEACHING A THINKING SKILL	TEACHING A TEST-TAKING SKILL
I. INPUT The skill or strategy is the lesson's focus. The skill is defined. Students are told why the skill is important and when it will be needed. Previous experiences are recalled. The teacher or a skilled person models it. Related vocabulary is introduced in each step. Students discuss it. (Costa, 1991, p. 77)	The test-taking skill or concept is taught explicitly so the information is mentally processed in a variety of ways. Prior experiences are woven into the lesson. Use of the skill is modeled. The vocabulary is related to use of the skill. Activities involve individual and group members in discussions of the skills used.
II. PROCESS The skill is experienced using known content. Students think about the test skill or strategy and verbalize their thinking during the experience. The learners analyze their thinking about the skill in individual and group activities. The steps used applying the skill are sequenced. (Costa, 1991, p. 78)	The test-taking skill is used with formal and informal tests using known content. When the information is processed, the learners talk through their step-by-step thinking. They rehearse, analyze, and summarize the information to personalize the skill so it will be used automatically when needed.
III. OUTPUT The skill is applied in new settings or contexts. Students think about their thinking while completing each task to refine the skill's use. The skill is applied in various ways in the classroom and in real-life situations. (Costa, 1991, p. 78)	The learners apply and adapt the test-taking skill in a different way and often in a new setting. Students think about their use of the skill in formal and informal tests. The information related to the skill's use becomes a part of the individuals' repertoire of test-application strategies and daily use outside the classroom.
IV. REVIEW Students review and apply each skill in future lessons and experiences throughout the year. (Costa, 1991, p. 78)	The skill is used as needed in formal and informal tests to demonstrate ownership and understanding by the productive learners. (Costa 1991, 77-78)

learn so students will be able to learn more (Gill 1993). Students have to take tests throughout their entire educational career. To be successful, they must have a thorough knowledge of test-taking skills and know how to apply them in and out of the classroom. Thus, students must be taught how to regulate and control their learning with appropriate strategies.

Students must be taught how to identify their emotions and how to control and use them appropriately for test success.

Goleman's Emotional Intelligence Theory

Emotional intelligence plays a major role in each student's test success. Emotions evident during tests include nervousness, anxiety, excitement, worry, frustration, and fear of failure. These negative emotions block thinking processes. A major component of emotional intelligence is self-awareness, which is defined by Goleman as "self-reflective, introspective attention to one's own experience, sometimes called *mindfulness*" (1995, 315). Students must be taught how to identify their emotions and how to control and use them appropriately for test success.

Sousa's Perspective of Transfer

Transfer is the ability to learn in one situation and apply the new knowledge—possibly in a modified or generalized form—in other situations (Sousa 1995). A variety of enriched learning experiences must be provided to enhance transfer of test-taking skills to subject areas. Students need to be taught how to connect test-taking skills to all tests, to subject-related lessons, and to daily experiences outside the classroom.

Gardner's Multiple Intelligences Theory

The multiple intelligences theory was introduced in 1983 by Howard Gardner, professor of education at Harvard University, following an in-depth study of cognitive development in young people. Most tests target two intelligences: verbal/linguistic and logical/mathematical. The other intelligences, which are often not targeted in tests, are musical/rhythmic, visual/spatial, bodily/kinesthetic, interpersonal, intrapersonal, and naturalist. However, each intelligence can be used in the problem-solving process embedded in tests. Teachers can implement activities designed for the intelligences to assist students as they internalize the use of test-taking skills. Carolyn Chapman's book, *If the Shoe Fits...How to Develop Multiple Intelligences in the Classroom* (1993), is filled with exciting, practical ideas to help students learn facts and concepts. The "how to" advice, strategies, and activities can be adapted to teaching test-related skills.

Sternberg's Aspects of Intelligence

Dr. Robert Sternberg (1985) has identified *analytical, creative,* and *practical* abilities as three aspects of intelligence. Teachers can apply these abilities to the testing scene as another way of approaching testing in brain-compatible classrooms.

1. An individual's analytical skills include the ability to critique, evaluate, and judge critically. Students who are strong in these areas usually perform well in traditional classrooms and perceive a test as a positive event.

2. The creative aspect of intelligence includes the ability to create, design, brainstorm, invent, and use the imagination. Students who have creative intelligence usually do not perform well on formal tests. Teachers should design instruction to teach content information and test-taking skills in varied, stimulating ways to meet the needs of creative minds. This knowledge then can be transferred to the subject area and skills being tested.

3. The practical aspect of intelligence is knowing how to apply what one knows. Other definitions include common sense, progressive thinking, and the ability to cope in new situations. The practical thinker is likely to perceive the test as a waste of time. The application of test-taking skills to content and life skills outside the classroom will help this learner understand the purpose of testing and make the experience more meaningful for the student. Attitude plays a major role in test success for the practical thinker. This student is more likely to succeed on tests when he or she is encouraged to say, "I am going to do my very best!" and "I will celebrate what I learned and show the world I can do well on this test."

TIPS FOR TEST SUCCESS IN THE BRAIN-COMPATIBLE CLASSROOM

Teachers can use the following tips to promote brain-compatible testing practices in their classrooms.

1. Vary Instructional Strategies to Teach Content

Teachers can relay meaningful content to students by designing strategies and activities to help students retain and retrieve more information. Each student has areas of strength for learning, and he or she needs to know how to use his or her strengths to learn test-taking strategies and skills. Teachers can use differentiated instruction to help students identity and apply the tools needed for test success.

Teachers also can teach students that the purpose of each lesson is to place information in memory for later use at school and in the world outside the classroom. Learners need to know that retrieval of this information for tests will be an easy process when the activities and strategies to jog the memory are applied (Chapman and King 2000). Students also need to know that memory is more accessible when information is learned with mnemonics, color coding, graphic organizers, raps, jingles, rhymes, role-playing, movement, and other activities designed for active participation.

Each student has areas of strength for learning, and he or she needs to know how to use his or her strengths to learn test-taking strategies and skills.

2. Practice Application of Test-Taking Skills

Teachers can practice test-taking skills with students in all subjects throughout the school year. Strategies to teach procedures, vocabulary, test format, listening, and content need to become routine in the learner's repertoire of knowledge. The more automatic these skills are, the better test-taker the individual becomes. Students must model, rehearse, apply, and practice skills for memorization on a regular basis. Teachers can create multiple-choice samples using meaningful content in daily lessons and activities to demonstrate how answers need to be attacked. This is an effective way for students to learn the ins and outs of testing.

3. Improve Student Behaviors during Test Performance

Teachers should observe each student's emotional and physical reactions to routine assessments during chapter, unit, and six-week tests throughout the year. As each test period approaches, teachers can address individual habits and problems that may hinder a student's top performance and guide the student to correct this behavior. For example, if a student becomes sick or talks inappropriately when a test is given, he or she may be experiencing test anxiety. He or she can learn strategies to correct the behavior and to be more comfortable and confident in future assessments and evaluations. Behaviors that hinder a student's test performance need to be identified and corrected during the year so they are less likely to occur in future tests.

4. Bridge the Testing Scenario to Real-Life Experiences

Teachers should design activities to help students see the value of learning each test- taking skill. These skills should be applied in content areas and to real-world experiences. The lessons should be tied to the learner's prior knowledge and to future use of the new information. For example, when students realize that obtaining a driver's license depends on a test, they exhibit a stronger desire to learn the necessary skills.

Teachers can create pleasant and exciting tests to be taken for fun during the week before major tests, and stress self-improvement rather than competition. Teachers can create fun tests by

- Sponsoring taste tests with unfamiliar foods in the cafeteria
- Using physical fitness tests and games to increase individual competencies in gym classes
- Using game formats such as Name the Composer or Name That Tune in music classes
- Organizing a celebration for the entire school each day before the test

Teachers can organize a celebration by stressing to students the value of doing their best on the test to "show what they know" and grow stronger as a learner. Teachers can start the celebration by having the entire school sing-along to a song such as "I'm Great and Getting Greater" (Chapman 1999) as it is played or sung over the intercom. Students can also be asked to share test cheers or theme songs they create over the loudspeaker. These activities can help teachers communicate to students the value of tests in individual improvement and success.

5. Teach Test-Taking Skills as an Integral Part of Curriculum throughout the Year

Teachers can consciously and explicitly teach testing skills and processes throughout the year using subject integration. Students need to learn and internalize strategies through meaningful, personal experiences and transfer these strategies to various test formats. These strategies include making a best guess, attacking a passage, skimming, backsolving, and making predictions.

6. Talk Step-by-Step Thinking

Teachers can model inside thinking by orally walking students through each step in a problem. Teachers also can routinely ask learners to think through their answers aloud when answering questions and problem solving. It is the process—not the product—that should be emphasized by teachers so that students realize the importance of knowing and using steps to find solutions.

7. Establish an Appropriate, Effective Testing Environment

Teachers can establish an appropriate and effective testing environment that is comfortable and nonthreatening for effective learning. Students are not brain-compatible are not afraid to take risks and to strive to do their best in brain-compatible classrooms. Teachers and students need to develop personal bonds based on mutual respect, rapport, and genuine interest. When this relationship exists, students are motivated to meet established expectations to please the teacher.

Visuals create a team spirit and fuel students' desire to excel.

Teachers can "dress" the school and classroom for test success by displaying banners, mobiles, and posters featuring raps, songs, and jingles written by students. These visuals create a team spirit and fuel students' desire to excel. Pencils, notepads, rulers, or bookmarks with special logos such as "Zap the Test" and "Smart Pencil" are excellent motivators.

Teachers can present tests as opportunities for students to "show off" what they have learned throughout the year. Since the achievement test is an assessment of what has been learned, students should perceive each test as a time to celebrate their abilities and hard work. Pep rallies, test-success parties, and grand finale celebrations provide students with positive experiences to associate with tests.

8. Provide Perks during Tests

Teachers can ask students to create a personal "cool test kit" or "lucky bucket" to hold items such as a lucky eraser, tissues, a bottle of water, green peppermint candy (promotes thinking), a snack, and a note of encouragement from parents. It is important that teachers let students choose things that make them feel good or that they feel bring them luck. Wearing a favorite T-shirt or a special color may help students create feeling of luck, too. These choices will not only meet some of the students' physical needs, but will also give them things to enjoy during a stressful event. These materials need to be accessible to students during tests and transitions. This technique will work if students are taught to use these items appropriately throughout the year.

9. Create Unified Support with School, Home, and Community

Teachers can work to establish a positive learning environment in students' homes and community. This can be accomplished when teachers communicate the value of removing negativity from the testing scenario to everyone involved in the students' educations. Parent workshops, weekly newsletters, and classroom meetings should be held to address recent brain research and the prevalent need for positive approaches to tests. Teachers should emphasize the value of establishing relaxed, comfortable, nonthreatening learning environments at home. They should give parents guidelines and checklists designed to help them prepare their students for tests. Included in such guidelines should be a vocabulary of terms and phrases for positive communication; nutrition tips; physical exercise advice; and recommendations for mental relaxation, thinking exercises, and prompts to express high expectations and avoid undue anxiety and stress. Teachers can obtain community support for implementing positive approaches to tests through local newspapers, cable programs, and web pages.

10. Use Test Data as a Positive Tool

Teachers should use test results in positive ways. Teachers can examine students' areas of strength and weakness to plan appropriate curriculum design and to meet differentiated learner needs. This test data can be shared with students and parents. Teachers also should emphasize the use of test summaries for improvement and celebrations of learning.

CONCLUSION

The authors designed this article as a valuable source for setting the stage for testing using positive learning environments in the classroom, throughout the school, and in the home. It is hoped that teachers will use the activities and strategies for teaching test-taking skills to prepare students emotionally, physically, and mentally for tests. The activities presented to teach test-taking skills incorporate active participation, multiple intelligences, and other meaningful learning techniques to teach test-taking skills. These approaches will help students become self-regulated learners who possess a large repertoire of strategies for test success.

REFERENCES

Caine, R. N. and Caine, G. 1994. *Making connections: Teaching and the human brain.* Menlo Park, CA: Innovative Learning Publications.

Chapman, C. 1999. *Making the shoe fit: A walking journey of learning. Songs by Connie Ryals, Sonya Bailey, and Carolyn Chapman.* Thomson, GA: Creative Learning Connection, Inc.

Chapman, C. 1993. *If the shoe fits...How to develop multiple intelligences in the classroom.* Arlington Heights, IL: IRI/SkyLight Training and Publishing, Inc.

Chapman, C. and R. King. 2000. *Test success in the brain-compatible classroom.* Tuscon, AZ: Zephyr Press.

Clovis, D. L. 1999, April. Take out your No.2 pencils: Taking the stress out of standardized tests. *Scholastic Instructor*, 27–28.

Costa, A. 1991. *The school as a home for the mind.* Arlington Heights, IL: SkyLight Training and Publishing, Inc.

Costa, A. 1985. Towards a model of human intellectual functioning. In *Developing minds: A resource book for teaching thinking*, edited by A. Costa. Alexandria, VA: Association for Supervision and Curriculum Development.

Esa, B. 1999. Interview by Rita King. Knoxville, Tennessee.

Gardner, H. 1993. *Frames of mind: The theory of multiple intelligences.* NY: Harper-Collins.

Gill, J. H. 1993. *Learning how to learn: Toward a philosophy of education.* Atlantic Highlands, NJ: Humanities Press.

Goleman, D. 1995. *Emotional intelligence: Why it can matter more than IQ.* New York: Bantam Books.

Hoff, K. 1999. Interview by Rita King. Smyrna, Tennessee.

Leech, M. 2000. Interview by Rita King. Murfreesboro, Tennessee.

Sousa, D. A. 1995. *How the brain learns.* Reston, VA: National Association of Secondary School Principals.

Sternberg, R. J. 1985. *Beyond IQ: A triarchic theory of human intelligence.* NY: Cambridge University Press.

Section 6

The Humility of Continuous Learning: The Human Capacity for Self-Renewal

It is what we think we know already that often prevents us from learning—Calude Bernard (1813–1878 French Physiologist)

Intelligent people are in a continuous learning mode. Their confidence, in combination with their inquisitiveness, allows them to constantly search for new and better ways to do things. People with this habit of mind are always striving for improvement, always growing, always learning, always modifying, and thus, always improving themselves. They seize problems, situations, tensions, conflicts, and circumstances as valuable opportunities to learn.

A great mystery about humans is that we confront learning opportunities with fear rather than with mystery and wonder. We seem to feel better when we know rather than when we learn. We defend our biases, beliefs, and storehouses of knowledge rather than inviting the unknown, the creative, and the inspirational. Being certain and closed gives us comfort while being doubtful and open gives us fear.

One of the worst things educators can do is to think that they "know it all" about reading and math. The current emphasis on phonics as the only way to go is an example. Herbert Ginsburg and Dorothy Strickland both invite us to remain open to new learnings about mathematics for young children and about our directions in reading instruction.

Professor Reuven Feuerstein describes the mediated learning experience as a strategy for helping others remain open to new learnings; that true learning occurs when one learns how to learn.

Finally, Wilson and Greenberg introduce Katherine Greenberg's Cognitive Enrichment Advantage (CEA) Approach and how it relates to Reuven Feuerstein's theory of mediated learning experience.

These authors suggest that only by being open to new learnings and being willing to challenge their beliefs, methods, and ideologies can educators truly become educated.

Challenging Mathematics for Young Children

by Herbert P. Ginsburg, Robert Balfanz, and Carole Greenes

This article is about *Big Math for Little Kids,*™ a curriculum designed for young children (preschoolers and kindergartners). Based on psychological research, principles of mathematics education and pedagogy, our curriculum engages all young children—lower- and middle-class, white and black, minority and mainstream children roughly 4 and 5 years of age—in "Big Math," that is, challenging forms of mathematical learning. This article begins by describing research on young children's mathematical competence that provides the psychological basis for our work; next it describes the pedagogical principles guiding development of the curriculum and ensuring that it is developmentally appropriate; and then it provides a brief description of *Big Math for Little Kids*™.

YOUNG CHILDREN'S MATHEMATICAL INTERESTS AND ABILITIES

Over the past 30 years or so, developmental and educational psychologists have conducted a body of research that provides remarkable insights into unsuspected competencies in young children (Ginsburg, Klein, and Starkey 1998). The research shows that mathematical thinking begins in infancy, when babies can see that there is more here than there, and that adding makes more and subtracting less. Before entering school, children are capable of informal addition and subtraction. To add, children typically combine two groups of objects, imaginary or real, and count them all to get a sum. To subtract, children take some objects away from the larger group and then count what is left to get the remainder. Further, young children un-

---

derstand key *ideas* underlying addition and subtraction. They know that adding makes more and subtracting less. Of course, there are important limitations to children's approach to addition and subtraction. They can deal only with small numbers and their methods can be inefficient (as when they add 7 + 1 by counting "one, two, three, four, five, six, seven, eight"). Nevertheless, it is fair to say that young children possess a remarkable degree of competence in key aspects of informal mathematics.

Although providing new insight into young children's thinking, this body of research leaves several questions unanswered. Most of the research on preschoolers has examined their performance on tasks devised by and imposed on them by researchers. These tasks mostly revolve around the three C's—counting, computation, and conservation (Piaget's famous problem in which children are asked to determine whether two lines of, say, seven objects, initially identical in appearance, are still equivalent in number despite being moved around, in full view of the child, so that they now look different, one line now being longer than the other). Although informative, this kind of research cannot provide insight into children's spontaneous mathematical interests. What kinds of mathematical issues engage their interest in everyday life? What mathematical investigations do they choose to engage in? And how do children learn in these situations?

Another largely unresolved issue has to do with the mathematical abilities of different groups of children. We know that in elementary school and beyond, lower-class children generally, and African-Americans and Latinos in particular, demonstrate lower academic achievement than do their middle-class peers (Natriello, McDill, and Pallas 1990) How can we explain this widely observed social class disparity in performance? There are of course many possibilities, ranging from the "savage inequalities" of education (Kozol 1991) to differences in the intellectual abilities of the social classes and ethnic groups. One explanation that psychologists have often proposed (Griffin and Case 1997) is that poor children enter school with inadequate cognitive abilities. We wished to learn whether a difference in basic mathematical competence manifests itself as early as the preschool and kindergarten years. If so, what is the nature of the difference? Are poor children a little slower than their middle-class peers or do they suffer from a basic cognitive deficiency in mathematical thinking?

To answer our two basic questions, we carried out, with the generous support of the Spencer Foundation, a series of psychological investigations of young children. One kind of research involved "naturalistic" observation describing the mathematical activities "spontaneously" undertaken by 4- and 5-year-old children—African-American, Latino, and White, from lower-, middle-, and upper-class groups—during their free play. This type of research allowed us to determine the mathematical content of children's everyday activities, to examine how they learn in the course of free play, and to identify possible social class differences in everyday mathematical behavior. In effect, this kind of research allowed us to "ask" children what kinds of mathematical activities they consider to be developmentally appropriate and to make some inferences about their abilities and learning styles.

The second type of research involved intensive clinical interviews on basic mathematical concepts in the same groups of children described above. The clinical interview method involved great flexibility; it permitted the examiner to adjust the questioning in order to overcome young children's discomfort, to put them at ease, and to discover the ways in which they interpret the problem and the methods they use to solve it. This research allowed us to focus on key mathematical concepts and to gain insight into young children's mathematical competence—the best they can do under favorable testing conditions.

Naturalistic Observation

Our basic plan was to obtain videotapes of young children's everyday behavior during "free play." We began by introducing the video camera and cordless microphone to the children in four daycare centers in order to make them comfortable with the equipment. Then we randomly selected a target child from the 4- and 5-year-old rooms in each of the daycare centers. We placed a cordless microphone on the target child and videotaped his or her activity for 15 minutes during the free play time, usually 8:30 to 9:00 and 10:00 to 11:00. Anything a child did was recorded.

The participants were 80 children ranging in age from 4.17 to 6.00 years in four daycare centered located in Manhattan. Of the 80 children, 30 were from lower-class families, African-American and Latino. The second group included 30 children from middle-class families, again mostly African-American and Latino, and a few

Whites and Asians. The last group, which we called upper-class, consisted of 20 White children from affluent families. We considered families to be "lower class" if they qualified for subsidized daycare according to the local governmental guidelines. Families were considered "middle class" if they failed to qualify for such subsidy and if one or both parents was working. Families were "upper class" if they could afford to send their children to a very expensive preschool in one of the most affluent areas of New York City. All of the daycare centers had roughly the same kinds of materials and room arrangement—block area, Legos™, etc.—although the more affluent centers had a greater variety and quantity of materials.

We divided the videotaped episodes of each child's play into 15 one-minute segments and then coded each into several categories of mathematical content—whether the target child engaged in mathematical activity and if so, what kind of mathematical activity it was. Here is a definition and example of each activity:

- *Classification:* Systematic arrangement in groups according to established criteria. In cleaning up, a child spent time carefully sorting the different blocks by shape and color so as to return them to the proper shelves.
- *Dynamics:* Exploration of the process of change or transformation. A child began with 10 objects, removed one, counted the remainder, and repeated this action until none was left. Apparently he was interested in the effects of repeated subtraction by one.
- *Enumeration:* Numerical judgment or quantification. Several children disputed how many figures were depicted in a picture.
- *Magnitude Comparison:* Comparison of two or more items to evaluate relative magnitude. Children discussed who was more frightened by a story or whether one child's block construction was larger than another's.
- *Pattern and Shape:* Exploration of patterns and forms. A child carefully constructed identical houselike figures in which triangles of the same size and shape were placed in the same positions over identical rectangles.
- *Spatial Relations:* Exploration of positions, directions, and distances in space. A child gave directions to a friend to go to a particular location in order to find an object "behind" another.

These categories represent what we think are key aspects of everyday mathematical behavior. In doing these things, children are, of course, not using formal, written school mathematics. Rather, they are engaged in informal mathematical thinking in order to cope with the ubiquitous mathematical content that permeates all environments. In all places and cultures children are faced with the necessity to categorize things, to find out how many there are, to compare quantities, to see what things look like, and to determine where they are.

When children engage in free play, how much of their time is devoted to mathematical activities? At the outset, this might appear to be an absurd question. When children play, they do not appear to be doing mathematics. But our results show otherwise. The percentage of minutes (15 minutes for each of 80 children, for a total of 1,200 minutes) in which at least one mathematical activity occurs is 46.6. In other words, during free play, children engage in mathematical activity—of course, as we define it—during about half of the total amount of minutes.

Consider next social class differences. Do children from different social class groups engage in different amounts of mathematical activity? The answer is that social class was insignificantly related to frequency of mathematical activity: lower- and middle-class children had virtually identical averages (44.0 and 44.5 respectively) and the somewhat older upper-class children slightly more (53.7). Statistically removing the effect of age, we find a lack of social class differences in children's overall level of mathematical activity.

We also examined the relative frequency of different types of mathematical activity—specifically the average percentage of minutes during which a particular category of mathematical activity occurred. The most frequently occurring mathematical activity was Pattern and Shape (an average of 25 percent of the 15 minutes) and then Magnitude Comparison (13 percent), followed by Enumeration (12 percent), Dynamics (6 percent), Spatial Relations (5 percent), and finally Classification (2 percent). Clearly, the "leaders" were Pattern and Shape, Magnitude Comparison, and Enumeration, each occurring a goodly portion of the time. Moreover, a very similar rank order was shown by all social class groups.

How do children learn during "free play"? At this point, we can make these preliminary observations. During free play, children's learning takes many forms. Sometimes children spend long periods of time alone, concentrating on a problem. Thus, a child may exert intense concentration on constructing a geometric figure with attribute blocks. No one sets the task for the child, and the child gets help from no one in completing it. On other occasions, children work side by side at a task, like building with large blocks, and help each other: one child may explicitly provide information another does not have or one child may model an activity for the other. Children seem to recognize who is expert in a particular activity and are often willing to accept that child's assistance. On still other occasions, children compete at a task. Sometimes the effect is destructive, as when one child knocks over another's structure or when one child belittles another's work. Sometimes, the result of competition is effective, as when children learn to construct a high block tower in order to show off and best their peers. We do not yet know how frequent are these various activities or how important they are for children's long-term learning. But we are certain about one thing: Most of children's free play occurs in the absence of the teacher. This is perhaps not surprising, because teachers generally see this activity as the children's time for choice and hence largely leave them alone, usually intervening only to resolve a behavior problem.

Most of children's free play occurs in the absence of the teacher.

Clinical Interviews

In this part of the investigation, individual children from the same groups described above were interviewed for about 30 minutes by one of seven different clinical interviewers, all graduate students at Teachers College, each of whom was carefully trained for this task. Each interviewer was provided with a protocol that was to be used as a guide, although the actual questions could vary depending on the child's level of mathematical competence, linguistic understanding, motivation, and/or interests.

After a warm-up task, each child participated in a series of addition, subtraction, and representation tasks, examples of which included the following:

- *Addition:* "Let's pretend you have X pennies in one hand, and Y pennies in the other hand. How many pennies do you have altogether?"
- *Subtraction:* "There are X children in the playground and Y children leave the playground to go home and do their homework. How many children are left in the playground?"
- *Representation:* The interviewer made paper and pencil available to the child for the solution of the following task: "Suppose we

are having a party. At the party you get X presents. Then you get Y more presents. How many presents do you have altogether?"

The data concerning children's responses to various problems were first analyzed according to use of strategy and then to understanding of principle. In solving the problems described above, the children used a wide variety of strategies, ranging from pushing objects aside to representing them symbolically. To obtain an index of children's performance, we developed a score depicting overall strategy level. This was done by grouping strategies into four levels of developmental sophistication in which lower levels represent a relatively concrete approach to the task whereas higher levels rely more heavily on abstract reasoning. The results showed that the average strategy level is weakly associated with social class. Lower-class and middle-class children's strategy levels were about the same, and differed only slightly from those of upper-class children.

The children's responses were also scored for understanding of a key principle, namely reversibility—the understanding that if you first subtract by some amount and then return the same amount, the initial number is unchanged (e.g., if 3 of 4 children first leave and then return to the house, there must be 4 children in the house: you do not have to calculate the result). The results showed that understanding of reversibility was clearly linked to social class. Almost all upper-class children understood the concept; lower- and middle-class children performed at lower levels.

These results are extremely interesting with regard to social class differences. In general, lower- and middle-class children showed similar levels of understanding and used similar strategies. Lower-class children can hold their own at this age level; they are not far behind, and indeed in some areas they are not behind at all. The upper-class children were the only group showing signs of somewhat superior understanding and strategy use. Why? Of course, these children are in some respects very privileged: they get the best of everything—computers, books, toys. But in addition to this, the upper-class children were selected for nursery school admission on the basis of intelligence and other tests. Children judged less intellectually able often are turned away from this school. Would a randomly selected group of upper-income children perform better than the others? Our evidence does not speak to this point. But the basic results are clear: lower- and middle-class children show themselves to be capable of the basic concepts and strategies of informal arithmetic.

PRINCIPLES FOR TEACHING MATHEMATICS TO YOUNG CHILDREN

Our research shows that young children—all young children—are capable of and often interested in various mathematical activities. Some of these activities are surprisingly complex and challenging, like constructing symmetries in three dimensions or trying to count beyond 100. In effect, through their often joyful choices, the children are "telling" us that engagement in challenging mathematics is "developmentally appropriate." Young children do not have to be protected from the study of mathematics nor made ready for learning (Greenes 1999).

Our research shows that young children—all young children—are capable of and often interested in various mathematical activities.

How can adults help? Clearly, our children deserve more than mindless drill of academic seatwork of the type that characterizes too many elementary school classrooms. Such activities would only serve to dampen children's interest in mathematics at an even earlier age than is unfortunately typical (around the third grade in schools employing such methods).

But should the teacher do nothing but let the children play? After all, we have shown that their play is interesting and important. Although preferable to subjecting children to a mindless curriculum, leaving children to play by themselves has the unfortunate result of neglecting many interesting opportunities for engaging children in creative learning. Unguided play does not teach children everything they need to know or could enjoy learning. Often, free play leads to dead ends and wrong results. For example, children sometimes try to count very high in free play but cannot succeed unless adults provide necessary information.

Consequently, it is the responsibility of adults (Dewey 1976) to provide guidance that can help young children to learn even more than they manage to learn on their own. This guidance should be developmentally appropriate in the sense suggested by the National Association for the Education of Young Children, namely that it should involve a balance of structure and exploration. "Children benefit from engaging in self-initiated, spontaneous play and from teacher-planned and -structured activities, projects, and experiences" (Bredekamp and Copple 1997, 23).

Given our view that young children are already engaged in interesting mathematical activities in everyday life, and that they can benefit from adult guidance, we set out to develop a challenging mathematics curriculum—*Big Math for Little Kids*™—with the following characteristics:

- It exploits and builds upon the informal mathematics that all children construct in everyday life. Informal mathematics is a solid foundation on which at least some formal mathematics can be built (Baroody 1987; Ginsburg 1989; Resnick 1989).
- It presents the study of mathematics both as a separate "subject" and as an integrated part of other preschool activities. Sometimes, the curriculum presents "math activities," like counting or studying shapes. Sometimes, it blends the mathematics into such activities as stories, songs, block building, and the like.
- It helps children to explore mathematical ideas in depth. The goal is to explore by mathematical ideas over a lengthy period of time through extended activities.
- It engages the child in thinking like a mathematician—making interesting conjectures, engaging in problem solving, looking for patterns.
- It aims at taking young children to advanced levels and to investigate complex ideas. For example, instead of limiting the study of shape to the standard circle, square, and triangle, the program introduces symmetries. Instead of teaching counting to 20 or 30, the program helps children to count into the hundreds. Why? Because they want to and are capable of it. Moreover, mastering challenging tasks fosters feelings of confidence and competence (Stipek 1997).
- It encourages the rudiments of a reflective, metacognitive approach to early mathematics: self-awareness, verbalization-communication, checking/monitoring one's work, generalization, seeing relations, and appreciating abstractions. This is consonant with children's spontaneous efforts and with the Vygotskian approach of helping the child to develop "scientific" concepts (Vygotsky 1986).
- It prepares children for the informal symbolism of mathematics by establishing clear links between informal mathematics and some basic formalisms. The program does not have a heavy emphasis on symbolism, but is not afraid to introduce it if it can be made meaningful.

• It employs large group activity, small groups, and individual exploration. Young children need to learn how to behave and learn in large groups. They profit from the greater degree of teacher attention possible in small groups. And they need time for individual learning and exploration.

The goals of *Big Math for Little Kids*™ are to foster young children's enthusiastic and joyful mathematics learning and to help them prepare for later learning in school. The program can be of special value for poor children who are at heightened risk of school failure and failing schools.

DESCRIPTION OF THE CURRICULUM

With the generous support of the National Science Foundation, *Big Math for Little Kids*™ is undergoing development in three major sites, an inner-city Baltimore church serving African-American children; a publicly supported school serving low-income children, mostly immigrants, in Chelsea, Massachusetts; and a Catholic school serving low- and middle-class children of various ethnicities in New York City. Although the curriculum was designed primarily for 4- and 5-year-old children, it appears to be useful for 3-year-olds as well. During the first two years of the project, 1998–2000, the various activities are being developed, tried out in at least one of the sites, and then revised. Prototypes of parent and teacher preparation materials are also being developed. From 2000 to 2002, the curriculum will be field tested at various preschools and daycare centers around the country.

The curriculum is organized into six major strands or basic ideas.

• *Number:* This strand covers such topics as counting (into the hundreds), enumerating objects, and the meaning of number (cardinality).

• *Shape:* These activities focus on identifying and constructing various shapes in both two and three dimensions, and exploring their properties, including symmetry.

• *Putting together and taking apart:* This set of activities focuses mainly on adding and subtracting, and also deals with the relations between sets and subsets.

• *Spatial relations:* This strand covers relations such as in front of, behind, and left-right, as well as maps—all of which are important for navigating in the world.

• *Measurement:* The exact quantification of physical attributes (such as length, weight, and temperature) as well as time and money are explored in this strand.

• *Patterns and predictions:* These activities introduce the child to patterns involving shapes, numbers, and sounds, and encourage detection and use of patterns for the purpose of prediction.

The strands are covered in two ways—one involves systematically organized activities and the other daily "past-times." In working with organized activities, the teacher introduces the six strands, in the sequence described above, over the course of a year. Of course, the level at which teachers cover the material differ according to the age and ability of the children. Nevertheless, in all cases, the teacher employs activities designed to be continued over a fairly lengthy period of time in order to introduce children in a systematic way to the various "big ideas" or strands.

The teacher employs activities designed to be continued over a fairly lengthy period of time in order to introduce children in a systematic way to the various "big ideas" or strands.

For example, *Bag It* is a deceptively simple activity in which the teacher begins by presenting children with a collection of plastic ziplock baggies on which are written the numerals 0, 1, 2, 3. The teacher shows how to read the numerals written on each bag and explains that a special number of things should be placed in each. She then presents them with a collection of small objects—buttons, toy cars, miniature people, or similar objects available in the room. The first task is to place in each bag the appropriate number of objects. To do this, each child has to read the numeral on the bag, count out or otherwise determine the corresponding number of objects, carefully place them in the bag, and zip it up. After this has been done, the teacher shows them some "counting bins," boxes on which are written the numerals 0, 1, 2, 3. The job now is to place the plastic bag in the correct bin. This requires reading and matching the numeral on each. This basic task can of course be extended to larger numbers. After a while, children become quite proud of their ability to count out 20 or even 100 objects in the bag.

Variations on the task can also be introduced to teach other aspects of number. For example, children are asked to take out two bags from the same bin, empty each bag onto a different mat, and match the objects one-to-one to verify that the number of objects is the same. In this way, children learn to use one-one correspondence to establish equivalence of number, and in the process learn that the type or size of object does not affect number.

Another variation on the task involves taking out from the bins bags whose numbers differ by one. The children have to compare the objects in the bags, again by one-one correspondence, to learn what has more and which less.

Note that these variations on *Bag It* all require some time to learn; they are not activities to be done once and only once for 5 minutes. They all involve some deep mathematical ideas. The goal is not simply to count accurately or to read the numeral; rather, it is to learn something important about what a number is and how it compares with other numbers. Although the variations are math "lessons," they all involve manipulatives—something that is true of virtually all of our activities except for those involving learning the counting words. The variations can be placed in a meaningful sequence, so that notions of more and less then can be discussed after the basic idea of same number. The activities do not shy away from written symbols, although they are always introduced in a meaningful context where the child can figure out what they mean.

Big Math for Little Kids™ does not involve discrete bits and pieces: it is a coherent system.

Activities like these are presented in an ordered sequence increasing in complexity. Thus, the teacher may employ various forms of *Bag It* for 3 weeks, and then follow up with other number activities for the next month. Then the teacher might do the strand on shapes for two months. From the point of view of the teacher, these sequenced activities, usually introduced each day in circle time and then pursued in small groups, are "math lessons," designed to elaborate on key mathematical ideas, like number or shape. But the children usually do not think of these activities as math. For the children, they are games that usually involve playing with blocks, shapes, or other manipulatives. In fact, after several months of our curriculum, a child asked one of us, "When we are going to learn math?"

No doubt many preschool teachers and programs employ some activities of these types. We believe that one distinctive feature of *Big Math for Little Kids*™ is that the activities are arranged systematically, lead to deep exploration of complex topics, and are pursued intensively throughout the year. *Big Math for Little Kids*™ does not involve discrete bits and pieces: it is a coherent system. And besides being conceptually rich, the activities are a great deal of fun. The children we work with enjoy the activities and get engrossed in them. In fact, when working on the activities, the children often display a very lengthy attention span.

The daily "past-times" are not necessarily tied to the current big idea being taught. Suppose that the children have already spent a considerable amount of time doing numbers and have now moved on to systematic activities designed to teach shapes. At the same time, the teacher may introduce short past-times of various sorts during various times of day. Some past-times revolve around snack-time, others around line-up, and still others around reading and singing. For example, at snack time, the teacher may engage in the common activity of asking children to count the children who need plates, distribute the right number of plates, etc. All this may serve the function of reviewing, practicing, and consolidating some basic counting activities and ideas about one-one correspondence that the children have already learned. Another example is lining up, which always presents the teacher with an opportunity to review counting, ideas of in front, in between, behind, and the like.

We are also exploring various songs and books that may be used to teach, review, or practice various mathematical concepts. Past-times are not organized into sequences, and they do not necessarily coincide with the current strand being taught. Instead, they are daily activities, not usually seen as "math," that easily lend themselves to enjoyable mathematical extensions and that reinforce the idea that math is always with us, sometimes in unexpected places.

In brief, *Big Math for Little Kids*™ offers both systematically organized sequences of activities and daily past-times to introduce challenging mathematical ideas. We feel confident that our evaluations will confirm that all young children can learn a good deal from it.

REFERENCES

Baroody, A. J. 1987. *Children's mathematical thinking.* New York: Teachers College Press.

Bredekamp, S., and C. Copple (Eds.). 1997. *Developmentally appropriate practice in early childhood programs* (Rev. ed.). Washington, DC: National Association for the Education of Young Children.

Dewey, J. 1976. The child and the curriculum. In *John Dewey: The middle works, 1899-1924. Volume 2: 1902-1903,* edited by J. A. Boydston. Carbondale, IL: Southern Illinois University Press.

Ginsburg, H. P. 1989. *Children's arithmetic: How they learn it and how you teach it.* 2d ed. Austin, TX: Pro Ed.

Ginsburg, H. P., A. Klein, and P. Starkey. 1998. The development of children's mathematical thinking: Connecting research with practice. In *Handbook of child psychology: 5th Ed., Vol. 4.* 401–76. *Child Psychology and Practice,* edited by I. Sigel and A. Renninger. New York: John Wiley and Sons.

Greenes, C. 1999. Ready to learn: Developing young children's mathematical powers. In *Mathematics in early years,* edited by J. Copley. Reston, VA: National Council of Teachers of Mathematics: 39–47.

Griffin, S., and R. Case. 1997. Rethinking the primary school math curriculum: An approach based on cognitive science. *Issues in Education* 3: 1–49.

Kozol, J. 1991. *Savage inequalities: Children in America's schools.* New York: Crown Publishers.

Natriello, G., E. L. McDill, and A. M. Pallas. 1990. *Schooling disadvantaged children: Racing against catastrophe.* New York: Teachers College Press.

Resnick, L. B. 1989. Developing mathematical knowledge. *American Psychologist* 44: 162–169.

Stipek, D. 1997. Success in school—For a head start in life. In *Developmental psychopathology: Perspectives on adjustment, risk, and disorder,* edited by S. S. Luthar, J. A. Burack, D. Cicchetti, and R. R. Weisz. Cambridge, England: Cambridge University Press.

Vygotsky, L. S. 1986. *Thought and language.* (A. Kozulin, Trans.). Cambridge, MA: The MIT Press.

Reinventing Our Literacy Programs

Books, Basics, Balance

by Dorothy S. Strickland

"We really want to make some changes, but it's all so confusing. Should we stop teaching phonics? What about spelling and grammar? My teachers love all the new trade books, but they say they're not sure what to do with them. And what about that invented spelling? To tell you the truth I can't make head or tail out of it. Somebody really needs to write a manual for the whole language method."

This was, in its essence, said to me by an elementary school principal in a large, suburban community that views itself as forward looking. No doubt some will find these comments amusing. Others will wonder how it is possible for an administrator to be so uninformed. Ten years ago, I certainly would have been at least slightly amused. Today, however, I find such comments unsettling because they are not as uncommon as one might believe.

Even the comments of those who are better informed often reflect a kind of bewilderment in their search for consistency and order. A classroom teacher recently complained to me, "Dr. Strickland, every time I think I'm on the right track, I read an article that seems to contradict a lot of what I'm doing. Even you experts don't agree. It's making me crazy."

After more than 3 decades in literacy education, it is clear to me that new insights into emergent literacy, the writing process, response to literature, and whole language have brought research and practice together in ways I never before thought possible. Nevertheless, even

---

From Reinventing our literacy programs: Books, basics, balance by Dorothy Strickland. *The Reading Teacher* 48(4), pp. 294–302.

with all of the excellent professional materials and workshops available, the progress being made in literacy today is often coupled with uncertainty and confusion.

In this article I address some of the frustrations teachers and administrators encounter as they seek to make changes in their literacy programs. I deal with recurring themes that emerge as I interact with practitioners throughout the United States and Canada, primarily those who struggle toward more holistic instruction and have difficulty maintaining a sense of equilibrium as they move ahead. My hope is that they will recognize that change ranges along a continuum and become inspired to continue taking advantage of new knowledge in the field. I also hope that administrators and parents will find ideas here that help them rethink their personal conceptions of an effective literacy curriculum. Finally, I offer this article as a means for teachers, parents, and administrators to exchange ideas about what literacy learning in school should and could be.

I focus on three areas of concern: *books,* referring to the challenges faced by teachers as they attempt to move from total reliance on traditional basal reading programs and content area textbooks to greater use of authentic literature; *basics,* referring to concerns about addressing such skills as phonics, spelling, and grammar; and *balance,* referring to the search for bridges between the conventional wisdom of the past and the need to take advantage of new research and wisdom particularly as it relates to issues such as grouping, direct versus indirect instruction, and assessment.

BOOKS: TO BASAL OR NOT BASAL, IS THAT REALLY THE QUESTION?

"These books are beautiful. Now what do I do with them?"

New Directions

Textbooks continue to be important classroom resources, but they are no longer the dominant materials for learning literacy or learning in the content areas. Students share and respond to authentic literature in all areas of the curriculum. Response to literature takes many forms including group discussion, writing, art, and drama. Fiction and nonfiction trade books, poems, textbooks, and other materials are discussed in terms of their content and literary qualities. Throughout the grades, teachers read aloud to children every day and give them time to read materials of their choice (Cullinan, 1992; Huck, 1992; Norton, 1992).

The Issues

Incorporating literature into the curriculum poses numerous challenges. Many teachers lack experience with extensive use of literature in the curriculum. They are limited both in their knowledge of available trade books and in the ways to use them. As a result, they frequently turn to district or commercially prepared guides that may be little better than the old basals they were meant to replace (Hepler, 1988). Some districts suffer such severe budget constraints that teachers lack the materials needed to conduct literature studies. Rigid assignment of books to particular grade levels may impede rather then encourage the use of literature across the curriculum. Even in better literature-based programs, the use of nonfiction tends to lag behind that of fiction. Concerns about how literature-based programs will meet the needs of diverse populations (Freeman, Freeman, & Fennacy, 1993) and how schools will cope with the possibility of greater censorship of books (Shannon, 1989) are also prevalent.

Incorporating literature into the curriculum poses numerous challenges.

Ideas to Consider

- *Collaborate with others to keep up with the literature for children and adolescents and explore creative ways to use it.* Many teachers participate in Teachers As Readers groups that meet regularly to discuss fiction and nonfiction literature and their uses in the classroom. Some find help in the professional literature on constructing their own literature study guides (Hepler, 1988; Routman, 1991). Thinking through the potential uses of a given book puts the teacher in charge of situating it within the curriculum. It also provides the background knowledge needed to evaluate those commercial guides that might be considered worth using.

When specific books are assigned for study at certain grade levels, it may cause conflicts among teachers who wish to use the same book at other levels. When teachers focus on certain genres and writing forms at particular grade levels, however, it contributes to a sense of order in the curriculum and offers some assurance that a core of strategies and content will be addressed over time. This should never preclude the study of these forms or genres at other grade levels. For example, in depth focus on the friendly letter as a writing form of literature may be emphasized at a specific grade level, but this does not exclude them at other levels. A limited number of suggested titles and activities might be developed and shared locally among teachers as a base for extension at the classroom level.

- *Explore many resources to get more literature into the classroom.* In many districts, commercially developed, literature-based programs act as a bridge to more holistic practice. These programs provide an entry to a wider use of tradebooks and offer greater teacher flexibility than traditional basals of the past. They should be used in combination with many other resources for literacy, particularly tradebooks, across the curriculum. In the face of shrinking resources, teachers can use their old basals creatively by treating them as anthologies for student-run discussion groups, for example, physically tearing them apart and saving worthy selections to supplement the independent reading program. School book clubs, such as Scholastic and Trumpet also provide an excellent means of acquiring multiple copies of current and classic selections of fiction and nonfiction (Strickland, Walmsley, Bronk, & Weiss, 1994).
- *Capitalize on the diversity among the readers, what they read, and how they respond.* One of the advantages of a literature-based curriculum is that if offers opportunities to broaden the range of materials introduced to children. As the demand for good children's literature has increased, so has the response by publishers to provide books on a variety of levels that feature characters, settings, and authors of diverse backgrounds.

Diversity has always been a major challenge to teachers, even in classrooms that appear relatively homogeneous. Teachers can explore and share ideas on dealing with diversity of all types: abilities, interests, and cultural and linguistic backgrounds. Most particularly, teachers need to provide more open ended literacy tasks where varied response is expected and where students are assessed primarily in terms of their individual progress and less in terms of a fixed standard.

One means of providing for diversity is to layer instruction in numerous books that children may be engaged with simultaneously: (a) one book might involve children in an extended whole group read aloud (by the teacher), using varied means of response; (b) sets of titles might involve students in small response group activities; (c) still other books might be used as resources for individual inquiry and report or independent reading for pleasure. At times, all of these books might relate to a particular theme or genre. This allows students to ponder a variety of viewpoints on a single theme and to talk across texts, some of which might have been written by members of the class.

- *Develop a schoolwide or districtwide policy regarding censorship and book selection before it becomes an issue.* Schools moving toward greater use of trade books would do well to prepare themselves for concerns by teachers and parents regarding the content of specific books. Discussing criteria for book selection and putting a policy in place for dealing with complaints about particular books will help teachers to act with assurance and avoid potential confrontations regarding censorship.

Research suggests we must redefine what is basic to becoming literate.

BASICS: REDEFINING WHAT IS BASIC

"You mean I don't have to worry about skills?"

New Directions

Research suggests we must redefine what is basic to becoming literate. A literacy curriculum that emphasizes what is basic values and builds on the knowledge that students bring to school, emphasizes the construction of meaning through activities that require higher order thinking, and offers extensive opportunities for learners to apply literacy strategies and their underlying skills in the context of meaningful tasks.

These understandings about the basics build upon a growing body of knowledge indicating that reading and writing are closely related processes within a language superstructure in which all of the elements of language are inextricably linked. Thus, when reading and writing are segmented into component parts, the discrete elements no longer function as they do when they are embedded within the acts of reading and writing. Readers and writers bring a great deal of existing knowledge to these processes. Even preschool children have some knowledge of literacy before formal schooling and, like all learners, use their knowledge about the world and about literacy to construct meaning. Finally, in order to become literate, learners must engage in literate acts (Donaldson, 1978; Goodman & Goodman, 1979; Smith, 1982; Wells, 1986).

The Issues

Differences of opinion about defining and teaching the basics remain key issues of curriculum reform. The basics usually refer to what many consider to be the fundamental skills or components of reading and writing. Using this definition, direct instruction in phonics is emphasized for beginning readers with discrete instruction in comprehension "skills" such as "finding the main idea" and "noting details" stressed for readers who are developing fluency. In writing instruction, the basics include a focus on grammar, spelling, and the mechanics of written composition such as capitalization and punctuation. A basic skills curriculum will stress the teaching of each distinct skill in a fixed sequence from basic to higher order levels. This notion of what is basic has been ingrained in school curricula for many years, providing a convenient mechanism for dividing curricular content among various grade levels. It is the basis of the content of standardized tests and the categories of evaluation on report cards.

In an attempt to apply current knowledge about literacy learning and teaching, today's educators are shifting the emphasis away from teaching discrete skills and toward a focus on strategies—the strategic use of skills through meaningful use. "The learner must know how and why to apply the skill; that is what elevates the skill to the strategy level" (Routman 1991, p. 135). Any teacher who has observed a youngster demonstrate competence in a specific skill via a worksheet only to find the skill inaccessible during actual reading or writing knows the difference between learning a skill and being skillful.

It is easy to understand why tension exists between those who wish to hold on to the conventional wisdom and "logic" of a discrete basic skills approach and those who do not. Yet, moving toward a more holistic approach does not involve the abandonment of the old basics. It involves a different view of how knowledge and use of these basics are demonstrated. For example, rather than display a knowledge of phonics through workbooks and worksheets, a holistically oriented teacher is more concerned with the application of phonics as demonstrated though children's invented spellings and through the strategic use of phonics for unlocking unknown words. Similarly, knowledge of the conventions of grammar and correct spelling are assessed through their use in the context of written composition rather than through tests on discrete skills.

Obviously, the issues go well beyond merely defining what is basic to what a new definition entails. At the heart of the confusion is the difficulty encountered when schools attempt to envision a more holistically oriented curriculum through a skills oriented lens, creating an inevitable mismatch between instructional goals, strategies, and methods of assessment.

Ideas to Consider

- *Get the change process started by establishing a forum for sharing ideas.* Districts that attempt to make changes in their curriculum would do well to initiate small discussion groups, where teachers and administrators spend time reading, viewing, listening, and discussing professional literature, video tapes and audio tapes, and reflecting on their own current practices related to learning and teaching. This kind of group rethinking and renewal in a nonthreatening manner helps to establish the groundwork for any major changes that might follow. My experience suggests that this should not totally exclude the introduction of some instructional strategies for people to consider as the discussion evolves. Teachers enjoy collecting and trying out new ideas. Some become impatient if nothing appears to be forthcoming that is immediately useful for the classroom. Nevertheless, establishing a collective mind set or vision of what teaching and learning should be should precede major changes.
- *Scrutinize your curriculum guides and the "real" curriculum occurring in the classrooms.* Once the door is open to rethinking the status quo, several things can occur to help everyone move gradually and consistently toward change. A review of curriculum guides may result in clustering lists of discrete skills under new, more inclusive headings. This makes them more manageable as objectives for instruction in classrooms that focus on process.

For example, rather than list 15 or 20 discrete word recognition skills, collapse them under a more general statement: "Students make use of a variety of word recognition strategies to aid reading comprehension." More specific word recognition objectives might be geared to particular grade levels and stated so that instruction and assessment are inherently linked. For example, at second grade: "Uses the following word recognition strategies alone or in combination: skips unknown word to get more information, rereads sentence for contextual information; uses picture clues, uses phonics clues." These strategies are easily documented over time.

- *Don't be afraid to establish benchmarks.* Communication among teachers, parents, and administrators may break down in the absence of guidelines for typical literacy experiences and expectations about competence at specific grade levels. These should be stated in terms of the processes in which students engage rather than as an accumulation of knowledge about literacy. For example: "Children will read and write for several different purposes." A district might want to specify one or two of these purposes at each grade level. Assessment would be based on evidence garnered from lists and samples of students' reading and writing in reading logs and writing folders. The quality of the work would be evaluated according to criteria described and agreed upon by teachers at that grade level.

- *Curriculum guides should be used to cross check coverage, not to prescribe or constrain it.* All teachers should be intimately familiar with the curriculum guides related to their grade levels. Unfortunately, it is virtually impossible to create a curriculum document that does not appear to address even the most global objectives in a linear way, causing some to think that the order in which they are listed in the guide is *the order* in which objectives are to be taught. Properly used, a curriculum guide for literacy instruction should serve as a framework for integrating the language arts with each other and with the content areas. Rather than proceed through the document in a particular order, teachers should regularly cross check what they are actually teaching with what is included in their curriculum documents to determine whether or not the strategies and skills included there are being addressed.

Ironically, even the most skills-oriented teachers with whom I have worked agree that by teaching this way they cover the skills to an even greater extent than when they were addressing each in order, checking it off, and moving on to the next. When teaching holistically teachers constantly address, review, and assess skills through the strategies children use as they read and write each day. Perhaps more important, strategies and skills that need more or less attention are constantly revealed to both teacher and learners. Learners become aware of the importance of a skill by experiencing its need rather than by simply being told "This is something you need to know." Where there is a need to highlight specific strategies and skills, direct instruction may be provided in whole or small group minilessons or through an individual conference.

- *Don't waste time debating whether or not to teach phonics, spelling, grammar, and other "skills" of literacy.* Obviously, young children cannot read or write without encountering the use of phonics, grammar, spelling, and other conventions of written language. Do spend time discussing how to teach them in a way that contributes to the learners' self-improvement. Keep in mind that these conventions and enablers to reading and writing are not reading and writing nor are they precursors to involvement in reading and writing as meaningful acts.

Teach these skills through meaningful use. Anything less is not only misleading, it contributes to the kind of educational fraud that results in children and their parents believing that phonics is reading and in young adults graduating from high school having completed thousands of worksheets yet unable to read and write.

- *Differentiate instruction. What is basic for one student may not be basic for another.* Inherent to effective teaching are the notions of access to excellence and differentiated instruction. For example, all students may be given a similar prompt to think about as they read and respond in their logs. Or they may be given specific information and asked to create a math problem for others to solve. In each case, all children would be expected to respond with creativity and excellence. However, it is obvious that there would be variability in the quality of the responses. Holistically oriented teachers not only expect variability, they encourage it. The point is to stretch each child to his or her maximum potential (to coin a phrase), something we never did very well with the skills-based curricula where all children were expected to perform in precisely the same way within the exact same time frame.

BALANCE: MAKING INFORMED DECISIONS

"Now that I have choices, I'm really confused."

New Directions

Thoughtful educators find that new research findings compel them to rethink some of their most entrenched ideas about instruction. For example, a great deal is known today about some of the most troublesome areas of curriculum decision making: grouping, structure, direct vs. indirect instruction, and assessment.

Long-term ability *grouping* within a grade level does not yield sufficient results to outweigh the possible risks to the self concepts of poor readers. Ability grouping results in less instructional time and less learning for low ability groups. Assignment to instructional groups should be based on need or purpose at a given point in time (Allington, 1993; Hiebert, 1983; Slavin, 1987).

How individuals view structure or order in the curriculum or classroom is largely dependent on the way in which they view teaching and learning. Brian Cambourne (1992) suggests that those who use the term *laissez-faire* in a negative sense regarding whole language are conveying an implicit negative message that "for effective learning to occur it must be directed from some source external to the learner" (p. 48). Reading and writing are social processes—dynamic and interactive. They involve making decisions and solving problems, much of which occurs through constructive interaction with others.

Goodman (1986) makes the point that "there is no one-to-one correspondence between teaching and learning" (p. 39). Overreliance on *direct instruction* may actually interfere with language learning and impede students' growth as independent learners. Schools must provide low-risk learning environments, where instruction is organized to encourage interaction and group dynamics with many opportunities for indirect learning and teaching.

Assessment and evaluation involve different audiences requiring different kinds of information (Farr, 1992). Assessment involves the gathering of data relevant to student performance. Evaluation involves the use of that information to inform and guide instruction. Effective classroom assessment and evaluation view reading and writing as process, make use of varied contexts, are developmentally and culturally appropriate, occur continuously over time, and are integral to instruction (Harp, 1993).

The Issues

Restructuring the use of time, type of tasks, and the modes of instruction are major issues of curriculum reform. For example, some teachers have misinterpreted the use of holistic approaches to literacy learning as meaning all whole group or all individualized instruction. Unfortunately, this kind of thinking ignores one of the key principles of literacy learning: that it is social and dynamic. Scheduling the day, using large blocks of time with a more seamless flow of activities, rather than a series of abrupt divisions between each subject also represents a challenge.

Making greater use of indirect instructional techniques, such as collaborative group learning, sustained silent reading and writing, and inquiry approaches to themes, does not come easy to teachers whose primary mode of instruction consists of dispensing knowledge through text and lecture.

Issues surrounding assessment and evaluation affect all of the other aspects of literacy instruction. In school moving toward more holistic instruction, the mismatch between instruction and assessment causes tremendous anxiety among teachers and administrators. School boards and the general public continue to look to norm-referenced tests for information about school achievement. There is, however, a growing awareness of the limitations and negative consequences of norm-referenced tests: they do not capture the higher level literacy abilities needed for participation in today's workplaces and communities; they have not evolved with our research-based understanding of the reading process; and they are poorly aligned with classroom instruction that reflects this research. These tests have an undue influence on instructional content, resulting in the narrowing and fragmentation of the curriculum. Moreover, they yield few meaningful results for teachers seeking information on the effectiveness of their instruction (Valencia, Hiebert, & Afflerbach, 1994).

Issues surrounding assessment and evaluation affect all of the other aspects of literacy instruction.

Dissatisfaction with the use of norm-referenced, standardized tests has brought about a search for alternative measures. Generally termed authentic or performance assessment, these procedures are more likely to represent activities that reflect the actual goals and instructional activities of the classroom and the real world outside the classroom. However, even some of the so-called authentic tests are far from the kind of instruction found in a good writing process classroom, where students are allowed to write over an unspecified period of time, collaborating with peers, revising, editing, and even putting a piece aside temporarily or permanently in favor of a new topic or approach.

Most discouraging are those instances where teachers use various means of integrating instruction and assessment, such as running records and the analysis of readers response logs, only to find that scores on standardized tests are given the most weight by parents and administrators in judging student progress and making decisions about retention and promotion.

Ideas to Consider

• *Work together to establish frameworks for planning and organizing instruction.* As with other aspects of our lives, structure is important in the classroom. Skillful teachers provide a rather predictable day, establishing classroom routines with children. Having established an instructional framework, children are grouped in a variety of ways: whole group, small group, and one to one—and for a variety of purposes—response groups, research groups, interest groups, special needs, and so on. Grouping is based on instructional needs and long-term ability grouping is avoided.

In my experience, helping teachers to conceptualize an instructional framework for a reading/writing workshop is the first critical step. Once that overall structure is in place, daily planning and instruction seem to follow in a very consistent manner—each new set of activities builds upon the previous ones. Inevitably, content area activities begin to find their way into the reading/writing workshop. As the overlap of process (the language arts) and content (science, social studies, and so on) occurs, a seamless day begins to emerge naturally (Strickland, 1992).

• *Make the most of direct and indirect instruction.* As I observe skillful teachers work, it occurs to me that they rely heavily on a series of well conceived, ongoing opportunities for indirect instruction throughout the day. They also tend to be masterful at capitalizing on opportunities that were not planned. In these classrooms, direct instruction even takes on an interactive quality, involving teacher demonstrations, modeling, and rehearsing with what students will eventually be expected to do independently.

• *Chart the kind and quantity of assessments in place and their usefulness.* Many school districts with which I have worked over the past several years have reduced the number of norm-referenced tests given at the elementary levels, sometimes eliminating all such tests before third grade. These have been replaced by a variety of performance based assessment procedures that are closely linked to the curriculum. The hope is to gather information that is more balanced toward classroom observation but also useful to school administrators and the general public as they seek to compare their schools with others across the nation. Moving in this direction requires extensive professional development for all concerned—teachers, administrators, and school boards. It also requires extensive efforts to help parents understand the changes in assessment, evaluation, and reporting that eventually occur.

A criterion that I have set for inservice workshops is to balance the teaching strategies I share with specific suggestions for assessment. I recommend the same approach when school districts develop curriculum guides. Every goal and objective should be placed side by side with suggestions for instruction and informal strategies for assessment. Too often, suggestions for assessment are placed at the back of the guide in a separate section. Suggestions for gathering and analyzing data should also be included.

Every goal and objective should be placed side by side with suggestions for instruction and informal strategies for assessment.

CONCLUSION

Obviously, this article is not for the born-again whole language teacher. Neither is it for the intransigent educator who readily admits, "I watch all these new fads come and go. I never change a thing. Sooner or later they'll come back around to my way of doing things."

Rather, this article is addressed to the great majority of teachers who are at different points along a continuum of thoughtful change. For them, I offer a few final words of encouragement:

First, be reassured that you don't need to change everything overnight. Real change takes time.

Second, get in touch with what you believe about teaching and learning. Your belief system provides the foundation for everything you do. Examine it and give it care and nurturing. But always keep the door open for new ideas and insights.

Third, don't be afraid to question new ideas; but do it with an open mind, one that truly is searching for some answers, not merely looking for loopholes in a theory.

Fourth, get used to living with a degree of ambiguity. You're really making progress when each question answered stimulates no more than two or three new ones.

Fifth, work with other members of your staff to set long term goals and establish a shared vision of where you want to be. Then work together to take consistent, reasonable steps to accomplish them.

Sixth, keep in mind that it is probably not a good idea to attempt too many changes at once and that some will take longer to make progress in than others. Even so, it is not unreasonable to ask everyone to make some changes and continue to build on these each year.

As teachers of reading, we have recently been challenged to prepare students for "the literacy of thoughtfulness," a literacy that involves being able to think, know, understand, and learn in ways that go beyond the mere accumulation and storage of information and that requires the ability to collaborate and support others in ways that extend beyond commonly held notions of "teamwork" (Brown, 1991). I agree; this is a worthy goal. I would only add that these ideas apply not just to our students but to those who teach them.

REFERENCES

Allington, R. (1993). Reducing the risk: Integrated language arts in restructured elementary schools. In L. Morrow, L. Wilkinson, & J. Smith (Eds.), *The integrated language arts: Controversy to consensus* (pp. 193–213). New York: Allyn & Bacon.

Brown, R. (1991). *Schools of thought: How the politics of literacy shape thinking in the classroom.* San Francisco: Jossey-Bass.

Cambourne, B. (1992). Does whole language necessitate a laissez-faire classroom? In O. Cochrane (Ed.), *Questions and answers about whole language.* (pp. 46–51). Katonan, NY: Richard C. Owen.

Cullinan, B. (1992). *Invitation to read: More children's literature in the reading program.* Newark, DE: International Reading Association.

Donaldson, M. (1978). *Children's minds.* New York: W.W. Norton.

Farr, R. (1992). Putting it all together: Solving the reading assessment puzzle. *The Reading Teacher, 46,* 26–37.

Freeman, D., Freeman, Y., & Fennacy, J. (1993). California's reading revolution: A review and analysis. *The New Advocate, 6,* 41–60.

Goodman, K. (1986). *What's whole in whole language.* Portsmouth, NH: Heinemann.

Goodman, K. S., and Y. A. Goodman. (1979). Learning to read is natural. In L. B. Resnick & P. A. Weaver (Eds.), *Theory and practice of early reading* (Vol. 1, pp. 137–154). Hillsdale, NJ: Erlbaum.

Harp, B. (Ed.). (1993). *Assessment and evaluation in whole language programs.* Norwood, MA: Christopher-Gordon.

Hepler, S. (1988). A guide for the teacher guides: Doing it yourself. *New Advocate, 1,* 186–195.

Hiebert, E. (1983). An examination of ability grouping for reading instruction. *Reading Research Quarterly, 18,* 213–255.

Huck, C. (1992). Literature and literacy. *Language Arts, 69,* 520–526.

Norton, D. (1992). *The impact of literature-based reading.* New York: Macmillan.

Routman, R. (1991). *Invitations.* Portsmouth, NH: Heinemann.

Shannon, P. (1989). Overt and covert censorship of children's books. *The New Advocate, 2,* 97–104.

Slavin, R. (1987). Ability grouping and student achievement in elementary schools: A best-evidence synthesis. *Review of Educational Research, 57,* 293–336.

Smith, F. (1982). *Understanding reading.* New York: Holt.

Strickland, D., S. Walmsley. G. Bronk, and K. Weiss. (1994). Making the most of book clubs. *Instructor, 103,* 44–47.

Strickland, D. (1992). Organizing a literature-based reading program. In B. Cullinan (Ed.), *Invitation to read: More children's literature in the reading program* (pp. 110–121). Newark, DE: International Reading Association.

Valencia, S., E. Hiebert, and P. Afflerbach. (Eds.). (1994). *Authentic reading assessment.* Newark, DE: International Reading Association.

Wells, G. (1986). *The meaning makers: Children learning language and using language to learn.* Portsmouth, NH: Heinemann.

Mediated Learning Experience

Professor Reuven Feuerstein Responds to Some Critical Questions

by Reuven Feuerstein

What is the difference between learning and mediated learning? Learning adds something new to your repertoire. A new word or skill, or even concept. This appears to be a simple form of learning, and it happens for people in a quasi-pervasive way. One hears, one sees, one imitates. In response, one is modified, or better said, one's perception of the experienced stimuli is modified to a certain extent by this exposure. But true learning, with attributes of deeper meaning for the individual's cognitive structure is not simply modified by *what you do*. True learning occurs when one learns *how to learn,* the process and nature of that which has been learned. This is a very different kind of learning. This learning is done simply by being exposed to and having experienced a stimuli or event, but in order to become meaningful, it requires the acquisition of strategies—going beyond the learning that occurs through direct exposure to objects and events in one's experience, with a mediator who focuses the learner on how to learn. This is the essential focus and benefit of mediated learning experience (MLE).

Mediated learning is an experience that the learner has that entails not just seeing something, not just doing something, not just understanding something, but also experiencing that thing at deeper levels of cognitive, emotional, attitudinal, energetic, and affective impact through the interposition of the mediator between the learner and the experienced object or event (stimuli). In such a context, learning becomes a deeply structured and, often, a pervasive and generalizable change.

In order to be a mediator, one does not simply content oneself to act as an educational pipeline or conduit of information and data. To be a mediator means that you have a unit of information in your repertoire, and you convey it "through the pipeline" until it reaches the learner. The mere conveyance of the information does not affect the mediator, does not affect the mediatee (the learner), except by adding another element to the existing repertoire of knowledge. Then the quality of mediation is added. The mediator changes, transforms in aspect and process as a part of the conveyance. As a teacher, you become physically and vocally animated, your eyes glow, you act exaggeratedly interested and energetic. "I want you to know this! I want you to see it! Look at it. . . . This is important, interesting, etc.!" Now, instead of simply providing the access (acting as the pipeline), you are influencing the intensity, flow, directionality, importance, excitement, and impact of the information that comes to the learner. Thus, these qualities of mediated learning experience transform the information that impinges on the learner, and enters his or her repertoire in a totally different way.

Knowing that the brain is affected by external learning experiences, such as with MLE, we are now on the verge of great discoveries.

How does mediated learning change a person?

There are three partners in the interaction in a mediated learning experience—the mediator, the stimuli that are being mediated, and the mediatee. All three are transformed by the intention to mediate. This creates a great change in the mediatee regarding the way the MLE is reacted to, the way the experience is registered, and the way it will be subsequently used and experienced. One of the most interesting and exciting aspects of MLE considered from this perspective is that the quality of interaction not only changes the structure of behavior of the individual, not only changes the amount and quality of his repertoire, but—according to increasingly powerful sources of evidence from the fields of neurophysiology and biochemistry—changes the structure and functioning of the brain itself in very meaningful ways. Knowing that the brain is affected by external learning experiences, such as with MLE, we are now on the verge of great discoveries.

What impact does brain research have on the process of study of MLE?
The process of change in the brain occurring as a consequence of MLE can now be studied. Not just what stimuli changes it, but what are the ingredients? And what is the interaction between the brain as an organ and the environment—both internal and external—that creates the proliferation of synapses, of new connections of organization in the neural structures? At this point there is a great deal that we do not know but now are in the position to find out. We are on the verge of great discoveries in this field. It is my belief that mediated learning, as we have conceptualized and implemented it in practice, theorizing that structural changes can and do occur, can now be corroborated by the advancing available science, perhaps even in ways beyond our first conceptions. We are now more than ever in a position to confirm that MLE is a quality of interaction that is responsible for the types of changes we observe in individuals following exposure to it.

What is Instrumental Enrichment?
The Instrumental Enrichment Program is a form of mediation, formally solidified into a systematic series of activities, providing two kinds of experiences. First, there are exercises that the learner completes. The doing of the exercises creates processes of thinking that are translated into action as the tasks are responded to. The activities are designed to translate the action of the learner into problem-solving behavior, into processes of perception, exploration, and systematic manipulation of data according to well-designed parameters of tasks (the Cognitive Map) and developmental functions (the Cognitive Functions); for example, the processes of looking for spatial and temporal indicators and identifiers of the particular event (presented in the task). When did it happen? Where did it happen? Processes of before and after, and processes requiring the use of more than one source of information. The need for precision and accuracy in responding, the recognition of potential to elaborate the process through searching for rules, justification of logical evidence, and the like.

A great wealth of opportunities for active operational thinking has been built into the exercises of the program—the student must define the problem, compare various attributes—and the student, in completing the exercises, activates his or her cognition on both executive levels. Not only on perceptual, elaborational, understanding, and input levels, but also on output levels (responding and communicating—labeling, projecting, transporting, and generalizing responses). The whole system is activated. The hands, eyes, ears, and everything in between for the learner is in some way activated. This is one part.

The second part is related to the first. The learner is activated, and feels challenged, wanting to know and do more. An important goal of mediation is to create and to activate the learner's need system. This provokes mediation. "Can the student tell me what is the meaning of this particular dot (in the Organization of Dots instrument)? Why is this dot in an inappropriate place?" And the teacher responds, "Aah, you've discovered it. Wonderful! What made you feel that this dot is not in the right place?" "Because it doesn't fit into the thing we must do here in this frame." And the teacher continues, "Ah ha! You've compared, and you've found an error. You are right, you have made an important discovery. Perhaps this error is here so that you could find it."

An important goal of mediation is to create and to activate the learner's need system.

In this way, mediation is a process of discovery, of finding rules and developing insight, enabling the learner to transform and elaborate his or her experience to further, more elaborated cognitive structures. This is the second major goal of the Instrumental Enrichment Program. Other important subgoals of the IE program are the correction of deficient cognitive functions, the acquisition of a vocabulary, concepts, and operations necessary for efficient problem solving, the development of intrinsic motivation through the development of expanded need systems and interest in the mastery of tasks, and the creation of more reflective thinking and insight. The program is thus used to create in the learner a plasticity, flexibility, and orientation in order to become a more independent, autonomous, and efficient learner.

What is the place of content learning in the Instrumental Enrichment (IE) Program?

One of the great debates that we have been engaged in with our colleagues in the field of cognitive processes and development is the extent to which cognition should be infused in specific academic or culturally related content. There are many who take the position that "you cannot teach children thinking, build intelligence, and so on, by using content-free exercises. You must teach them content and introduce specific formal aspects into the content" according to the parameters of the particular content domain. But it is our experience that if one links thinking processes too tightly to content, it stays content oriented.

Children do not easily detach learning from the context. So one must be very careful to ensure that the content does not become a kind of "golden cage" containing or restricting the information that the child has learned. Rather, the processes of learning should be related or linked to various kinds of content, as examples and flexible adaptations of what has been learned. It is for this reason that Instrumental Enrichment is best taught by a teacher who also is engaged with students in content instruction, so as to bring elements of content into conjunction with Instrumental Enrichment learning through the process of bridging. Research has shown that when the teacher who teaches content also teaches Instrumental Enrichment, the outcome effects of the program for the students are significantly enhanced.

The processes of learning should be related or linked to various kinds of content, as examples and flexible adaptations of what has been learned.

We also want teachers who teach in the subject matter areas to be knowledgeable of what students are learning in Instrumental Enrichment. This capitalizes on the student who comes into the classroom with a tool (from IE) that has not yet been used in context; for instance, organizing a diagram, identifying a rule or principle, trying out a new strategy in response to a curriculum (content) demand. In such a situation, the teacher should be aware and not consider this a bizarre incident, but rather accept and assimilate it into the context of the classroom. We have observed some teachers who react by saying, "Why does this student challenge what is occurring in the classroom as irrelevant? What does he or she mean by irrelevant?" In one such situation, a boy stood up and said, "I'm sorry, this information is irrelevant to what we are now studying." Teachers who have had this experience, without orientation and preparation, and a readiness to accept and utilize such learning in their students, may react quite negatively: "How dare you teach these children things that then become a source of criticism?" Our response is "We are sorry for the discomfort. The Instrumental Enrichment Program gives students tools to judge situations."

What is the contribution of standardized tests? How do children who have experienced mediated learning of cognitive functions fare on these tests?

A standardized test, conforming to psychometric objectives and properties, does not do justice to the child, to the subject, or to the science of understanding the human being. To give but one of many possible examples: a standardized test often requires the child to respond rapidly. A certain response must be formulated within a given standard of time. In Instrumental Enrichment, we teach the students to inhibit their tendency to respond impulsively—"Just a moment, let me think" becomes an ingrained motto of the program. Our children are taught to take their time, not to respond impulsively. Throughout, and in a variety of task modalities, we caution them: "Don't respond before you are sure, so that your response corresponds to your thinking. Your output should not do harm to your thinking. First think, then decide, then control, and say to yourself, 'Yes, it's right.'" All this takes time, so under certain circumstances our children, rather than performing within expected time constraints on the standardized test, may do less well, even though their level of understanding and processing may be within or above expectations.

Our children are taught to take their time, not to respond impulsively.

However, and notwithstanding conditions such as those just described, children who have experienced mediated learning and the Instrumental Enrichment Program do fare better on standardized tests. They do better in a variety of performance areas, compared to similar students who have not had such exposure. What is even more important is the ability to assess retention effects of such learning.

If you assess a child on something that has been learned today, at a given point in time, there is no expectation that when assessed four weeks later the child will be able to remember what he was assessed for. There is the expectation that there will be some degree of decline in what has been learned. In the situation of IE, on the other hand, if you examine the child well after the program has been concluded, a very unusual and unexpected thing happens. In comparison to a student who has not had IE, when looking at the child even two or three years later, you will see strong differences in favor of the child who has had IE. Not only that, but the differences between the child and the non-IE exposed child increase with time. And suppose you stop exposing the child to the program, and after a period of time you want to see what remains in the child's repertoire from the program exposure . . . will the child retain the effects one or two years after the program has stopped? Well, the data on this is consistent, and amazing. In every study of these phenomena, there is strong evidence of a "residue effect" and indications that the learning experienced in the program continues to generalize to a variety of outcome effects—cognition, academics, and a growing body of evidence on socialization factors. The differences between the children who have had Instrumental Enrichment and those who have not increase over time, after termination of the intervention, to the point that the differences may double or even triple. And the evidence further suggests that these are lasting effects.

This usually is not the situation when two groups exposed to different treatment effects are compared: as long as the "experimental" group is exposed to the treatment, the differences occur and hopefully strengthen, and then when treatment is withdrawn the differences decline, manifesting what is known as a "regression toward the mean." But in the case of Instrumental Enrichment, there is no regression to the mean. On the contrary, there is a rise, a consistent rise after cessation of the program, to the point that there is a real divergence in means. It can be explained as follows: If what you learn has changed your style of learning, has changed the way you experience the world, and then you have the opportunity to experience it more and more, each time you experience it you add something rather than lose something.

Can the processes of mediated learning and Instrumental Enrichment change brain structure?

Not long ago, in an earlier period in our work, we spoke modestly and cautiously about changes in the structure of cognitive behavior. We hoped that these changes did not restrict themselves to the level of behavior but went to the structure of the brain itself. However, we didn't dare say this for fear of being viewed as heretical. Now, with advances in the science of neurophysiology and neurobiology, evidence is mounting that there are in fact many changes in the brain that occur as a result of exposure to an active interaction with MLE, and that clearly this behavior affects the brain. However, this science is still at its relative beginnings, and we still do not know specifically what types of exercises, what types of stimuli, what types of interaction affect the brain in what ways. We pose mediated learning experience and the types of activities in Instrumental Enrichment as modalities of activation of the brain, of mobilization of the mental processes, as a high-powered quality of interaction that may be an ingredient responsible for changes in the structure of the brain.

We have come to realize and want others to know that the idea of "potential" itself is a very restricting, limiting concept.

What about educators who believe that an individual's intelligence is fixed?

We have come to realize and want others to know that the idea of "potential" itself is a very restricting, limiting concept. You hear people say, "Well, he has used up all of his potential," as if there is a certain store of capacity, like a bank account, and when it is expended (reached) there is no more. Others may say, "Listen, we can only do what the potential allows!" So "potential" has become a synonym for the existence, in the individual, of a certain limited amount of mental power with which the individual arrived into this world, which is not always fully materialized, which we can help materialize, but once fully materialized there is nothing much left to do.

In the last few years we have developed a very different type of definition, not only of intelligence but of a variety of other types of modal behavior—emotional, affective, intellective types of behavior. And we emphasize the modifiability of the human being, and the ways in which all of these characteristics, these modes of acting, are modifiable. We return to the conclusion that we have to relate to these behaviors as states and not traits, and as such they are amenable to change. Thus, to be in the forefront of the fight for modifiability, we must look for definitions that will make modifiability an acceptable term and encourage actions consistent with this belief: "I am in a state that makes me behave this way." A state may seem to be permanent, may be of long duration, may be resistant to change, but basically—and essentially—it is a state that is delimited by certain conditions, and under certain conditions may be modified. When these conditions change—often as a consequence of our very hard work—"all of a sudden" we see these people in very different states.

So when we speak of states, we focus more on "propensity," or the energetic aspect of change. Potential is a trait—you arrive with it, you bring it with you into the world. Propensity is an energy, a tendency, a trend, that is available to modifiability. We speak in this respect not to a capacity to become modified but about an energy that makes you become able to be modified.

Potential is a trait—you arrive with it, you bring it with you into the world. Propensity is an energy, a tendency, a trend, that is available to modifiability.

Advice to educators who want to "teach for intelligence?"

First and foremost, teachers must know more about the process of learning and what affects this process. Then they must become familiar with those functions whose absence or deficiency hampers the process of learning, with the characteristics of the tasks of learning (as in the Cognitive Map) so as to effectively orient the learning process for the student, and to understand the relationship between the learner's need system as developed by the cognitive processes, affecting the intrinsic and extrinsic motivational systems of the learner. To do so makes the teachers more able to use themselves as mediators and to make children more permeable, more ready, more curious, more interested, to make the children more able to mobilize their human propensities to learn and grow and change.

Unfortunately, educational systems often create teachers who acquire characteristics of learned helplessness, turning potentially beautiful, inventive, ingenious people into passive acceptors of the status quo. And this has a pernicious effect throughout the whole educational process. We must empower the teacher—create a transformation from passive acceptance to active modification. The Instrumental Enrichment Program has this effect on those teachers who are trained to use it. Another thing we do is to teach teachers to use our dynamic approach to assessment, the Learning Propensity Assessment Device (LPAD), not to turn them into psychologists, but to give them the feeling that they can change the child, that they can understand in a deeply meaningful way how the child learns, and how the child can be modified in his or her cognitive structures. And in the process of interaction, with the child and the tools of the LPAD, they learn a great deal . . . they change their whole perspective on the teaching/learning process and their interaction with it. This then affects their readiness and their feeling of having a real access to the soul, to the destiny of the child. And once a teacher succeeds, the pleasure they experience—on both professional and personal levels—transforms them. It is not an exaggeration to say that in no other way can this type of pleasure be experienced.

Learning to Learn

The Cognitive Enrichment Advantage Approach

by Donna Wilson and Katherine H. Greenberg

Sue is a second grader who had difficulty with organization and planning skills before her school began to use the Cognitive Enrichment Advantage (CEA) learning to learn approach (formerly known as the COGNET Education Model). The following conversation occurred as she was helping her father organize his tools.

Sue: "Dad, you can do better if you use systematic Exploration and Planning. They will help you organize this stuff."

Father: "I need to what? Hey, Mom, what in the world is Susie talking about?"

Mother: "I didn't hear her. What did you say, Sue?"

Sue: "I told Dad he should use systematic Exploration and Planning to get organized."

Father: "Where is she learning these skills and vocabulary?"

Mother: "At school. Her teacher and others have begun using a learning to learn approach called the Cognitive Enrichment Advantage or CEA. They are planning to hold a meeting soon to see if parents want to join them by helping our children learn to learn at home."

Sue: "In my class we're building a learning community and using Building Blocks of Thinking and Tools of Learning to make strategies so we don't have trouble learning."

Mother: "So...what did you tell Dad?"

Sue: "I just told him that if he uses systematic Exploration and Planning he will be able to decide on a strategy for organizing his stuff. Maybe he needs Self-Regulation, too!"

The parents in this scenario are particularly proud of their daughter's understanding and application of new skills learned through CEA. Sue had been having an increasing number of problems in school. Prior to participation in CEA's learning to learn approach, Sue often had trouble with attention, organization, and using strategies to approach tasks. She was beginning to doubt her ability to succeed in school and was becoming anxious and fearful of challenges. As Sue developed the ability to think about her thinking, as well as the feelings and motivation that connect to cognition and learning, she began to understand how to maintain inner control over her learning. Sue's parents and teachers reported the changes that occurred as Sue was able to complete tasks both at home and at school; tasks she had struggled with before participation in CEA (Wilson 1996).

AN OVERVIEW OF THE COGNITIVE ENRICHMENT ADVANTAGE LEARNING TO LEARN APPROACH

CEA is a comprehensive approach to learning to learn developed by Katherine Greenberg, Ph.D. at The University of Tennessee, Knoxville (Greenberg in press a, Greenberg in press b). It is designed to facilitate the building of learning communities among teachers and students in the classroom, and among families, educators, and others who have a shared purpose of helping students become effective lifelong learners. Through CEA, students are helped to develop knowledge about thinking, feeling, and motivation that they can use to build the personal learning strategies necessary for effective independent and interdependent learning. As a result, students can receive a cognitive enrichment advantage to help them better adapt and contribute responsibly to an ever-changing world. CEA is comprised of three key components adapted by users to meet their learner's specific needs. These components are the following:

1. A CEA classroom community for learning to learn with practices supported by theories and research from the fields of cognitive education and cognitive psychology, and compatible with brain research.

2. A CEA family-school partnership for learning to learn has been shown to increase student success in learning in and out of school and helps family members and educators understand each others' expectations for learning, and to build a shared purpose.

3. A supportive network of users that connects participants with other CEA implementers in diverse settings throughout the world.

Although influenced by many of the ideas from the new field of cognitive education, CEA is based primarily upon Feuerstein's theory of mediated learning experience (Feuerstein, Klein, and Tannenbaum 1990; Feuerstein 1980). Feuerstein's ideas help explain two aspects of learning to learn that are becoming increasingly important in today's world: the importance of culture in learning and the need for an explicit understanding of how to learn.

The Role of Mediated Learning Experiences in an Ever-Changing World

Based upon his work with young immigrants to Israel who had suffered greatly from the Holocaust in Europe or cultural upheaval in Morocco, and also from his experiences with adolescents displaying moderate to severe disabilities in learning, Feuerstein developed his ideas about the importance of mediated learning experiences (Feuerstein 1980). These learning experiences are not as common as those in which learners are directly exposed, without assistance, to stimuli in the environment. Instead, mediated learning experiences are a special type of interaction through which those with more knowledge share a system of cultural meanings and values about how to learn with those with less knowledge.

Parents, teachers, and others naturally act as mediators of learning experiences because of their need to share information about how one behaves in the world. As they mediate, they share tacit (nonexplicit, implied) knowledge about how to learn that encompasses thinking, feeling, and motivation. However, learning problems often interfere with school success when there is a cultural mismatch in the classroom—when teachers and students do not fully understand each other's assumptions about how learning is supposed to occur. Problems also occur when students are less open to mediated learning due to disabilities, especially when teachers and parents do not know how to refine mediated learning experiences to provide the kind of cognitive enrichment that can result in more effective learning. Many teachers today use some cognitive education techniques in the classroom. However, long-term benefits are limited unless the approach incorporates explicit knowledge about thinking, feelings, and motivation that can be used by the student to develop personal learning strategies (Ashman and Conway 1997; Schunk and Zimmerman 1994).

As the world becomes more complex, the ability to engage in effective lifelong learning is becoming a necessity. Today, all learners can benefit from a cognitive enrichment advantage that occurs through the mediation of explicit knowledge about thinking, feeling, and motivation. This is especially true for nontraditional and underachieving learners. Due to increased cultural diversity and dependence upon a global economy, independent and interdependent learning skills are needed by young and old alike regardless of their level of learning or career focus. When mediated learning is combined with the building of a learning community in the classroom and in family-school partnerships, then all learners have a better opportunity to become effective independent and interdependent lifelong learners.

As the world becomes more complex, the ability to engage in effective lifelong learning is becoming a necessity.

As with Sue in the scenario, other students who have had difficulty learning often become motivated and successful when they develop metacognitive awareness that can serve as a system from which to build personal strategies for learning. A seven-year series of studies examined the effects of CEA (then known as COGNET) on the academic achievement of elementary school students—primarily in Title I Schoolwide Project Schools—as a part of the USDE Follow Through Program (Greenberg, Machleit, and Schlessmann-Frosst 1996). COGNET was one of the national Follow Through education models from 1988-1991. In the studies, Follow Through schools used CEA and similar schools served as comparison schools. Students considered at-risk for academic failure who attended schools using CEA for two or more years made much greater educational gains than students in the comparison schools. Furthermore, one of the CEA schools demonstrated significant decreases in the percent of students scoring below average on achievement tests as the students moved from first to fourth grade. Other studies in elementary schools and informal reports from teachers of older students supported the positive impact of CEA. These results led to the validation of CEA (under the name of COGNET Education Model) by the former National Diffusion Network in 1995.

Interviews were also conducted with parents who participated as partners with educators in the use of CEA. These parents made highly positive comments about the importance of the partnership they built with their children's schools. One important theme shared by many of the parents related to their desire for more opportunities to learn and use CEA with their children. One parent explained that CEA helped her understand her role as a partner with the school and helped her child understand the purpose of school (Greenberg 1992).

One parent explained that CEA helped her understand her role as a partner with the school and helped her child understand the purpose of school

THE CEA FAMILY-SCHOOL PARTNERSHIP FOR LEARNING TO LEARN

Maximizing learning potential and valuing cultural differences provides a clear moral purpose for schools in today's world. Family-school partnerships are an important component of this moral purpose, as the theory of mediated learning experiences makes clear. Cultural mismatch (whether due to such factors as racial or ethnic differences, socioeconomic status, or family style differences) can only be overcome when family members work with educators to help children understand and respect the subtle or dramatic differences between home and school expectations for how to go about learning. The higher degree to which family members and educators understand each other's expectations for learning, the better they can overcome barriers to effective family-school partnerships and the better they can provide children with a cognitive enrichment advantage (Gestwicki 1996; Henry 1996).

The most important feature of CEA partnerships is their adaptability to meet the particular needs of a given school. While some CEA partnerships may emphasize parent-volunteer programs in the school, others may focus on self-improvement programs for parents, and all CEA partnerships include a focus on the parent's role as the primary mediator of learning experiences in the child's life. CEA provides these partnerships as a basis for developing a shared purpose and two-way communication for helping students learn to learn. CEA also provides a shared vocabulary that family members and educators can use with students that relates to knowledge for thinking, feeling, and motivating learning. In the expanded CEA version, the family-school partnership approach can be used to help teachers and parents better understand the similarities and differences in their expectations for specific children's learning in home and school settings.

Building Blocks of Thinking and Tools of Learning

Students, educators, and family members participating in CEA develop a shared vocabulary for 12 Building Blocks of Thinking (cognitive processes that foster effective thinking), and 8 Tools of Learning (affective/motivational factors that foster independent and interdependent learning). Teachers integrate minilessons for Building Blocks of Thinking and Tools of Learning into school activities. Family members using CEA adapt suggestions for mediating Building Blocks of Thinking and Tools of Learning to fit their culture and personal worldview.

The Building Blocks of Thinking and Tools of Learning are organized into categories to facilitate the remembering of labels and to develop further understanding of how thinking, feeling, and motivation work together to provide a cognitive enrichment advantage. Tables 1 and 2 display labels, definitions, and categories for Building Blocks of Thinking and Tools of Learning.

THE CEA CLASSROOM COMMUNITY ATMOSPHERE

The CEA classroom approach can help educators create or deepen an open classroom atmosphere that facilitates mediated learning. By establishing what CEA calls a *laboratory for learning* in the classroom, members of this learning community establish shared standards that help students feel accepted, safe, and challenged—ready to seek out mediated learning experiences.

These standards

- Expect all students to learn
- Respect all students for their efforts to learn
- Encourage thinking that leads to effective learning
- Support learning opportunities (no co-opting or depriving a student of a learning opportunity)
- Value the process of learning at least as much as the product
- Honor effective independent and interdependent lifelong learning
- Treat the classroom as a laboratory for learning, not a stage for producing right answers.

(Greenberg, in press a)

CEA Building Blocks of Thinking
(cognitive processes that foster effective thinking)

Building Blocks for Approaching the Learning Experience

Exploration	*To search systematically for information needed in the learning experience.*
Planning	*To prepare a detailed method for approaching the learning experience.*
Expression	*To communicate ideas and actions carefully in the learning experience.*

Building Blocks for Making Meaning of the Learning Experience

Working Memory	*To use memory processes effectively.*
Making Comparisons	*To discover similarities and differences spontaneously among some parts of the learning experience.*
Getting the Main Idea	*To identify spontaneously the basic thought that holds related ideas together.*
Thought Integration	*To combine pieces of information into a complete thought and hold onto them while needed.*
Connecting Events	*To find relationships spontaneously among past, present, and future learning experiences.*

Building Blocks for Confirming the Learning Experience

Precision and Accuracy	*To know there is a need to correctly understand and use words and concepts correctly and to seek information spontaneously when the need arises.*
Space and Time Concepts	*To understand how things relate in size, shape, and distance; how events occur in time and order; and how to use this information effectively in the learning experience.*
Selective Attention	*To choose between relevant and irrelevant information and to focus on the information needed in the learning experience.*
Problem Identification	*To experience a sense of imbalance spontaneously and define its cause when inconsistencies occur in the learning experience.*

Table 1

Cognitive Enrichment Advantage Tools of Learning

(affective/motivational approaches that foster independent and interdependent learning)

Tools for Understanding Feelings within the Learning Experience	
Inner Meaning	*To seek deep, personal value in learning experiences that energize thinking and behavior and lead to greater commitment and success.*
Feeling of Challenge	*To energize learning effectively in new and complex experiences.*
Awareness of Self-Change	*To recognize and understand feelings about personal growth and to learn to expect and welcome change and development.*
Feeling of Competence	*To energize feelings, thoughts, and behaviors by developing beliefs about being capable of learning and doing something effectively.*
Tools for Motivating Behavior within the Learning Experience	
Self-Regulation	*To reflect on thoughts and actions as they occur to energize, sustain, and direct behavior toward successful learning and doing.*
Goal Orientation	*To taking purposeful action in consistently setting, seeking, and reaching personal objectives.*
Self-Development	*To value personal qualities and to enhance personal potential.*
Sharing Behavior	*To become interdependent by sharing thoughts and actions effectively, by enhancing collaborative learning, and by participating actively as a learner and peer-mediator.*

Table 2

Because the CEA classroom approach encourages inquiry and cooperative/collaborative learning, students have many opportunities to reflect upon the need for Building Blocks of Thinking and Tools of Learning and to try out learning strategies they have developed. CEA teachers/mediators report that many students quickly and frequently transfer their knowledge about Building Blocks of Thinking and Tools of Learning to new situations, just as Sue did in the scenario. Students also have opportunities to serve as peer mediators for each other and to become more effective as both independent and interdependent learners.

Using Cognitive Enrichment Advantage

The CEA approach has been used in a variety of sites in the U.S., as well as in Belgium, Brazil, Canada, Chile, South Africa, and the United Kingdom. CEA is intended for use in schools that have a commitment to long-term solutions, rather than quick fixes. Educators and family members develop a two-year plan for implementation, and educators participate in a CEA Level I workshop. Teachers/mediators also participate in coaching sessions and support meetings with colleagues throughout the initial two years of use. Early in the second year, educators take part in a Level II workshop. Through the family-school partnership, plans are made for parent activities that may include joint workshops with teachers that provide opportunities for two-way conversations about home and school learning expectations and a discussion of how family members can use CEA in the home.

Cognitive Enrichment Advantage materials include the following:

- *Cognitive Enrichment Advantage Teachers Handbook*, a 200-page guide to the classroom approach (Greenberg, in press a) with an in-depth overview of CEA, recommendations for how to use and adapt the classroom approach, and information about each Building Block of Thinking and Tool of Learning.
- *Cognitive Enrichment Advantage Minilessons* (Greenberg in press c), with 229 minilessons about Building Blocks of Thinking, and Tool of Learning, and general aspects of learning to learn that can be integrated into individual, large and small group, and curricular and daily living skills school activities.
- *Cognitive Enrichment Advantage Family-School Partnership Handbook,* which includes an overview of CEA, commonly held school expectations for children's use of Building Blocks and Tools, and information about each Building Block of Thinking and Tool of Learning suggestions for how family members might talk about them with children during family activities.

Two additional books are in progress, one for those in leadership roles in the use of the CEA classroom approach and/or in developing the family-school partnership, and another book for CEA certified consultants.

Because of the comprehensiveness of the CEA approach, educator materials are available for workshop participants only. These materials are to be used as resources by those who have firsthand experience with CEA practices. The *Cognitive Enrichment Advantage*

Family-School Partnership Handbook is available with or without workshop participation. Family members and educators who participate in partnership workshops, however, will gain a much deeper understanding of this component of CEA. These workshops are designed separately for each group based upon needs and shared purposes.

EXPECTED OUTCOMES

Based upon results and ongoing efforts in many schools, use of the complete CEA approach helps schools and family members take steps to achieve the following outcomes:

1. Students develop an awareness of how to become responsible members of society who can adapt and contribute to an ever-changing world.
2. Professional educators develop or renew visions for developing school and classroom learning communities.
3. Family members and educators develop an understanding of how thinking, feeling, and motivation work together to bring about effective lifelong independent and interdependent learning, and how they can use mediated learning experiences based upon their own expectations for learning to provide students with a cognitive enrichment advantage.
4. Teachers/mediators further develop knowledge about a classroom atmosphere that facilitates mediated learning opportunities through inquiry learning and cooperative/collaborative learning activities.
5. Students, educators, and family members develop a shared purpose for school that values cultural diversity and learning to learn.
6. Educators and family members develop and sustain family-school partnerships that include the involvement of parents in school activities and a coordinated approach to helping students learn how to learn in school and home settings.
7. All participants can choose to become a part of the world of CEA users who support each other through a variety of community-building activities.

CONCLUSION

The CEA approach is unique in many of the ways it strives to teach for intelligence. It is highly comprehensive, designed to be embedded into the school curriculum, and can be modified to meet specific needs of family-school partnerships. Furthermore, the CEA approach views learning to learn holistically by focusing on affect, motivation, and cognition as they relate to each other. This approach integrates and refines many practices demonstrated as effective in the field of cognitive education and utilizes methods that appear to ovecome problems that often occur in thinking skills programs that rely on the teaching of expert strategies. Although long-term studies have demonstrated the effectiveness of CEA in increasing academic performance of students, research on various aspects of the CEA approach continues. For example, studies are currently being planned to focus on the use of CEA with adults in basic education programs in prison schools in Canada. It is especially important to document the experiences of educators, schools, and family-school partnerships to determine how best to adapt the CEA approach in ways that can effectively meet specific needs of given communities. The learning problems of students like Sue, as described at the beginning of this article, can only be met through a comprehensive, systemic approach based upon careful evaluation.

REFERENCES

Ashman, A., and R. Conway. 1997. *An introduction to cognitive education.* New York: Routledge.

Feuerstein, R. 1980. *Instrumental Enrichment.* Baltimore, MD: University Park Press.

Feuerstein, R., P. S. Klein, and A. Tannenbaum. (Eds.). 1990. *Mediated learning experience (MLE): Theoretical, psychosocial and learning implications.* London: Freud Publishing House, Ltd.

Gestwicki, C. 1996. Home, school and community relations. 3rd ed. New York: Delmar Publishers.

Greenberg, K. H. in press a. *Cognitive Enrichment Advantage teacher handbook.* Arlington Heights, IL: Skylight Professional Development.

Greenberg, K. H. in press b. *Cognitive Enrichment Advantage family-school partnership handbook.* Arlington Heights, IL: Skylight Professional Development.

Greenberg, K. H. in press c. *Cognitive Enrichment Advantage minilessons.* Arlington Heights, IL: Skylight Professional Development.

Greenberg, K. 1992. COGNET: Mediating the learning network. In *Follow Through: A bridge to the future.* Austin, TX: Southwestern Educational Development Laboratory.

Greenberg, K., Machleit, S., and Schlessmann-Frosst, A. 1996. Cognitive enrichment network education model (COGNET). Urbana, IL: ERIC Clearinghouse on Elementary and Early Childhood Education. Resources in Education (RIE). (PS024949)

Henry, M. 1996. *Parent-school collaboration: Feminist organizational structures and school leadership.* Albany, NY: State University of New York Press.

Schunk, D. and Zimmerman, B. (Eds.). 1994. *Self-regulation of learning and performance: Issues and educational applications.* Hillsdale, NJ: Lawrence Erlbaum Associates.

Wilson, D. 1996. The school psychologist as co-teacher: Using COGNET as a means to teach thinking skills. *Journal of Cognitive Education* 5(2): 171–183.

Authors

Richard Allington is the Fien Distinguished Professor of Education at the University of Florida. He co-directs a national research project studying exemplary elementary teachers through the National Research Center on English Learning and Achievement.

Robert Balfanz received his Ph.D. in Education from the University of Chicago in 1995. He is a research scientist at the Center for Educating Students Placed At Risk at Johns Hopkins University. Robert worked at developing the Everyday Mathematics Curriculum of the University of Chicago School Mathematics Project. At present, Robert is working on Mathematics Programs for preschool and middle school children.

Meir Ben-Hur is a consultant and facilitator trained in the practices of mediated learning and learning potential assessment. He has over twenty years of classroom teaching experience, ranging from teaching high school mathematics to college and university professorships. A recipient of Professor Reuven Feuerstein's training, he has worked as a trainer with Feuerstein all over the world.

Ron Brandt is an education writer and consultant and was formerly the editor of Educational Leadership and other publications of the Association for Supervision and Curriculum Development (ASCD). He is a commentator on school improvement and reform, and is especially interested in the use of knowledge from cognitive research and neuroscience to improve school learning. His most recent book are *Powerful Learning and Assessing Student Learning: New Rules, New Realities,* both published in 1998.

Kay Burke is the senior vice-president of academics at SkyLight Professional Development. She has presented over 600 keynote addresses, seminars, and courses throughout the United States, Canada, and Australia and trains educators in classroom management, authentic assessment, student portfolios, and professional portfolios. She is the author of numerous books including *The Mindful School: How to Assess Authentic Learning* and *Designing Professional Portfolios for Change.*

Geoffrey Caine is an education consultant specializing in brain-based learning and teaching. He is an adjunct faculty member at the University of Redlands Whitehead Center for Lifelong Learning in California, where he teaches philosophy and management.

Renate Caine, an expert in brain research, is a professor of education at California State University-San Bernardino and former Executive Director of the CSUSB Center for Research in Integrative Learning and Teaching.

Carolyn Chapman is an international consultant and trainer for IRI/ Skylight. Her workshops on multiple intelligences, integrating the curricula, and authentic assessment support schools in the process of change. Some of her other areas of expertise are developing lifelong readers and writers, portfolio as a process, cooperative learning, and multiple intelligences centers and projects. Carolyn is the author of *If the Shoe Fits . . . : How to Develop Multiple Intelligences in the Classroom* and co-author of *Multiple Assessments for Multiple Intelligences* and *Multiple Intelligences Centers and Projects.*

Arthur Costa is Emeritus professor of Education at California State University, Sacramento, and Co-Director of the Institute for Intelligent Behavior, in Berkeley, California. He has served as a classroom teacher, curriculum consultant, an assistant superintendent for instruction, and as Director of Educational programs for the National Aeronautics and Space Administration. He has made presentations and conducted workshops in all fifty states as well as Mexico, Central America, South America, Canada, Australia, New Zealand, Africa, Europe, Asia, and the Islands of the South Pacific. Dr. Costa served as the president of the California Association for Supervision and Curriculum Development and was the national president of the Association for Supervision and Curriculum Development from 1988 to 1989.

Jennifer P. Day is a former elementary school teacher and reading specialist. She is currently a doctoral candidate at the University of Albany, State University of New York, and a research assistant at the Center for English Learning and Achievement. Her research interests include the needs of struggling readers and the influence of policy on teachers and teaching. She is currently working on her dissertation on the effects of educational policies in shaping more- and less-effective teachers.

Professor Reuven Feuerstein is an eminent cognitive psychologist, known for his groundbreaking research in cognitive mediation. He established that "all children can learn" while working with culturally deprived, mentally handicapped, and autistic children. Rejecting the idea that intelligence is fixed, Professor Feuerstein developed a curriculum to build the cognitive functions of students diagnosed by others as incapable of learning. This program, Instrumental Enrichment, provides students with the concepts, skills, strategies, operations, and techniques necessary to become independent thinkers. Feuerstein's Instrumental Enrichment instruments are taught today in more than twenty-nine languages.

Robin Fogarty, a leading proponent of the thoughtful classroom, trains teachers throughout the world in cognitive strategies and cooperative interaction. She has taught all levels from kindergarten to college, served as an administrator, and consulted with state departments and ministries of education in the United States, Russia, Canada, Australia, New Zealand, and the Netherlands. Dr. Fogarty is the author, co-author, and editor of numerous publications in professional education.

Herbert Ginsburg is the Jacob H. Shiff Professor of Psychology and Education at Teachers College, Columbia University. For the past thirty years, he has conducted research on cognitive development, particularly the development of children's mathematical thinking, both within the United States and in various countries around the world. He has used the knowledge gained from research to develop several kinds of educational applications, including mathematics textbooks and video workshops designed to enhance teachers' understandings of children's learning of mathematics. He is now studying preschoolers' mathematical thinking.

Katherine Greenberg is the founder of COGNET, A former U.S.D.E. follow-through project director, and a professor of educational psychology at the University of Tennessee, Knoxville. She has provided COGNET consultation across the United States and in six other countries. As a Fulbright Research Scholar, she worked for nine months with Reuven Feuerstein in Israel.

Carol Greenes is Professor, Mathematics Education and Associate Dean, Research and Development, and Advanced Academic Programs in the School of Education at Boston University. Dr. Greenes has written and collaborated on numerous books, programs, monographs, and articles in the areas of early childhood education, mathematical problem solving, and mathematics for children at both ends of the achievement spectrum. Dr. Greenes is senior author of *Hot Math Topics,* the *TOPS Beginning Problem Solving Program,* and *Groundworks: Algebraic Thinking.*

Jane Healy is an educational psychologist, lecturer, consultant with over thirty years of experience as an educator interested in brain development and learning. She is the author of *Endangered Minds* and *Your Child's Growing Mind.* Her latest book is *Failure to Connect: How Computers Affect Our Children's Minds for Better and Worse* (Simon & Schuster, 1998).

Clifford Hill is Arthur I. Gates professor of Language and Education at Columbia University, where he also chairs the Department of International and Transcultural Studies at Teacher College. In addition, he directs the Program in African Languages in the School of International and Public Affairs.

Rita King is an international consultant for Creative Learning Connection. Her expertise includes test success, multiple intelligences, brain-compatible learning environments, parent involvement and self-directed learners. Her passion is to make a difference for today's learners and educators through her powerful courses, seminars, and workshops. Rita has served as a teacher, director of laboratory experiences for education majors and principal. Currently she is an adjunct professor in the Department of Educational Leadership at Middle Tennessee State University. Rita co-authored *Test Success in the Brain-Compatible Classroom* with Carolyn Chapman. The book will be published in the spring.

Donna Ogle is a professor in the Reading and Language Department of National-Louis University in Evanston, Illinois. Her major work has been in strategic reading and staff development for instructional change. The KWL strategy, which she developed for expository reading and learning, is widely used throughout the world. Donna is active in professional leadership, having served on the Board of Directors for both the National Reading Conference and the International Reading Association for teacher educators in Russia. She is also active in the National Urban Alliance for Effective Teaching.

Joseph Renzulli is Professor of Gifted Education and Talent Development at the Neag Center, University of Connecticut, where he also serves as Director of the National Research Center of Gifted and Talented. He has served on numerous editorial boards in the field of gifted education and has served as a senior research associate for the White House Task Force on Education for the Gifted and Talented.

Peter Senge is a senior lecturer at the Sloan School of Management at Massachusetts Institute of Technology and chairperson of the Social Organizational Learning (SOL). Dr. Senge has lectured extensively throughout the world, translating the abstract ideas of systems theory into tools for better understanding of economic and organizational change. His areas of special interest focus on decentralizing the role of leadership in organizations so as to enhance the capacity of all people to work productively toward common goals.

Robert Sternberg is IBM professor of Psychology and Education in the Department of Psychology at Yale University. Sternberg is the author of more than 650 publications. He has won numerous awards from various educational organizations and is Fellow of the American Academy of the Arts and Sciences, American Association for the Advancement of Sciences, American Psychological Association, and American Psychological Society.

Dorothy Strickland is State of New Jersey Professor of Reading at Rutgers University. A former classroom teacher, she is past president of the International Reading Association (IRA). She is active in the National

Council of Teachers of English (NCTE) and the National Association for the Education of Young Children. She received IRA's Outstanding Teacher Educator of Reading Award and is the current president of the IRA Reading Hall of Fame. She received the 1994 NCTE Rewey Belle Inglis Award for Outstanding Women in the Teaching of English and the 1998 Outstanding Educator of Language Arts.

Robert Sylwester is an emeritus Professor of Education at the University of Oregon who focuses on the educational implications of new developments in science and technology. He has written several books and over 100 journal articles. His most recent books are *Student Brains, School Issues* (1998, SkyLight Training and Publishing, Inc.) and *A Biological Brain in a Cultural Classroom: Applying Biological Research to Classroom Management* (2000, Corwin Press). The Education Press Association of America gave him Distinguished Achievement Awards for this 1994 and 1995 syntheses of cognitive science research, published in Educational Leadership. He has made over 1000 conference and inservice presentations on educationally significant developments in brain/stress theory and research.

Donna Wilson, consultant for SkyLight Professional Development, uses her multicultural experiences to integrate learning throughout schools, universities, and communities. Her expert insight into how children learn stems from years of teaching elementary grades, serving as a school psychologist, and advocating teacher preparation for the classroom.

Pat Wolfe is a former teacher of Kindergarten through 12th grade and county office administrator. Over the past 12 years, as an educational consultant, she has conducted workshops for thousands of administrators, teachers, boards of education, and parents in schools and districts throughout the United States and internationally. Her major area of expertise is the application of brain research to educational practice. She is an author and has appeared on numerous videotape series, satellite broadcasts, radio shows, and television programs. Dr. Wolfe is a native of Missouri. She completed her undergraduate work in Oklahoma and her postgraduate studies in California. She presently resides in Napa, California.

Acknowledgments

Grateful acknowledgment is made to the following authors and agents for their permission to reprint copyrighted materials.

SECTION 1

Peter Senge for "Systems Change in Education." © 1998 by Psychology Press. Reprinted with permission.

Geoffrey and Renate Caine for "Unleashing the Power of Perceptual Change." © 1999 by Geoffrey Caine and Renate Caine. Reprinted with permission.

Arthur L. Costa and Robert J. Garmston for "Changing Curriculum Means Changing Your Mind." Adapted from Thinking Magazine, October 1998, pp. 14-17.

SECTION 2

Meir Ben-Hur for "Learning and Transfer—A Tautology." © 2000 by SkyLight Training and Publishing Inc. Reprinted with permission of SkyLight Professional Development.

Pat Wolfe and Ron Brandt for "What Do We Know from Brain Research?" © 1998 by Pat Wolfe and Ron Brandt. First printed in Educational Leadership, November 1998. Reprinted with permission of Pat Wolfe and Ron Brandt.

Association for Supervision and Curriculum Development and Robert Sylwester for "Art for the Brain's Sake." © 1998 by Association for Supervision and Curriculum Development. Reprinted with permission.

SECTION 3

SkyLight Professional Development and Robin Fogarty for "Memory, the Thing I Forget With." © 2000 by SkyLight Training and Publishing. Printed with permission of SkyLight Professional Development.

Robert J. Sternberg for "Creativity Is a Decision." © 2000 by Robert J. Sternberg. Printed with permission.

Pat Wolfe for "Revisiting Effective Teaching." First printed in Educational Leadership, November 1998, pp. 61-64. © 1998 by Pat Wolfe. Reprinted with permission.

Donna Ogle for "Multiple Intelligences and Reading Instruction." © 2000 by Donna Ogle. Printed with permission.

SECTION 4

American Association of School Administrators and Jane Healy for "The Mad Dash to Computer. Enriching or Eroding Intelligence?" Appeared in The School Administrator, April 1999. © by American Association of School Administrators.

Ron Brandt and Phi Delta Kappa for "Educators Need to Know About the Human Brain." Appeared in Phi Delta Kappan, November 1999, vol. 81, no. 3, pp. 235-238. © 1999 by Ron Brandt.

Joseph S. Renzulli for "Raising the Ceiling for All Students." © 2000 by Joseph S. Renzulli. Printed with permission.

SECTION 5

Kay Burke for "Learning Standards." Adapted from The Mindful School: How to Assess Authentic Learning, Chapter 1. © 1999, 1994, 1993 by SkyLight Training and Publishing Inc. Reprinted with permission.

Jeni Pollack Day and Richard L. Allington for "What Sorts of Standards for Teachers? Focusing on Exemplary Elementary Teaching." © 2000 by Richard L. Allington and Jeni Pollack Day. Printed with permission.

Clifford Hill for "Constructivist Assessment in Early Childhood Education." From presentation at the Teaching for Intelligence Conference in San Francisco, April 1999. © 1999 by Clifford Hill. Printed with permission.

Carolyn Chapman and Rita King for "Test Success in the Brain-Compatible Classroom." © 2000 by Carolyn Chapman and Rita King. Printed with permission.

SECTION 6

Herbert P. Ginsburg, Robert Balfanz, and Carole Greenes for "Challenging Mathematics for Young Children." © 2000 by Herbert P. Ginsburg, Robert Balfanz, and Carole Greenes. Printed with permission.

Dorothy Strickland and the International Reading Association for "Reinventing Our Literacy Programs: Books, Basics, Balance." From The Reading Teacher 48(4), pp. 294-302. © 19995 by International Reading Association. Reprinted with permission of Dorothy Strickland and the International Reading Association. All rights reserved.

Reuven Feuerstein for "Mediated Learning Experience. Professor Reuven Feuerstein Responds to Some Critical Questions." © 2000 by SkyLight Training and Publishing Inc. Printed with permission of SkyLight Professional Development.

Donna Wilson and Katherine H. Greenberg for "Learning to Learning. The Cognitive Enrichment Advantage Approach. © 2000 by SkyLight Training and Publishing Inc. Printed with permission of SkyLight Professional Development.

Index

There are
one-story intellects,
two-story intellects, and three-story
intellects with skylights. All fact collectors, who
have no aim beyond their facts, are one-story men. Two-story men
compare, reason, generalize, using the labors of the fact collectors as
well as their own. Three-story men idealize, imagine,
predict—their best illumination comes from
above, through the skylight.

—*Oliver Wendell Holmes*